# NOTABLE NATURAL DISASTERS

# NOTABLE NATURAL DISASTERS

## Volume 1

## Overviews

*Edited by*
**Marlene Bradford, Ph.D.**
*Texas A&M University*

**Robert S. Carmichael, Ph.D.**
*University of Iowa*

SALEM PRESS, INC.
Pasadena, California   Hackensack, New Jersey

∞ The paper used in these volumes conforms to the American National
Standard for Permanence of Paper for Printed Library Materials, Z39.48-
1992 (R1997).

These essays originally appeared in *Natural Disasters* (2001). New essays
and other material have been added.

**Library of Congress Cataloging-in-Publication Data**

Notable natural disasters / edited by Marlene Bradford, Robert S.
Carmichael.
    p. cm. — (Magill's choice)
Includes bibliographical references and index.
    ISBN 978-1-58765-368-1 (set : alk. paper) — ISBN 978-1-58765-369-8
(vol. 1 : alk. paper) — ISBN 978-1-58765-370-4 (vol. 2 : alk. paper) —
ISBN 978-1-58765-371-1 (vol. 3 : alk. paper) 1. Natural disasters. I. Bradford,
Marlene. II. Carmichael, Robert S.

GB5014.N373 2007
904'.5—dc22
                                                                2007001926

# CONTENTS

# PUBLISHER'S NOTE

Some books about natural disasters focus on science, using examples of events or lists without extended descriptions. Disaster chronologies list events and generally do not provide a comprehensive look at underlying scientific principles and other general concerns. *Notable Natural Disasters* addresses both aspects of natural disasters in an accessible manner that is scholarly, not sensationalized. This three-volume set combines clearly explained scientific concepts with gripping narrative details about 100 memorable disasters in history. In addition, *Notable Natural Disasters* is illustrated with 170 photographs, maps, tables and diagrams to aid the reader.

This affordable subset of *Natural Disasters* (2001) has been rearranged and thoroughly updated with new bibliographic sources and entries on recent disasters: the 2002-2003 SARS epidemic, the 2003 Europe heat wave, the Fire Siege of 2003 in Southern California, the 2003 Bam earthquake in Iran, the Indian Ocean tsunami in 2004, Hurricane Katrina in 2005, the Kashmir earthquake of 2005, and the 2006 Leyte mudslide in the Philippines.

## ■ DEFINITION AND SCOPE

For this set, a natural disaster is defined as an event caused, at least in part, by uncontrollable forces of nature. For example, the overviews on "Fog" and "Icebergs and Glaciers" discuss collisions and crashes in which those natural conditions were a factor, although human error played a role. Similarly, "Explosions" addresses only accidental ignitions. Decisions were also made regarding scope and focus. For example, only wildfires affecting cities or whole regions are addressed in the "Fires" overview and among the events, rather than tragic blazes in single buildings such as hotels or theaters.

In selecting the 100 events covered here, further questions were asked. Is a "great" disaster measured by numbers of people killed and injured, or by the amount of disruption caused? When does a local tragedy become an event of broader significance? Why are some disasters more heartbreaking or spectacular, and thus more memorable, than others?

# ■ OVERVIEWS

Volume 1 begins with disaster overviews by type:

| | |
|---|---|
| Avalanches | Heat Waves |
| Blizzards, Freezes, Ice Storms, and Hail | Hurricanes, Typhoons, and Cyclones |
| Droughts | Icebergs and Glaciers |
| Dust Storms and Sandstorms | Landslides, Mudslides, and Rockslides |
| Earthquakes | |
| El Niño | Lightning Strikes |
| Epidemics | Meteorites and Comets |
| Explosions | Smog |
| Famines | Tornadoes |
| Fires | Tsunamis |
| Floods | Volcanic Eruptions |
| Fog | Wind Gusts |

Each essay explains the disaster in scientific terms. First, a few sentences define the natural phenomenon and its importance. Then the factors involved (animals, chemical reactions, geography, geological forces, gravitational forces, human activity, ice, microorganisms, plants, rain, snow, temperature, weather conditions, wind) and the regions affected (cities, coasts, deserts, forests, islands, lakes, mountains, oceans, plains, rivers, towns, valleys) are listed.

Several subsections of text follow. "Science" explains the science behind the phenomenon in general terms understandable to the layperson. "Geography" names and describes the continents, countries, regions, or types of locations where this disaster occurs. "Prevention and Preparations" describes any measures that can be taken to prevent or predict the disaster. The steps that can be taken in advance to avoid or minimize loss of life and property are discussed, including drills, warning systems, and evacuation orders. "Rescue and Relief Efforts" explains what is done in the aftermath of the disaster to find and treat casualties. The typical wounds received and any special challenges faced by rescue workers are addressed. The efforts of relief organizations and programs are highlighted. "Impact" describes the typical short-term and long-term effects on humans, animals, property, and the environment of these disasters.

Most overview essays also include a section called "Historical Overview," offering a broad sense of the disaster type beginning with the first recorded occurrences and offering highlights of notable events up to the present day, and a box called "Milestones," listing major events, such as significant disasters, relevant scientific discoveries, and establishment dates for programs, organizations, and classification systems. All overviews end with an annotated bibliography of further sources for readers to consult.

## ■ THE DISASTERS

The overviews are followed by entries on the 100 worst disasters in history. These narrative-style essays offer facts, figures, and interesting stories. Events were chosen based on loss of life, widespread destruction, and notable circumstances. They range in time from 65,000,000 B.C.E. to 2006 and cover five continents.

Each event entry begins with a year and a general description of location or the popular designation for the disaster. Then the most accurate date and place for the event is identified. Magnitude on the Richter scale, either official or estimated, is given for earthquakes. The best speed estimate is listed for hurricanes, if available. For tornadoes, the most reliable F-rating is offered. Measure on the Volcanic Explosivity Index is provided for some eruptions. Estimated temperature in Fahrenheit or Celsius is listed for heat waves. "Result" lists the best figures for total numbers of dead or injured, people left homeless, damage, structures or acres burned, and so forth.

Each entry then provides readers with an account—before, during, and after—of the disaster, including both broad scientific and historical facts and narrative details. A section at the end of each entry entitled "For Further Information" lists books, chapters, magazines, or newspapers offering specific coverage of that particular event.

## ■ SPECIAL FEATURES

At the back of volume 3, a Glossary defines essential meteorological and geological terms, a Bibliography offers sources for more material about natural disasters, a list of Organizations and Agencies provides information about warning and relief efforts. The Time Line records major disasters and related milestones. The Category

List breaks the 100 events into disaster types, and the Geographical List organizes the events by region, country, or state. A comprehensive subject Index concludes the volume.

All articles are written by experts in the various fields of meteorological and geological studies; every essays is signed, and their names and affiliations are also listed in the front matter to volume 1. Special acknowledgment is extended to the Consultants, Marlene Bradford, Ph.D., and Robert S. Carmichael, Ph.D. for their knowledge and enthusiasm.

# CONTRIBUTORS

Amy Ackerberg-Hastings
*Iowa State University*

Richard Adler
*University of Michigan-Dearborn*

David Barratt
*Asheville, North Carolina*

Mary Etta Boulden
*Middle Tennessee State University*

Marlene Bradford
*Texas A&M University*

John A. Britton
*Francis Marion University*

Jeffrey L. Buller
*Georgia Southern University*

Edmund J. Campion
*University of Tennessee*

Robert S. Carmichael
*University of Iowa*

Nicholas Casner
*Boise State University*

Gilbert T. Cave
*Lakeland Community College*

Paul J. Chara, Jr.
*Loras College*

Monish R. Chatterjee
*Binghamton University, SUNY*

Jaime S. Colome
*Cal Poly State University, San Luis Obispo*

M. Casey Diana
*University of Illinois at Urbana-Champaign*

Gordon Neal Diem
*ADVANCE Education and Development Institute*

Margaret A. Dodson
*Boise Independent Schools, Idaho*

Colleen M. Driscoll
*Villanova University*

John M. Dunn
*Forest High School
Ocala, Florida*

Mary Bosch Farone
*Middle Tennessee State University*

Bonnie L. Ford
*Sacramento City College*

Soraya Ghayourmanesh
*Nassau Community College*

Sheldon Goldfarb
*University of British Columbia*

Nancy M. Gordon
*Amherst, Massachusetts*

Robert F. Gorman
*Southwest Texas State University*

Daniel G. Graetzer
*University of Washington Medical Center*

Hans G. Graetzer
*South Dakota State University*

Don M. Greene
*Baylor University*

Johnpeter Horst Grill
*Mississippi State University*

Irwin Halfond
*McKendree College*

C. Alton Hassell
*Baylor University*

Charles Haynes
*University of Alabama*

Diane Andrews Henningfeld
*Adrian College*

Mark C. Herman
*Edison Community College*

Jane F. Hill
*Bethesda, Maryland*

William Hoffman
*Fort Myers, Florida*

Robert M. Hordon
*Rutgers University*

Raymond Pierre Hylton
*Virginia Union University*

Karen N. Kähler
*Pasadena, California*

Victor Lindsey
*East Central University*

Donald W. Lovejoy
*Palm Beach Atlantic University*

David C. Lukowitz
*Hamline University*

Dana P. McDermott
*Chicago*

Michelle C. K. McKowen
*New York City*

Louise Magoon
*Fort Wayne, Indiana*

Carl Henry Marcoux
*University of California, Riverside*

Howard Meredith
*University of Science and Arts of Oklahoma*

Randall L. Milstein
*Oregon State University*

Lauren Mitchell
*Pasadena, California*

William V. Moore
*College of Charleston*

Otto H. Muller
*Alfred University*

Anthony Newsome
*Middle Tennessee State University*

Robert J. Paradowski
*Rochester Institute of Technology*

Nis Petersen
*New Jersey City University*

Erika E. Pilver
*Westfield State College*

Steven J. Ramold
*University of Nebraska-Lincoln*

Donald F. Reaser
*The University of Texas at Arlington*

Betty Richardson
*Southern Illinois University, Edwardsville*

Edward A. Riedinger
*Ohio State University Libraries*

Charles W. Rogers
*Southwestern Oklahoma State University*

Billy Scott
*Fordham University*

Rose Secrest
*Chattanooga, Tennessee*

James B. Seymour, Jr.
*Texas A&M University*

R. Baird Shuman
*University of Illinois at Urbana-Champaign*

Gary W. Siebein
*University of Florida*

## Contributors

Donald C. Simmons, Jr.
*Mississippi Humanities Council*

Roger Smith
*Portland, Oregon*

David M. Soule
*Compass Point Research*

Kenneth F. Steele, Jr.
*University of Arkansas*

Joan C. Stevenson
*Western Washington University*

Dion C. Stewart
*Adams State College*

Toby R. Stewart
*Adams State College*

Eric R. Swanson
*University of Texas at San Antonio*

Sue Tarjan
*Santa Cruz, California*

Robert D. Ubriaco, Jr.
*Illinois Wesleyan University*

Rosa Alvarez Ulloa
*San Diego, California*

Winifred Whelan
*St. Bonaventure University*

Edwin G. Wiggins
*Webb Institute*

Mary Catherine Wilheit
*Texas A&M University*

Richard L. Wilson
*University of Tennessee at Chattanooga*

Lisa A. Wroble
*Redford Township District Library, Michigan*

Jay R. Yett
*Orange Coast College*

# COMPLETE LIST OF CONTENTS

## Volume 1

# Volume 2

Contents. . . . . . . . . . . . . . . . . . . . . xxvii
Complete List of Contents. . . . . . . . . . . . . xxix

■ **EVENTS**

■ INDEXES

# Volume 3

Contents . . . . . . . . . . . . . . . . . . . . . . . . . . xli
Complete List of Contents . . . . . . . . . . . . . . . . . . . xliii

## ■ APPENDIXES

## ■ INDEXES

# NOTABLE NATURAL DISASTERS

# Avalanches

**FACTORS INVOLVED:** Chemical reactions, geography,
geological forces, gravitational forces, human
activity, ice, plants, rain, snow, temperature, weather
conditions, wind
**REGIONS AFFECTED:** Cities, forests, mountains, towns,
valleys

## DEFINITION

An avalanche is a large amount of snow, ice, rock, or earth that becomes dislodged and moves rapidly down a sloped surface or over a
precipice. Avalanches are generally influenced by one or several natural forces but are increasingly being initiated by human activities.
Landslide avalanches are defined as the massive downward and outward movement of some of the material that forms the slope of an incline. Unqualified use of the term "avalanche" in the English lan-
guage, however, most often refers to a snow avalanche and generally
refers to movements big and fast enough to endanger life or property. Avalanche accidents resulting in death, injury, or destruction
have increased tremendously in direct proportion to the increased
popularity of winter recreational activities in mountainous regions.

## SCIENCE

The term "avalanche" relates to large masses of snow, ice, rock, soil,
mud, and/or other materials that descend rapidly down an incline
such as a hillside or mountain slope. Precipices, very steep or overhanging areas of earth or rock, are also areas prone to avalanche activity. Landslide avalanches are downward and outward movements
of the material that forms the slope of a hillside or mountain. General lay usage of the term "avalanche" often relates to large masses of
snow or ice, while the term "landslide" is usually restricted to the
movement of rock and soil and includes a broad range of velocities.
Slow movements cause gradual damage, such as rupture of buried utility lines, whereas high-velocity avalanches require immediate evacuation of an area to ensure safety.

A landslide avalanche begins when a portion of a hillside weakens

## MILESTONES

**218 B.C.E.:** Hannibal loses 20,000 men, 2,000 horses, and several elephants in a huge avalanche near Col de la Traversette in the Italian Alps.

**1478:** About 60 soldiers of the Duke of Milan are killed by an avalanche while crossing the mountains near Saint Gotthard Pass in the Italian Alps.

**September, 1618:** An avalanche kills 1,500 inhabitants of Plurs, Switzerland.

**1689:** A series of avalanches kills more than 300 residents in Saas, Switzerland, and surrounding communities.

**January, 1718:** The town of Leukerbad, Switzerland, is destroyed by two avalanches that leave more than 55 dead and many residents seriously injured.

**September, 1806:** Four villages are destroyed and 800 residents are killed when an avalanche descends Rossberg Peak in the Swiss Alps.

**July, 1892:** St. Gervais and La Fayet, Swiss resorts, are destroyed when a huge avalanche speeds down Mont Blanc, killing 140 residents and tourists.

**March, 1910:** An avalanche sweeps through the train station in Wellington, Washington State, destroying 3 snowbound passenger trains and killing 96.

**December, 1916:** Heavy snows result in avalanches that kill more than 10,000 Italian and Austrian soldiers located in the Tirol section of the Italian-Austrian Alps.

**January, 1951:** A series of avalanches leaves 240 dead; the village of Vals, Switzerland, is completely destroyed.

**January, 1954:** In one of the worst avalanches in Austrian history, 145 people are killed over a 10-mile area.

**1962:** Melting snow rushes down the second-highest peak in South America at speeds in excess of 100 miles per hour, killing around 4,000 in Peru.

**April, 1970:** A hospital in Sallanches, France, is destroyed by an avalanche that kills 70, most of them children.

**1971:** An earthquake unleashes a huge avalanche of snow and ice, killing 600 and destroying Chungar, Peru, and surrounding villages.

**1982:** Thirteen students and teachers are killed by an avalanche in Salzburg, Austria.

**June, 1994:** An earthquake in the Huila region of Colombia causes avalanches and mudslides that leave 13,000 residents homeless, 2,000 trapped, and 1,000 dead.

**November, 1995:** A series of avalanches kills 43 climbers in Nepal.

**March, 1997:** A park geologist and a volunteer are killed by an avalanche while working on a project to monitor Yellowstone National Park geothermal features.

**1998:** Three avalanches in southeastern British Columbia, Canada, leave 8 dead and several wounded.

**February, 1999:** The Galtür avalanche in Austria kills 38 and traps 2,000.

progressively to the point where it is no longer able to support the weight of the hillside itself. This weakness may be caused when rainfall or floodwater elevates the overall water content of the slope, thus reducing the sheer strength of the slope materials. Landslides are most common in areas where erosion is constantly wearing away at the local terrain, but they can also be initiated by events such as earthquakes and loud noises. Some landslides move only sporadically—during certain seasons of the year—and may lie dormant for decades, centuries, or millennia; their extremely slow movements may go unnoticed for long periods of time. Slow-moving landslides are distinguished from creep—the slow change of a mountain's or hill's dimensions from prolonged exposure to stress or high temperatures—in that they have distinct boundaries and have at least some stable ground.

Natural avalanches can be triggered when additional stressors are provided in the form of the added weight of additional snow, either fresh snowfall or windblown snow, or when the cohesive strength of the snowpack naturally decreases, which serves to weaken the bonds between particles of snow. Artificial avalanches may be triggered when humans, animals, or machinery begin the downslide, due to their contribution of additional stress to the snow. Many avalanches in outdoor recreational areas are triggered by the weight of a single skier or the impact of small masses of snow or ice falling from above. Explosives can also trigger an artificial avalanche, either intentionally or unintentionally. When explosives are detonated to knock down potentially dangerous snow at a prescribed time and location, such as for maintenance of highways or ski areas, the public is temporarily evacuated from the area.

Ground that has remained relatively stable for as little as one hundred years or possibly as long as tens of thousands of years may begin to slide following alteration of the natural slope by human development, such as during grading for roads or building projects on hillsides. Landslide avalanches can also be started by deep cutting into the slope and removal of support necessary for materials higher up the slope, or by overloading the lower part of the slope with the excavated materials. Some have occurred where development has altered groundwater conditions.

### GEOGRAPHY

Snow avalanches require a snow layer that has the potential for instability and a sloped surface that is steep enough to enable a slide to continue its downhill momentum once it has started. Slopes with inclines between 25 and 55 degrees represent the broadest range for avalanche danger, but a majority of avalanches originate on inclines between 30 and 45 degrees. Angles above 55 degrees are generally too steep to collect significant amounts of snow, as the snow tends to roll down the hillside very rapidly without accumulating. Slope angles of less than 25 degrees are generally safe, except for the remote possibility of very slow snow avalanches in extremely wet conditions.

When a layer of snow lies on a sloped surface, the constant force of gravity causes it to creep slowly down the slope. When a force imposed on a snow layer is large enough, a failure is triggered somewhere within the snow, thus stimulating the avalanche to begin to move rapidly downhill. There are two distinct types of failures that can occur within the snow prior to an avalanche. When a cohesionless snow layer rests on a slope steeper than its angle of repose, it can cause a loose snow avalanche, which is often also called a point-release avalanche. This can actually be triggered by as little as one grain of snow slipping out of place and dislodging other grains below it, causing a chain reaction that continues to grow in size as the accumulated mass slips down the hill. The point-release avalanche generally appears as an inverted *V* shape on the snow and is typically limited to only the surface layer of snow cover. In this type of avalanche, the snow has little internal cohesion, no obvious fracture line, and no clear division where the sliding snow separates from the layers underneath.

In contrast, when snow fails as a cohesive unit, an obvious brittle fracture line appears and an entire layer or slab of snow is set in motion. Because creep formation causes the snow layer to be stretched out along the slope, the fracture releases stored elastic energy. The release of this energy may cause the fracture to spread across an entire slope or basin. Failure may occur deep within the snow layer, allowing a good portion or nearly all the snow to be included in the avalanche. Slab avalanches are often larger and more destructive than point-release avalanches and can continue to slide on weaker layers underneath or actually upon the ground itself.

The specific shape of the slope may reflect the level of avalanche danger, with hazards being highest when snow accumulates on straight, open, and moderately steep slopes. One classic law of avalanches for mountaineers is that they face the least danger while moving on ridges, somewhat more danger while moving on the valley floor, and the most danger when moving directly upon the slope itself. Snow on a convex slope is more prone to avalanches, as it comes under tension because it tends to stretch more tightly over the curve of the hill. When coming down a convex slope, mountaineers may not know how steep the slope is until they pass the curve that temporarily obstructed their view and then discover that they are farther down on the face than is safe. Bowls and cirques (steep-walled basins) have a shape that tends to accumulate snow deposited by the wind. Once an avalanche begins, it most often spreads to the entire face and dumps large quantities of snow into the area below. Couloirs (mountainside gorges) are enticing to climbers because they offer a direct route up a mountain, but they are susceptible to snow movement because they create natural chutes. Forested slopes offer some avalanche protection, but they do not guarantee safety. While slides are less likely to originate within a dense forest, they have been known to crush through even very high-density tree areas. Shattered trees provide clear evidence that a previous avalanche has occurred on the mountainside. A slope that has only bushes and small trees growing on it may indicate that the incline has experienced avalanches so often that the timber is not being given a chance to regrow.

While avalanches can occur anywhere in the world where snow falls on slopes, some countries and regions are prone to such events. In Europe, the Alps—a mountain range stretching through Italy, Austria, Germany, Switzerland, and France—has experienced many devastating avalanches. The Andes mountain range in South America has produced avalanches in Peru. In North America, areas of the Pacific Northwest—particularly Washington State, British Columbia, and Alaska—are most often affected.

## PREVENTION AND PREPARATIONS

Snow avalanches are among the main hazards facing outdoor winter sports enthusiasts who drive through a mountain pass in an automobile or snowmobile, or hike, climb, snowshoe, hunt, or ski along a mountainside. The relative level of avalanche hazard and the conditions that occur to create the hazard at any given time are relatively easy for a trained professional to identify. The local news media generally report avalanche danger in heavily populated and well-traveled recreational areas. Unfortunately, there currently is no completely valid and reliable way to predict precisely where and when an avalanche will occur. Novice mountaineers can certainly benefit by being able to recognize the formation of different types of snow crystals and hazardous terrain and weather. They should keep in mind that avalanches can sweep even on perfectly level ground for more than 1 mile after the snow has reached the bottom of a slope.

Avalanche hazards can be assessed by examining the snow for new avalanches in the area. Cracks in hard snow may outline an unstable slab as snow settles with the weight of a person moving on it. The sound of a loud thump may indicate that a hard slab is nearly ready to release. Snow stability can be tested by probing with a ski pole to feel for layers of varying solidity or by digging a pit to examine the layers for weakness. Some excellent advice for winter travelers is to always stop to rest or set up camp outside the potential reach of an avalanche.

Avalanche research has consistently shown that approximately 80 percent of avalanches occur during or just after a storm. Avalanche

*Peru's Mount Huascarán during an avalanche.* (National Oceanic and Atmospheric Administration)

danger escalates when snowfall exceeds a level of 1 inch per hour or an accumulation of 12 inches or more in a single storm. Rapid changes in wind and temperature also significantly increase avalanche danger. Storms that begin with a low ambient temperature and dry snow on the ground and are followed immediately by a rapidly rising temperature are more likely to set off avalanche conditions. Snow that is dry tends to form poor chemical bonds and thus does not possess the strength to support the heavier, wet snow that rapidly accumulates on the surface. Rainstorms or spring weather with warm winds and cloudy nights creates the possibility of a wet snow avalanche and causes a "percolating" effect of the water into the snow.

The manner in which the sun and wind hit a slope can often provide valuable clues regarding potential avalanche danger. In the Northern Hemisphere, slopes that face south receive the most sun. The increased solar heat makes the snow settle and stabilize more quickly than on north-facing slopes. Generally speaking, south-facing slopes are safer in winter, but there are certainly many exceptions to this rule as determined by local factors. South-facing slopes also tend to release their avalanches sooner after a storm. Thus, slides that begin on southern slopes may indicate that slopes facing other directions may soon follow suit. As warmer days arrive near the end of winter, south-facing slopes may actually become more prone to wet snow avalanches, making the north-facing slopes safer. North-facing slopes receive very little or no sun in the winter, so consolidation of the snowpack takes much longer, if it occurs at all. Colder temperatures may create weak layers of snow, thus making northern slopes more likely to slide in midwinter. It is important to note that these guidelines should be reversed for mountainous areas south of the equator.

Windward slopes that face into the snow tend to be safer because they retain less snow—the wind blows it away. The snow that remains tends to become more compact through the blast of the wind. Lee slopes, which face the same direction the wind is blowing, collect snow rapidly during storms and on windy days as the snow blows over from the windward slopes. This results in cornice formation on the lee side of ridges, snow that is deeper and less consolidated, and the formation of wind slabs that can be prone to avalanches. Snow formation often indicates the prevailing wind direction, following the general rule that cornices face the same direction that the wind is blowing.

Attempts have been made to prevent avalanche damage by building artificial supporting structures or transplanting trees within anticipated avalanche zones. The direct impact of an avalanche has been effectively blocked by diversion structures such as dams, sheds, and tunnels in areas where avalanches repeatedly strike. Structural damage can be limited by the construction of various types of fencing and by building splitting wedges, *V*-shaped masonry walls that are designed to split an avalanche around a structure located behind it. Techniques have been developed to predict avalanche occurrence by analyzing the relationships between meteorological and snow-cover factors, which are often reported through the media. Zones of known or predicted avalanche danger are generally taken into account during commercial development of a mountainous area. The avalanche danger of unstable slope accumulations is often prevented through detonation, from explosives similar to grenades to the sending out of controlled acoustic waves.

### RESCUE AND RELIEF EFFORTS

Search and rescue experts recommend that, when individuals know they are about to become caught in an avalanche, they should make as much noise as possible and discard all equipment, including packs and skis. They should try to avoid being swept away by grabbing onto anything stable, such as large rocks or trees. Those who become caught in a slide should attempt to stay on the snow surface by making swimming motions with the arms and legs or by rolling. It is also recommended to attempt to close the mouth in the event that the head begins to fall below the snow surface. If victims anticipate becoming completely buried and no longer moving with the snow, they should attempt to create a breathing space by putting their hands and elbows in front of their faces and inhaling deeply before the snow stops in order to expand the ribs. All available oxygen and energy should be conserved if victims anticipate that rescuers will soon begin making appropriate search and rescue efforts.

Avalanche search and rescue efforts should begin as soon as possible by companions of the victim, who should generally anticipate that there will not be time for professional help to arrive. Despite the shock of the moment, rescue procedures should begin immediately by noting and marking—with an object such as a ski pole—three critical positions on the snow. These positions include the point where the victim was first caught in moving snow, the point where the victim disappeared beneath the snow surface, and the point where the moving surface of the avalanche eventually stopped. Accurately noting these three areas greatly reduces the area that needs to be searched, thus providing an increased chance of a successful search. Rescue beacons, small electronic devices which should be secured to all persons traveling together in a winter excursion party, have proven to be very effective tools in finding buried victims. The beacons can be switched to either transmit or receive signals at a radio frequency that is set to the transmit mode during the initial movement. Searchers who switch their beacons to receive mode immediately after an incident can often locate a buried victim in just a few short minutes. Procedures for avalanche rescue, such as setting up a probe line, have been established by search and rescue organizations and should be reviewed prior to a trip by all persons participating in winter activities within a potential avalanche zone.

## IMPACT

The impact pressures resulting from high-speed avalanches and landslides can completely destroy or harm human and animal life and property. About one-third of avalanche victims die from the impact; the remaining two-thirds die from suffocation and hypothermia. Movement of snow and other debris is most destructive when it is able to generate extremely high speeds. Small to medium avalanches can hit with impact pressures of 1 to 5 tons per square meter, which is generally enough force to damage or destroy wood-frame structures. Larger avalanches can generate forces that can exceed 100 tons per square meter, which is easily enough to uproot mature forested areas and destroy large concrete structures.

Measurements have shown that highly turbulent dry snow or dry powder creates avalanche speeds averaging 115 to 148 feet (35 to 45 meters) per second, with some velocities being clocked as high as 223 to 279 feet (68 to 85 meters) per second. These high speeds are possible only in dry powder avalanches because these avalanches incorporate large amounts of air within the moving snow, thus serving to reduce internal frictional forces. Wet snow avalanches comprise liquid or snow that is very dense, which creates less turbulent movement once the slide begins. With a reduction in turbulence, a more flowing type of motion is generated, and speeds are generally reduced to approximately 66 to 98 feet (20 to 30 meters) per second.

Persons who do not live in mountainous regions might mistakenly believe that damage caused by an avalanche is minimal when compared to the destruction caused by other environmental hazards such as tornadoes and floods. However, the frequency of accidents resulting in destruction, injury, or death has risen tremendously in direct proportion to the increased popularity of winter recreational activities in mountainous areas. An estimated 150 to 200 avalanche-related deaths occur per year, but it should be noted that these avalanche data are systematically and accurately recorded mainly in developed countries in North America, Europe, and northern Asia.

## HISTORICAL OVERVIEW

Considered one of the greatest military commanders in the history of the world, Hannibal and his North African army were no match for the natural forces unleashed in 218 B.C.E. when an avalanche descended upon his invading army of thirty-eight thousand soldiers, eight thousand horsemen, and thirty-seven elephants. The rapidly moving snowmass, which wreaked havoc at Col de la Traversette pass in the Italian Alps and claimed nearly 40 percent of Hannibal's fighting force, dealt the general one of the most devastating losses of his entire military career. The historic and horrendous tragedy experienced by Hannibal was also one of the first documented avalanches in European history.

Like so many before and since, Hannibal either was unaware of the dangerous physical environment created by the heavy snows or chose to ignore the danger. Thousands of avalanches occur annually worldwide, but most cause little damage. Each year, however, avalanches consistently claim about 150 lives and cause millions in property losses.

The European Alps, where the lives of Hannibal's troops were claimed, have been the site of the most deadly avalanches in recorded history, although the greatest number occur in the much more sparsely populated Himalayas, Andes, and Alaska. During World War I an estimated 40,000 to 80,000 soldiers were killed and maimed in the Alps by avalanches caused by the sounds and explosions of combat.

Such massive loss of life, however, is not representative of avalanche disasters. In a more typical year the country of Switzerland, for example, has an average avalanche death rate of fewer than 25. An 1892 avalanche that destroyed the Swiss resort towns of St. Gervais and La Fayet, killing 140 residents and tourists, was considered a fairly deadly and unusual occurrence. As one of the most avalanche-prone nations, Switzerland committed considerable resources after the early 1900's to identify ways to avoid the loss of property and life. The leading avalanche research center in Europe is the Swiss Federal Snow and Avalanche Research Unit, which takes considerable pride in its successful Avalanche Warning System. Similar research programs are located in the United States, Japan, and other countries.

Despite the best efforts and intentions of warning systems, avalanches continue to claim the lives of unsuspecting victims each year. Even the most highly trained and skilled scientists are often vulnerable to the deadly force of avalanches. Many of the individuals killed by the 1980 Mount St. Helens volcanic explosion and the resulting 250-mile-per-hour avalanche, the largest in recorded history, were scientists on location to study the volcano. In March, 1997, a park geologist and a volunteer were killed by an avalanche while working on a project to monitor Yellowstone National Park geothermal features.

As a result of years of research and data collection, however, scientists have identified ways of diminishing the potential for destruction and loss of life resulting from avalanches. Federal, state, regional, and local governments may coordinate efforts to detect and identify potentially unstable snow-covered slopes by monitoring weather conditions; geographic data available through photogrammetry, the science and art of deducing the physical dimensions of objects from measurements on photographs; and satellite imagery.

*Daniel G. Graetzer*
*Donald C. Simmons, Jr.*

**BIBLIOGRAPHY**

Armstrong, Betsy R., Knox Williams, and Richard L. Armstrong. *The Avalanche Book.* Rev. and updated ed. Golden, Colo.: Fulcrum, 1992. An excellent text highlighting the damage assessment of all major avalanches in North America.

Cupp, D. "Avalanche: Winter's White Death." *National Geographic* 162 (September, 1982): 280-305. A documentation of the March, 1982, avalanche tragedy at California's Alpine Meadows ski resort that claimed seven lives, with heroic rescuers saving the lives of four others. Also reports on how science attempts to deal with avalanches and to rescue quickly those caught in their paths.

Ferguson, Sue, and Edward R. LaChapelle. *The ABCs of Avalanche*

*Safety.* 3d ed. Seattle: Mountaineers Books, 2003. This very readable applied science text discusses different types of avalanches, how they form, and where they can be predicted to occur, in addition to giving general guidelines on safety when traveling in mountainous regions.

Fredston, Jill. *Snowstruck: In the Grip of Avalanches.* Orlando, Fla.: Harcourt, 2005. The author, an avalanche expert with the Alaska Mountain Safety Center, writes from her own experiences with forecasting, prevention, education, and rescue.

Graydon, E. *Mountaineering: The Freedom of the Hill.* Seattle: Mountaineers Books, 1992. A presentation of both introductory and advanced information on the sport of mountaineering, with much practical information on avalanches and other hazards of snow travel and climbing.

Jenkins, McKay. *The White Death: Tragedy and Heroism in an Avalanche Zone.* New York: Random House, 2000. Jenkins uses a description of the deaths of five climbers in Wyoming in 1969 to frame his natural history of avalanches.

Logan, Nick, and Dale Atkins. *The Snowy Torrents: Avalanche Accidents in the United States, 1980-86.* Denver: Colorado Geological Survey, Department of Natural Resources, State of Colorado, 1996. This government document examines avalanche occurrences in the United States between 1980 and 1986.

Mears, Arthur I. *Avalanche Forecasting Methods, Highway 550.* Denver: Colorado Department of Transportation, 1996. In this booklet Mears discusses avalanche control and his studies in Colorado performed in cooperation with the Federal Highway Administration.

National Research Council Panel on Snow Avalanches. *Snow Avalanche Hazards and Mitigation in the United States.* Washington, D.C.: National Academy Press, 1990. Edited by committee chair D. B. Prior and panel chair B. Voight, this government report assesses avalanches and other related natural disasters in the United States and the efficiency of relief efforts by the government.

Parfit, M. "Living with Natural Hazards." *National Geographic* 194 (July, 1998): 2-39. An excellent write-up on natural hazard areas within the United States and some personal histories of persons whose lives have been affected by them.

*Avalanches*

USDA Forest Service. *Snow Avalanche: General Rules for Avoiding and Surviving Snow Avalanches.* Portland, Oreg.: USDA Forest Service, Pacific Northwest Region, 1982. Provides general guidelines for both recreational and serious outdoor enthusiasts for avoiding and surviving snow avalanches.

# BLIZZARDS, FREEZES, ICE STORMS, AND HAIL

**FACTORS INVOLVED:** Geography, gravitational forces, ice, rain, snow, temperature, weather conditions, wind

**REGIONS AFFECTED:** Cities, coasts, deserts, forests, islands, lakes, mountains, plains, towns, valleys

## DEFINITION

Blizzards, freezes, ice storms, and hail are significant weather events that occur infrequently. When they do occur, they may seriously disrupt or curtail transportation, business, and domestic activities; destroy agricultural produce; cause tens of millions of dollars in damages; and result in significant loss of life to humans and animals. Blizzards, freezes, and ice storms are winter storms, while hail and hailstorms occur in the warmer weather of late spring, summer, and fall.

## SCIENCE

Blizzards, ice storms, and hail are significant weather events associated with dynamic interactions between masses of air. These interactions are influenced by altitude, latitude, temperature, moisture, geography, geology, cyclonic rotations, and the jet streams, as these air masses and the jet streams move from place to place.

Blizzards are severe winter storms that may occur when temperatures are 10 degrees Fahrenheit or lower, when winds blow at a minimum of 35 miles per hour, and when there is sufficient blowing or newly fallen snow to reduce visibility to less than 0.25 mile for at least three hours. Blizzards are produced by strong frontal cyclones that bring low temperatures and blowing snow. Blizzards in the Arctic, Antarctic, mountainous regions, or the continental tundra may have winds that blow in excess of 100 miles per hour, with subzero temperatures creating the legendary blizzards of the polar seas and polar areas.

Blizzard snow as well as the perpetual snow cover often found on

## MILESTONES

**1643-1653:** Europe experiences its severest winters after the Ice Age.

**July 13, 1788:** A severe hailstorm damages French wheat crops.

**early October, 1846:** An early blizzard in the Sierra Nevada traps the Donner Party.

**January 23, 1867:** The East River in New York City freezes.

**March 11-14, 1888:** The Great Blizzard of 1888 strikes the eastern United States; 400 die.

**February 17, 1962:** Major storms blanket Germany; 343 are killed.

**January 29-31, 1966:** The worst blizzard in seventy years strikes the eastern United States.

**February 4-11, 1972:** Heavy snow falls on Iran; 1,000 perish.

**December 1-2, 1974:** Nineteen inches of snow falls on Detroit in the worst snowstorm in eighty-eight years.

**January 28-29 and March 10-12, 1977:** Blizzards ravage the Midwest; Buffalo reports 160 inches of snow.

**January 25-26, 1978:** A major snowstorm strikes the midwestern United States, with 31 inches of snow and 18-foot drifts.

**February 5-7, 1978:** The worst blizzard in the history of New England strikes the Northeast; eastern Massachusetts receives 50 inches of snow, and winds reach 110 miles per hour. All business stops for five days.

**January 12-14, 1979:** Blizzards in the Midwest yield 20 inches of snow, with temperatures at -20 degrees Fahrenheit; 100 die.

**February 18-19, 1979:** Snow blankets the District of Columbia.

**March 1-2, 1980:** The mid-Atlantic region experiences a blizzard.

**February 5-28, 1984:** A series of snowstorms strikes Colorado and Utah.

**March 29, 1984:** A snowstorm covers much of the East Coast.

**January 7, 1996:** The East Coast is hit by another big snowstorm.

**May 10-11, 1996:** A sudden and intense blizzard on Mount Everest, Earth's highest peak, traps climbers, killing 9 and leaving 4 others with severe frostbite.

**April 1, 1997:** The April Fool's storm strikes the Northeast.

**January 5-12, 1998:** A major ice storm covers northeastern Canada.

**February-March, 1999:** Heavy snowfall in the Alps triggers avalanches.

**January 20-24, 2005:** A heavy blizzard blankets New England with snow up to 40 inches in some places, shutting down Logan International Airport in Boston.

**January 12-16, 2007:** A freezing winter storm moves across the United States causing extensive power outages and 65 related deaths, many of them in Oklahoma.

high mountaintops, even in the tropics, results from the condensation and freezing of moisture contained within air masses that are forced up and over the mountains in a process called orographic lifting. Snow may also form when mid-Atlantic cyclones and upper-air troughs move over mountainous locations.

A ground blizzard is one in which previously fallen snow is blown around, often accumulating in large snow drifts that may exceed 10 feet in height. A whiteout is an especially dangerous type of blizzard in which visibility may be reduced to the point where the horizon, one's surroundings, and the sky become indistinguishable. During such blizzards, exposed humans and animals often suffer from disorientation and loss of the sense of direction.

There are several meteorological mechanisms that produce snow, potentially resulting in blizzards. There must be a constant inflow of moisture to feed growing ice crystals within appropriate clouds in the upper atmosphere. Convection may lift some of the moisture to higher, cooler regions of the atmosphere, where condensation may produce snow—or rain that will become snow—as it falls through cold atmospheric regions. Ice crystals falling from higher clouds may "seed" lower clouds, resulting in snowfall. Polar air masses from the north pick up significant quantities of moisture when they blow across relatively warmer bodies of water, such as the Great Lakes. This moisture may then dissipate into huge volumes of snow downwind, on land, creating blizzards. The Pacific Ocean is the source of moisture for most snowfalls and blizzards west of the Rocky Mountains; the Gulf of Mexico and the tropical portion of the north Atlantic Ocean are generally the sources of moisture for snowfalls and blizzards in the central and eastern portions of the United States and Canada.

When deep low-pressure systems (hurricanes) form over the eastern United States and approach the Atlantic Ocean, they can grow explosively as they are moving offshore, parallel to the coastline. Because winds around a hurricane generally blow in a counterclockwise direction, snow or rain, or both, will be accompanied by strong northeast winds, creating in winter a type of blizzard known as a northeaster. In summer the same systems can bring torrential rains, which may last for many days. Most major snowstorms and blizzards of the mid-Atlantic and New England states come from northeasters. If the system as it moves parallel to the coast should move slowly, or stall completely, the affected land areas may be battered for hours—or even days—by blizzard conditions and large amounts of snow or rain.

Ice storms are among the most destructive of all winter storms. They are caused by rain (liquid water) falling from an above-freezing layer of upper air to a layer of below-freezing air on or near the earth's surface. The freezing rain coats everything with a layer of ice, called glaze. If the rain continues to fall, and continues to freeze, staggering amounts of ice may build up on roads, bridges, trees, utility poles, transmission towers, power lines, and buildings. The ice may vary in thickness from 0.04 inch to as much as 6 inches. Upon slight warming by the sun, ice on superstructures of bridges, buildings, power lines, and trees may loosen and fall in chunks or very large pieces known as ice slabs. This falling ice threatens the safety of anyone or anything below. Roads and bridges are generally closed when this danger exists. Ice storms cripple all modes of transportation, cause roadways and other thoroughfares to be closed, and create extremely hazardous conditions for humans and animals.

Hail is sometimes confused with sleet; they are not the same thing. Sleet is made of frozen raindrops that fall during winter storms. Hail is composed of balls of ice of varying shapes and sizes that fall from the interior of cumulonimbus clouds during thunderstorms. Thunderstorms are necessary for the production of hail. Atmospheric instability associated with thunderstorms creates the powerful updrafts and downdrafts necessary for the production of hail. Hail and hailstorms occur not during the winter but rather during the late spring, summer, and fall. During these seasons, heating of the earth's surface by the sun creates warm, rising air currents called thermals or updrafts, in a process called convection. The rising air masses contain moisture, salt particles from ocean spray, particles of kaolinite clay, volcanic dust, sulfur oxides, and other kinds of particles, which are collectively called aerosols.

As the rising air masses encounter the lower temperatures of the upper atmosphere, the moisture condenses, forming cumulonimbus clouds. Within these clouds are residual moisture present in a liquid, supercooled state; ice crystals; and aerosols. Supercooled water is water that remains in a liquid state at temperatures below which it would usually freeze. The name cumulonimbus means "heaped cloud which may produce precipitation." These clouds, also called thunderheads, are towering, often extending vertically thousands of feet into the atmosphere. To the observer on earth they often appear puffy and lumpy and, because of upper-level wind shear, develop anvil-shaped tops. Their undersides often look dark and foreboding. Cumulonimbi are the clouds of greatest vertical extent, often measuring 10 miles or more from top to bottom.

Drops of atmospheric moisture brought by updrafts into the cold interiors of cumulonimbus clouds become supercooled and may begin to coalesce with and freeze around existing ice crystals or aerosols. Ice tends to freeze around particulate matter or other ice crystals, both of which serve as freezing nuclei, or nucleating agents. A nucleating agent is a substance that catalyzes the freezing of supercooled water into ice. Aerosols serve as nucleating agents. Updrafts within the clouds may lift the newly formed ice pellets to higher, cooler levels containing more supercooled water, which freezes them further, making them larger and heavier. When they are heavy enough for their movement to overcome the strength of the updraft, and the downward acceleration of gravity becomes the predominant force, they fall out of a cloud as hailstones. Downdrafts within a cloud may also push hailstones out and downward. Prior to exiting a cloud, hail may be bounced in trampoline fashion up and down within a cloud by competing updrafts and downdrafts. With each ascent, more supercooled water may freeze onto the ice pellets, making them still larger and heavier. Hailstones freeze in layers that look much like those of an onion. An examination of a cut hailstone shows these concentric layers. The number of layers provides a record of the number of times the hailstone was tossed up and down within the parent cloud. Hail may pass through several developmental stages and appear in pea-sized pieces called graupel, or soft hail. Hailstones may also be the size of baseballs or grapefruit.

The most frequent time for the production of hail is between 3 and 4 P.M., with almost all hailstorms occuring between 2 and 6 P.M., times that correspond to the period of maximum heating of the earth's surface by the sun. The development of the largest hailstones requires powerful updraft velocities and many trips up and down within a cloud. The largest documented hailstone fell in Coffeyville, Kansas, in September of 1970. It had a circumference of almost 18 inches and weighed almost 2 pounds. An updraft velocity of almost 400 miles per hour would be required to create a hailstone that size. In the United States, weather observers and reporters report hailstone sizes either in inches or in descriptive terms such as "quarter" (1 inch), "chicken egg" (2 inches), and "softball" (4.5 inches).

No one knows the maximum potential size of a hailstone. There are undocumented reports of basketball-sized hail having fallen in Manhattan, Illinois. Downdrafts from clouds may be powerful enough to slam the surface of the earth with wind gusts that exceed hurricane force, damaging property and causing airplane crashes. Powerful downdrafts are called microbursts, and they are second only to pilot error as the leading cause of airplane crashes. The amount of hail produced at any one time can be staggering. There are confirmed records of hail accumulations several feet deep, covering many square miles. It is not uncommon for snowplows to be used during the summer to clear haildrifts from roads. Melting hail is responsible for stream flooding and extensive property damage in many areas subject to hailstorms.

There are periodic reports of falling hail containing unusual items such as toads, frogs, snakes, worms, peaches and other fruits, fish, and even ducks. An explanation for such events suggests that powerful updrafts in appropriate places could be strong enough to sweep up and convectively transfer these objects from the surface of the earth into cumulonimbus clouds, where they would be coated and recoated with ice prior to falling to earth.

### GEOGRAPHY
Blizzards occur in regions where there is an abundance of moisture that can be transformed into snow and where temperatures are low

enough to both encourage snow production and sustain falling or previously fallen snow. Additionally, blizzard-prone areas are affected by jet-stream-accompanied cyclonic events, such as cyclonic vorticity, troughs, and severe frontal cyclones, which may develop in conjunction with jet streams, causing higher-than-usual winds. These systems create storms at other times of the year; however, during winter months they result in heavy snowfall and other blizzard conditions. Blizzards occur most often in Canada, the northeastern U.S. plains states, the mid- and north Atlantic states, and downwind of the Great Lakes. Blizzards also occur in polar areas and at high altitudes at or near the summits of mountains, particularly in north, central, eastern, and western Europe.

Ice storms generally occur in a broad belt stretching from Nebraska, Oklahoma, and Kansas eastward into the mid-Atlantic and northeastern states. They can occur in any other places that experience winter weather. Ice storms are among the most devastating and deadly of all winter storms. A 1952 ice storm covered Louisiana, Arkansas, and Mississippi. It lasted from January 28 to February 4 and killed at least 22 people. During such storms an icy glaze of varying thickness coats all exposed surfaces and objects. During a November, 1940, storm in northeastern Texas, ice coatings of 6 inches and more were reported. Coatings 6 inches thick were also reported in a December, 1942, storm in New York State.

In February of 1994, an ice storm in the southeastern United States caused 9 fatalities and over $3 billion in economic damages. During that same storm, up to 4 inches of ice accumulated in some locations from Texas to North Carolina. Some utility customers were without power for a month; coping with lengthy power outages may create serious, life-threatening situations for the elderly, the very young, and the ill. An April, 1995, ice storm in Chicago resulted in the closing of Michigan Avenue, a main thoroughfare, because of great ice slabs falling from buildings and other high-rise structures.

Ice storms also cause trees to become overburdened with the weight of the ice, causing them to collapse onto power lines or other structures. When utility poles, transmission towers, and other such structures collapse because of accumulations of ice on trees, the fallen trees and utility poles and similar structures must be removed before any work on restoring power can begin. Lack of power seriously interferes with or shuts down computers, elevators, escalators, heating systems, and hospital operations, among other things. Freezing rain and ice storms occur an average of twelve days per year around the Great Lakes and the northeastern United States. Such storms also occur in Canada and Europe.

Almost 5,000 hailstorms strike the United States each year, with perhaps 500 to 700 of them producing hailstones large enough to cause damage and injury. Hail forms in thunderstorms, but not all thunderstorms produce hail. The state of Florida has the greatest annual number of thunderstorms but has the lowest hail rate in the United States. Hail is most frequently found in "Hail Alley," a region that covers parts of eastern Colorado, Nebraska, and Wyoming. Hail is also common in the high plains, the Midwest, and the Ohio Valley. Cheyenne, Wyoming, is the so-called U.S. hail capital. The Pacific shorelines of the United States have the least hail. Hail in that region is produced by thunderstorms that blow on shore during winter storms. Northern India has the greatest frequency of large hail

*Brattleboro, Vermont, is blanketed by snow during a 1941 blizzard.* (Library of Congress)

events. India also has the greatest number of human fatalities from hail. Hail belts around the world are generally found at mid-latitudes, downwind of large mountain ranges.

Hail occurs in Canada, central Europe, the Himalayan region, southern China, Argentina, South Africa, and parts of Australia. The highest documented frequency of hailfalls on earth has been in Keriche, Kenya, which averages more than 132 days of hail per year.

### PREVENTION AND PREPARATIONS

Humans cannot prevent blizzards, ice storms, or hail. In 1948 the work of scientist Vincent Schaefer showed that adding finely divided dry ice crystals to cold clouds could induce precipitation. Further studies showed that, in addition to dry ice, crystals of either silver iodide or sodium chloride added to appropriate clouds would also spur precipitation. Each of these techniques was used in major efforts to suppress hail formation and/or modify the storm-producing potential of clouds. However, much of this work was terminated because of the lack of consistent positive results. Some states, from Texas to North Dakota, would continue modest efforts to control hail production, funded by the states themselves or jointly with federal agencies.

There are several steps that may be taken to lessen damage, injury, and loss of life from blizzards, ice storms, and hail. A very common response by many people to impending severe weather is to ignore it or assume that they will not be directly affected. This attitude should be replaced with one of greater respect and appreciation for these winter events, which can kill and cause hundreds of millions of dollars in damages. Information and forecasts about impending severe weather events for any area are readily available, well publicized, and continuously updated by radio and television weather services. These events often last for considerable periods of time, cause power outages, and make local or long-distance travel extremely difficult or impossible. For these reasons, prior to the onset of severe weather one should ensure that sufficient food, medical supplies, auxiliary lighting devices, water, snow shovels, and ice-melting aids are on hand. Automobiles should be fueled and should contain emergency items, even though travel or driving within or through the impacted areas should be avoided.

The occurrence of blizzards, ice storms, and hail is often unpredictable. Before the onset of such weather, one should be certain that insurance policies are in place to cover damages to personal property, agricultural produce, and livestock. Anyone caught outdoors during such events should seek immediate shelter. If one is trapped within an automobile, the chance of survival is increased by remaining with the vehicle, unless a safe place is visible outside. One should keep hazard lights on, make certain of adequate ventilation within the automobile, and make certain that snow or ice does not clog the exhaust pipe.

Mountain climbers and skiers often protect themselves from violent blizzards by digging holes in the snow, crawling in, and curling up in a fetal position to conserve body warmth. Snow is an excellent insulator. There can be a temperature difference of as much as 50 degrees 7 inches below the surface of the snow.

## RESCUE AND RELIEF EFFORTS

Severe blizzards, ice storms, and hail may arise suddenly and be significantly more violent, extensive, or involved than previously forecast. Blizzards are one of the greatest potential killers of humans, livestock, and wildlife. They are often accompanied by freezing rain, hail, and sleet. During such events, humans, domestic animals, and livestock may be trapped away from adequate, safe environments and may require rescue and relief efforts from outside sources. Except for cases of the direst emergencies, rescue and relief efforts are generally mounted after the severe weather has subsided. Typical problems encountered during the storms are blocked, impassable roads and sidewalks; power outages; children, the elderly, and sick persons trapped in unheated dwellings; and travelers trapped in vehicles.

Most municipalities located within winter storm belts have dedicated public officials assigned to coordinate snow, ice, and hail removal and rescue efforts. Law enforcement agencies maintain law and order and prevent looting. Service organizations such as the National Red Cross and Salvation Army often have representatives available to assist in providing food, clothing, and shelter for those suffering from the effects of winter storms. When storm effects are very widespread, state governors may request that the president of the United States declare a state of emergency in the impacted area, making people and businesses in that area eligible for federal disaster relief funds. The National Guard is frequently called upon to aid travelers and others who face peril from blizzards and other severe winter storms. The Guard helps to maintain order and prevent looting. It also combats accumulations of snow, ice, and hail.

A 1979 blizzard that dropped more than 18 inches of snow in Cheyenne, Wyoming, and Denver, Colorado, moved eastward at a time when many people were traveling for Thanksgiving. The blizzard killed 125 people, and the National Guard rescued more than 2,000 travelers. Many were rescued by helicopter, while others were stranded in automobiles, hotels, motels, National Guard armories, and public buildings and auditoriums. An Ohio blizzard in January, 1978, stranded about 6,000 motorists. A state of emergency was declared, and the National Guard moved in to aid stranded motorists and exhausted utility repairpersons.

The most common hazards associated with severe winter storms are hypothermia, frostbite, broken bones, and other injuries caused by slips, falls, and vehicle accidents. Each year thousands of Americans, especially the elderly, motorists, and hikers, die from exposure to cold. Although relatively uncommon, concussive injuries from falling hail are sometimes reported. In July, 1979, at Fort Collins, Colorado, an infant was killed in his mother's arms as she tried to shield him from falling hail. A 1953 hailstorm in Alberta, Canada, killed 65,000 ducks. Rescue and relief efforts must be directed not only toward humans but also toward livestock and other animals. Failure to do so may result in staggering losses.

## IMPACT

Blizzards, ice storms, and hail cause hundreds of millions of dollars in damages; they also kill and injure hundreds of people each year. These storms can bring big-city traffic to a complete standstill, ground airplanes, make it difficult or impossible to get to or from work or school, and create power outages and food and fuel shortages. Additional hardships may result from heavy rains and flooding that often follow such storms. The impact on traffic is enormous. More than 85 percent of all ice storm deaths result from traffic accidents.

## HISTORICAL OVERVIEW

Throughout history, including modern times, blizzards and ice storms have been a serious threat to travelers. Travelers crossing the Alps have been trapped by sudden and unexpected snowstorms; this was the likely cause of death of a prehistoric man whose well-preserved remains were unearthed in the high Alps in the 1990's. The famous St. Bernard dogs, trained by the friars of the hospice founded around 982 c.e. by St. Bernard of Menthon, have rescued many travelers trapped in the mountain passes of Switzerland by sudden and unexpected snowstorms.

In the early fall of 1846, an unexpectedly early snowstorm in the Sierra Nevada trapped the Donner Party, a group of emigrants from the East seeking to reach California. The early storm was followed by many additional snowfalls, leading to the deaths of most of the members of the party. Some were believed to have resorted to cannibalism to relieve their hunger in the weeks immediately preceding their own deaths from starvation.

In the seventeenth century, Europe experienced what has been described as the most severe winters after the end of the Ice Age, particularly in the years 1643 to 1653. In the eighteenth century, severe weather played its part in initiating the French Revolution: A hailstorm damaged much of France's wheat crop in the summer of 1788, sparking strong inflation in the price of bread and rousing the anger of the working class.

Hailstorms occur mostly in the summertime as a result of unusual temperature inversions, and the threat they usually pose is the destruction of agricultural crops. The growth of major transportation capabilities has enabled the world to alleviate the risks of local starvation caused by such storms, but they can be devastating to local economies, particularly in parts of the world where the standard of living is low.

The nineteenth century experienced a period of lower average temperatures in winter that led to some startling developments. The lower temperatures and early frosts are believed to have played a part in the decline of agriculture in the Northeast. As evidence of the lower temperatures, the East River in New York City froze over in January of 1867. People used sleds for winter travel, and the frozen rivers and ponds provided ice that was cut, stored, and shipped south in the spring and summer in an era before mechanical refrigeration developed in the 1870's. The most striking event associated with this period of lower temperatures was the Great Blizzard of 1888, in which

Cattle in a Blizzard on the Plains, *drawn by Charles Graham from a sketch by H. Worrall. This drawing appeared in* Harper's Weekly *on February 27, 1886.* (Library of Congress)

more than 400 people died as a result of being trapped outside or in unheated buildings. All travel came to a halt for several days.

Nevertheless, modern technology enticed several adventurers to believe they could overcome the enormous risks involved in exploring the world's coldest continent, Antarctica. Although a Norwegian explorer, Roald Amundsen, had managed to travel overland to the South Pole and return safely in 1911, the following year another explorer of the Antarctic, Robert Falcon Scott, together with four companions, who managed to reach the South Pole a month after Amundsen, lost his life in a series of blizzards encountered on the return trip from the South Pole. People continuing a series of scientific expeditions and scientific observations carried out in Antarctica have due regard for the risks of winter weather.

In the middle of the twentieth century, colder weather hit the Northern Hemisphere, resulting in several blizzards of note. In February of 1962, a major storm centered in Germany led to the deaths of 343 people. Four years later, in January of 1966, the worst blizzard in seventy years struck the eastern United States. In 1972 heavy snow fell in Iran, a country whose climate normally does not experience such events except in the mountains to the north and east.

The development of predictive capabilities helped significantly to reduce the toll of such life-threatening storms. In 1960, the deployment of the first weather satellite made it possible to view the weather over large areas of the globe. These images enabled weather services all over the world to see major snowstorms and blizzards coming, and to alert travelers to the risks of travel. In 1967, the National Oceanographic and Atmospheric Administration (NOAA) began making public its maps of snow and ice cover all over the world. These maps later revealed that in the early 1970's the snow and ice cover had begun to grow, and by 1973 it exceeded by 11 percent its extent in 1970.

Scientists began learning about the earth's climate and weather from the ice cores extracted from Greenland glaciers as early as 1966. These were analyzed by Danish scientists, as well as climatologists from other countries, and revealed that snowfall has been a variable event throughout history. It is concentrated, however, at high latitudes and high elevations. The lower temperatures that occurred in late medieval times, for example, wiped out the Norse settlers who had established a colony in Greenland around 1,000 C.E. Thanks to ice cores, scientists now have a clear chronological picture of snowfall over the entire period since the end of the last ice age, some twelve thousand years ago.

Between 1978 and 1980, the United States was hit by a series of blizzards. The Midwest was blanketed in late January of 1978, and in early February of that year the northeastern part of the country was targeted. There was another blizzard in the Midwest the following January, and in February of 1979 more than 18 inches of snow piled up in the District of Columbia, bringing traffic to a halt. Washington, D.C., had not received that much snow since 1922. In March of 1980, the mid-Atlantic region was the victim of a blizzard. Twenty-eight inches of snow fell in tidewater Virginia, more than at any time in the preceding eighty-seven years. In April, 3 feet of snow fell in Colorado and Utah. The same storm became a blizzard in New England. Another year of heavy snowfall was 1984. In March, much of the East Coast was hit by heavy snows, leading to 8 deaths. The great popularity of skiing for recreation put many people at risk in these storms.

In January, 1985, a blizzard hit the Midwest, reaching as far south as San Antonio, Texas, which had a record snowfall of 13.5 inches. In

November and again in December the Midwest experienced a series of blizzards, leading to 33 deaths. In 1986, it was Europe's turn. In the last week in January deep cold and snow caused many rivers and canals to freeze, and 33 people died. In January, 1992, an unusual snowstorm hit the Middle East, where it rarely snows except in the mountains. Jerusalem received as much as 18 inches of snow; 2 feet of snow fell in Amman, Jordan. In 1993 winds of 109 miles per hour (the Weather Service defines a blizzard as a snowstorm in which winds exceed 35 miles per hour) powered a blizzard along the entire East Coast, from Florida to Maine. The storm caused 213 deaths.

In 1996, a snowstorm covered much of the East Coast, and many highways were closed for as much as two days. Seventeen inches of snow fell on the District of Columbia, and the federal government shut down for two days. Parts of Pennsylvania received 31 inches of snow in this storm, and a few areas in New Jersey were blanketed by up to 37 inches of snow. The elevated trains in New York City had to shut down for a time.

On April 1 of the following year, what became known as the April Fool's snowstorm hit the Northeast. A sudden change in the path of this storm caught weather predictors by surprise. In May of 1997, 7 climbers on Mount Everest perished in a blizzard as they neared the peak of the mountain. Nine climbers had been killed the previous May in similar circumstances. The severe weather of 1996-1997 also proved fatal to at least 240 Hindu pilgrims attempting a pilgrimage to a cave in Kashmir; they were caught in a freak snowstorm on August 25, 1996.

What was termed a once-in-a-century ice storm devastated much of the Northeast as well as eastern Canada between January 5 and January 12, 1998. The storm dragged down power lines in much of the region, and crews had to be imported from southern states to help repair the damage. Many residents were without power for several weeks. The ice storm of 1998 was described as the most destructive storm in Canadian history. The Adirondacks in New York, as well as northern Vermont, New Hampshire, and Maine, were also hit. Damages in Canada exceeded a half billion dollars, and insurance claims totaling more than $1 billion were filed in both countries. Seven people died in Maine as a result of this storm and 4 in New York State.

The threat posed by snow and ice was transferred to Europe in the early months of 1999. Heavy snows in the Alps in February and March, the heaviest in fifty years, triggered avalanches that trapped a number of skiers and other tourists. At least 31 people died in Austria and 18 in France. The lives lost in these events made it clear that people have yet to learn to heed the warnings that the weather services of the world are now able to provide: Travel remains a risky proposition under snowy and icy conditions.

*Billy Scott*
*Nancy M. Gordon*

## BIBLIOGRAPHY

Allaby, Michael. *Dangerous Weather: Blizzards.* Rev. ed. New York: Facts On File, 2003. Intended for students. Discusses the origins and history of severe winter storms. Includes helpful diagrams.

Battan, Louis J. *Weather in Your Life.* New York: W. H. Freeman, 1983. An introduction to meteorology and weather written for the layperson. Describes how the atmosphere influences humans and human behavior. Topics include weather forecasting; social implications of weather modification; and effects of blizzards, ice storms, and hail on air transport, agriculture, and human health.

Christian, Spencer, and Tom Biracree. *Spencer Christian's Weather Book.* New York: Prentice-Hall General Reference, 1993. A weather primer written for laypersons. Briefly introduces readers to major weather-related topics, including storms, atmospheric dynamics, weather reporting, and forecasting. Provides information for students and any others who might want to pursue a career in meteorology or weather reporting.

Eagleman, Joe R. *Severe and Unusual Weather.* 2d ed. Lenexa, Kans.: Trimedia, 1990. A detailed and thorough text that describes meterological phenomena that cause various kinds of storms. An excellent companion textbook to accompany courses in general meteorology or the earth sciences.

Erikson, Jon. *Violent Storms.* Blue Ridge Summit, Pa.: Tab Books, 1988. A story of weather through the ages, written in general terms. Discusses weather folklore, weather and the development of agriculture, inadvertent weather modification, rainmaking, and other aspects of voluntary weather modification. Provides a list and discussion of significant historical weather events.

Ludlum, David M. *National Audubon Society Field Guide to North American Weather.* New York: Alfred A. Knopf, 1997. A field guide for observing and forecasting weather. Contains more than 300 color photographs of cloud types, storms, and weather-related optical phenomena. The book has thumb-tab references, visual keys, and images of historic weather occurrences.

————. *The Weather Factor.* Boston: Houghton Mifflin, 1984. A collection of little-known facts about how weather and winter storms have influenced Americans from colonial times to modern times. Detailed accounts are provided about when and where storms occurred and descriptions of weather impact on events such as political campaigns, wars, sports events, and air transport.

Lutgens, Frederick K., and Edward J. Tarbuck. *The Atmosphere: An Introduction to Meteorology.* 9th ed. Upper Saddle River, N.J.: Prentice Hall, 2004. Explores basic principles and concepts of science for beginning students of meteorology.

Lyons, Walter A. *The Handy Weather Answer Book.* Detroit: Visible Ink Press, 1997. Contains photographs and tables to illustrate and explain items and events described in the text. Uses a question-and-answer format to introduce general weather-related topics.

# DROUGHTS

**FACTORS INVOLVED:** Animals, geography, human
activity, plants, temperature, weather conditions,
wind

**REGIONS AFFECTED:** Cities, coasts, deserts, forests,
islands, lakes, mountains, plains, rivers, towns, valleys

## DEFINITION

A drought is an extended period of below-normal precipitation. It is a dry period that is sufficiently long and severe that crops fail and normal water demand cannot be met.

## SCIENCE

Drought can be defined as a shortage of precipitation that results in below-normal levels of stream flow, groundwater, lakes, and soil moisture. It differs from other geophysical events such as volcanic eruptions, floods, and earthquakes because droughts are actually non-events—that is, they result from the absence of events (precipitation) that should normally occur. Drought also differs from other geophysical events because it has no recognizable beginning (as opposed to an earthquake) and takes time to develop. Drought may be recognized only when plants start to wilt, wells and streams run dry, and reservoir shorelines recede.

Most droughts occur when slow-moving subsiding air masses dominate a region. Commonly, air circulates in continental interiors, where there is little moisture available for evaporation, thereby providing little potential for precipitation. In order for precipitation to occur, the water vapor in the air must be lifted so that it has a chance to cool, condense into dust particles, and eventually, if conditions are favorable, precipitate. Clearly, there is little opportunity for these conditions to occur when the air is dry and descending.

Another climatological characteristic associated with droughts is that, following their establishment within a particular area, they tend to persist and even increase in areal extent. Air circulation is influenced by the drying-out of soil moisture and its unavailability for precipitation further downwind. Concurrently, the state of the atmo-

## MILESTONES

**1270-1350:** A prolonged drought in the U.S. Southwest destroys Anasazi Indian culture.

**1585-1587:** A severe drought destroys the Roanoke colonies of English settlers in Virginia.

**1887-1896:** Droughts drive out many early settlers on the Great Plains.

**1899:** The failure of monsoons in India results in many deaths.

**1910-1915:** First in a series of recurring droughts affects the Sahel region in Africa.

**1932-1937:** Extensive droughts in the southern Great Plains destroy many farms, creating the Dust Bowl, in the worst drought in more than three hundred years in the United States.

**1960-1990:** Repeated droughts occur in the Sahel, east Africa, and southern Africa.

**1977-1978:** The western United States undergoes a drought.

**1982-1983:** Droughts affect Brazil and northern India.

**1986-1988:** Many farmers in the U.S. Midwest are driven out of business by a drought.

**1998:** A drought destroys crops in the southern Midwest and causes ecological damage on the East Coast.

**1999:** A major drought strikes the U.S. Southeast, the Atlantic coast, and New England.

**2002:** A severe, long-term drought begins in Australia. Urban areas begin to feel its effects by 2006, as major cities pass heavy restrictions on water usage and Perth constructs a desalination plant.

sphere that produces the unusual circulation associated with droughts can induce surface temperature variations that in turn foster further development of the unusual circulation pattern. As a result, the process feeds on itself, making the drought last longer and intensify until major atmospheric circulation patterns change.

Drought-identification research has changed over the years from a time when the size of the precipitation deficit was the only factor considered, to the present, when sophisticated techniques are applied to the quantitative assessment of the deviation of the total environmental moisture status. These techniques facilitate better understanding of the severity, duration, and areal extent of droughts.

Early in the twentieth century, drought was identified by the U.S. Weather Bureau (now the National Weather Service) as any period of three weeks or more when the precipitation was 30 percent or more below normal. (Note that normal is defined as the average for a thirty-year period, such as 1951-1980 or 1961-1990.) The initial selection of three weeks for defining a drought was based entirely on precipitation. Subsequent research has shown that the moisture status of a region is affected by other factors besides precipitation.

Further developments in drought identification during the mid-twentieth century involved examination of the moisture demands that are related to evapotranspiration, the return of moisture to the atmosphere by the combined effects of evaporation and plant transpiration. Some drought-identification studies have examined the adequacy of soil moisture in the root zone for plant growth. The objective of this research is to determine drought probability based on the number of days when the moisture storage in the soil is zero. The U.S. Forest Service used evapotranspiration in developing a drought index for use by fire-control managers. The index was used to provide an indicator of flammability that could lead to forest fires. It had limited applicability to nonforestry users as it was not effective for showing drought as a measure of total environmental moisture stress.

W. C. Palmer developed a drought-identification index in 1965 that became widely adopted. The Palmer Drought Index (PDI) defines drought as the period of time, generally measured in months or years, when the actual moisture supply at a specified location is always below the climatically anticipated or appropriate supply of moisture. Evapotranspiration, soil moisture loss, surface runoff, and precipitation are the required environmental parameters. The PDI values range from +4.0, for an extremely wet moisture status, to −4.0, for extreme drought. Normal conditions have values close to zero. Although the PDI has been used for decades and recognized as an acceptable procedure for including evapotranspiration and soil moisture in drought identification, it has been criticized. For example, the method determines a dimensionless parameter ranging from +4.0 to −4.0 that cannot be compared to variables such as precipitation, which are measured in units (inches) that are immediately recognizable. In addition, the index is not very sensitive to short drought periods, which can negatively affect crops.

In order to overcome these problems with the PDI, other researchers have used water-budget analysis to identify changes in environmental moisture status. The procedure is similar to the Palmer method, as it includes precipitation, evapotranspiration, and soil moisture. However, the values for moisture status deviation are dimensional and expressed in the same units as precipitation—inches. Drought classification using this method yields values ranging from approximately +1.0 inch, for an above-normal moisture status, to −4.0 inches, for extreme drought. As in the PDI, the index is close to zero for normal conditions.

## GEOGRAPHY

Many regions of the world have regularly occurring periods of dryness. Three different forms of dryness have a temporal dimension; they are known as perennial, seasonal, and intermittent. Perennially dry areas include the major deserts of the world, such as the Sahara, Arabian, Kalahari, and Australian Deserts. Precipitation in these large deserts is not only very low (less than 10 inches per year) but also very erratic. Seasonal dryness is associated with those parts of the world where most of the precipitation for the year occurs during a few months, leaving the rest of the year rainless. Intermittent dryness pertains to those areas of the world where the total precipitation is reduced in humid regions or where the rainy season in wet-dry climates either does not occur or is shortened.

The major problem for humans is a lack of precipitation where it is normally expected. For example, the absence of precipitation for a week where daily precipitation is the norm is considered a drought. In contrast, it would take two or more years without any rain in parts of Libya in North Africa for a drought to occur. In those parts of the world that have one rainy season, a 50 percent decrease in precipitation would be considered a drought. In other regions that normally have two rainy seasons, the failure of one could lead to drought conditions. Thus, the very word "drought" itself is a relative term, since it has different meanings in different climatic regions. The deficiency of precipitation in one location is therefore not a good indicator of drought, as each place has its own criteria for identifying drought.

## PREVENTION AND PREPARATIONS

Droughts cannot be prevented, but their effects may be ameliorated. There are two main options for managing droughts: increasing the supply of water and decreasing the demand.

There are several supply enhancement measures that can be instituted. For example, reservoir release requirements can be relaxed. This occurred on the Delaware River during the severe drought of the early 1960's, when the required flow of 3,000 cubic feet per second at Trenton could not be met without jeopardizing the water-supply needs of New York City. Accordingly, the reservoir releases in the upper Delaware were temporarily relaxed. Many states require low flow or conservation flows to be maintained in the channel below a reservoir for waste assimilation and aquatic health. If a drought is severe enough, the conservation flows can be temporarily reduced or even eliminated. Other measures include the temporary diversion of water from one source, such as a recreational lake, to a water-supply reservoir. Interconnections with other water-supply purveyors may be encouraged or mandated. New sources of water could also be obtained from buried valleys that contain stratified glacial deposits with large amounts of groundwater.

Demand reduction measures include appeals for voluntary conservation. If these do not work, then mandatory water-use restrictions can be imposed. Bans on outside uses of water, such as lawn watering and car washing, are common.

## RESCUE AND RELIEF EFFORTS

Drought in the developed world affects crops and livestock but generally does not pose a threat to life, as it does in the developing world. Industrialized societies have existing transportation networks that enable supplies and foodstuffs to be shipped to affected regions. If there are crop and livestock losses, governments can provide disaster relief in the form of low- or no-interest loans to affected farmers, as happened in the eastern United States in the summer of 1999.

The situation in the developing world is much grimmer. Governments often lack the money and resources to distribute supplies to rural populations. Food supplies coming from overseas donors may not reach the intended victims because of inadequate transportation infrastructures. Some relief efforts that could be successful include drilling of deeper wells so as to tap undeveloped water sources. This takes much time, but the extra water may inadvertently encourage more people to stay in an area that may not be sustainable.

## IMPACT

Droughts have had enormous impacts on human societies since ancient times. Crop and livestock losses have caused famine and death. Drought has caused ancient civilizations to collapse and forced many people to migrate. Water is so critical to all forms of life that a pronounced shortage can decimate whole populations.

The effects of drought are profound, even during modern times. For example, the dry conditions in the Great Plains in the 1930's in conjunction with intensive farming resulted in the Dust Bowl, which at one time covered more than 77,000 square miles, an area the size of Nebraska. An estimated 10 billion tons of topsoil was blown away, some of it landing on eastern cities. The Sahel region south of the Sahara in Africa had a severe drought from 1968 to 1974, which decimated local populations. Famine and disease killed several hundred thousand people (100,000 in 1973 alone) and 5 million cattle that were the sole means of support for the nomadic populations.

## HISTORICAL OVERVIEW

Drought is the absence of precipitation. It is a problem particularly where precipitation is marginal, usually because of topographic factors. For example, precipitation is less than 20 inches a year over much of the Great Plains of the United States; the area farther west, until the Rocky Mountains are reached, normally has less than 10 inches per year. In this case, precipitation is low because the Rocky Mountains exist between the Great Plains and the Pacific Ocean: Oceans are the source of moisture that becomes precipitation— either rain or snow. The mountains force most rain clouds to drop their moisture before the clouds have passed over the mountains. This is why rainfall is high in the Pacific Northwest and low in the region to the east of the Rocky Mountains.

Precipitation is often marginal in areas where rainfall is seasonal. This condition prevails in much of Africa and in Asia, where precipitation occurs in the form of seasonal monsoons. For central Asia, precipitation that should come in the form of monsoons is interrupted by the Himalaya Mountains, which lie between central Asia and the Indian Ocean, the source of moisture in that region.

Precipitation is also affected by long-term climatic trends. In general, when the climate is warmer, it tends also to be drier; when the climate is colder, it tends to be wetter. Some climatologists believe that the recurring droughts in northern and eastern Africa reflect a warming trend in the climate. Mean temperatures in the 1990's were higher than any recorded after the end of the Ice Age. These climatological trends are believed to be responsible for a prolonged drought in the American Southwest that undermined the Anasazi Indian culture of that region beginning in the thirteenth century. It is also possible that a comparable drought in central Asia led to the wave of Mongol invasions of Europe in the thirteenth century and the Turkish invasions of the fourteenth century.

While droughts occur with fairly regular frequency in areas of marginal precipitation, they represent an important historical event when they last more than one year. This was the case of the droughts believed to be responsible for the elimination of the early English colonies in Virginia in the sixteenth century. Droughts played a somewhat similar role in the late nineteenth century in the Great Plains of the United States, where farming settlement had been heavily promoted by the government through low-cost sales of public land. The process of moving the roving Native American tribes to reservations had been predicated on the assumption that they would be replaced by permanent white settlers. However, after droughts hit the newly established farms between 1887 and 1896, many of the settlers abandoned their residences.

The twentieth century saw repeated recurring droughts in the sub-Saharan portion of Africa. One that occurred between 1910 and 1915 led many of the pastoral tribes inhabiting the area to move onto marginal land at higher elevation, land less able to support the tribes as their numbers grew. This same area was subjected to recurring droughts in the second half of the twentieth century, which spread to eastern Africa. Because this area has many subsistence farmers, who are unable to survive a lost harvest, the drought problem led to much unrest, with large numbers of people migrating in search of food. The conditions in the Sudan and in Somalia and Ethiopia resulted in repeated calls for emergency food supplies.

In South America, drought is not uncommon along the Pacific coastline, particularly in Chile and Peru. Because the winds tend to blow from east to west, little moisture is moved over the Pacific coastline of South America, and the Andes Mountains prevent moisture that arises from the Atlantic Ocean from reaching the lands to the west of the mountains. Droughts also affect parts of Brazil that are well inland from the Atlantic. Droughts in this area have been increasing since the seventeenth century; at least 8 occurred in the twentieth century.

Many parts of Australia also suffer from recurrent droughts. The continent is located outside the main global circulation patterns that bring clouds and rain to inland areas, with the result that only the fringes of the continent are used for intensive cultivation. Most of Australia is suited only to grazing herds that can utilize the sparse vegetation and then move on. In 2002, a severe, long-term drought began in Australia. By 2006, urban areas had begun to feel its effects. Major cities passed heavy restrictions on water usage and debated gray-water recycling programs. Alternate sources of water were sought. Brisbane hoped to set up larger dams and a pipeline, and Perth constructed a desalination plant.

Probably the most famous drought in American history was that which hit the southern part of the Great Plains region in the early 1930's. Lands that even under the best of conditions receive only marginal precipitation had been "broken to the plough" in the first two decades of the twentieth century. When precipitation failed to materialize in the early 1930's, many subsistence farmers were driven from the land in what came to be known as the Dust Bowl, as winds blew the unprotected soil off the land.

Another drought affected the Great Plains, even the northern Great Plains, in the late 1980's. Many farmers who had borrowed money to extend their farms were unable to pay back the loans and lost their farms when their crops failed. Another drought hit the southern Great Plains in 1998, destroying a large portion of the cotton crop in Texas. In 1999 the drought conditions moved to the southeastern United States, devastating crops in that region. Coupled with high temperatures, this drought captured public attention.

*Robert M. Hordon*
*Nancy M. Gordon*

**BIBLIOGRAPHY**

Allaby, Michael. *Droughts*. Rev. ed. New York: Facts On File, 2003. Intended for students. Discusses the origins and history of droughts. Includes helpful diagrams.

Benson, Charlotte, and Edward Clay. *The Impact of Drought on Sub-Saharan African Economies: A Preliminary Examination*. Washington, D.C.: World Bank, 1998. A look at the effects of often-occurring droughts on African life.

Bryson, Reid A., and Thomas J. Murray. *Climates of Hunger: Mankind and the World's Changing Weather*. Madison: University of Wisconsin Press, 1977. A descriptive discussion of the profound effect of climate on human societies, going back to ancient times.

Dixon, Lloyd S., Nancy Y. Moore, and Ellen M. Pint. *Drought Management Policies and Economic Effects in Urban Areas of California, 1987-92*. Santa Monica, Calif.: Rand, 1996. This report examines the impacts of the 1987-1992 drought in California on urban and agricultural water users.

Frederiksen, Harald D. *Drought Planning and Water Resources: Implications in Water Resources Management*. Washington, D.C.: World Bank, 1992. This short report of thirty-eight pages contains two papers on drought planning and water-use efficiency and effectiveness.

Garcia, Rolando V., and Pierre Spitz. *Drought and Man: The Roots of Catastrophe*. Vol. 3. New York: Pergamon Press, 1986. Food insecurity and social disjunctions caused by drought are discussed, using case studies from Brazil, Tanzania, and the Sahelian countries.

Tannehill, Ivan R. *Drought: Its Causes and Effects*. Princeton, N.J.: Princeton University Press, 1947. A classic technical but non-mathematical book on the climatology of droughts.

Wilhite, Donald A., ed. *Drought and Water Crises: Science, Technology, and Management Issues*. Boca Raton, Fla.: Taylor & Francis, 2005. Explains the role of science, technology, and management in resolving the issues associated with drought management.

Wilhite, Donald A., and William E. Easterling, with Deborah A. Wood, eds. *Planning for Drought: Toward a Reduction of Societal Vulnerability*. Boulder, Colo.: Westview Press, 1987. A collection of 37 short chapters on the large number of issues pertaining to drought, including social impacts, governmental response, and human adaptation and adjustment.

# Dust Storms and Sandstorms

**Factors involved:** Geological forces, human activity, plants, rain, weather conditions, wind
**Regions affected:** Deserts, plains, valleys

## Definition

Dust storms and sandstorms are composed of airborne and wind-blown clouds of soil particles, mineral flakes, and vegetative residue that impact climate, air temperature, air quality, rainfall, desertification, agricultural productivity, human health, and human habitation of the land.

## Science

Dust storms result from wind erosion, desertification, and physical deterioration of the soil caused by persistent or temporary lack of rainfall and wind gusts. Dust storms develop when wind velocity at 1 foot above soil level increases beyond 13 miles per hour, causing saltation and surface creep. In saltation, small particles are lifted off the surface, travel 10 to 15 times the height to which they are lifted, then spin downward with sufficient force to dislodge other soil particles and break down earth clods. In surface creep, larger particles creep along the surface in a rolling motion. The larger the affected area, the greater the cumulative effect of saltation and surface creep, leading to an avalanche of soil particles across the land, even during moderate wind gusts. The resulting soil displacement erodes the structure and texture of the remaining soils, reduces the moisture content of the soil, exposes bedrock, and limits the type of vegetation sustainable on the remaining soil.

Dust storms remove smaller and lighter soil particles, leaving behind the larger and denser particles and granular minerals associated with deserts, and erode rock surfaces, creating dust and granular particles. As soils become drier and more dense, and as ground cover is reduced, the number and intensity of subsequent dust storms increases. Arid or semiarid soil eventually becomes desert. Atmo-

*A dust storm approaches a Kansas town in 1935.* (National Oceanic and Atmospheric Administration)

spheric dust increases soil and air temperature by trapping heat in the lower atmosphere. Dust may also reduce soil and air temperature by reflecting the sun's heating radiation back into space. Changes in air temperature, coupled with dust in the atmosphere and drier land surfaces, reduce local rainfall, encouraging desertification.

Dust storms result from the dislodging of small, light soil particles, mineral flecks, and decomposing vegetation matter. Dust storms rise miles into the atmosphere and have both local and global impacts. Sandstorms result from dislodging larger, heavier particles of soil and rock. They tend to occur in conjunction with desert cyclones. Sandstorms remain close to ground level and have primarily local impacts. Dust and sandstorms may occur simultaneously.

There are many types of dust storms. Haze reduces visibility to three-fourths of a mile or less and results from persistent wind gusts across arid soils or across temporarily dry or disturbed semi-arid soils. Dust devils lift silt and clay particles several hundred yards into the air. Tornadoes generate local vortices that lift silt, clay, mineral flecks, and vegetation residue more than a mile high and transport it hundreds of square miles. Cyclones form at the leading edge of thunderstorm cells, extending across a front of several hundred miles, generating winds up to 150 miles per hour, and lifting particles and debris several miles into the upper atmosphere and jet stream for distribution around the globe.

## GEOGRAPHY

Dust storms and sandstorms of global significance originate in the arid deserts and semiarid lands covering 36 percent of the earth's land surface. Major deserts are located in northern Africa, northeast Sudan, southwest Africa, the Arabian Peninsula, southwest Asia, the Middle East, northern and western China, central Australia, southwest North America, parts of southern and western South America, the Caucasus of Russia, central Spain, and the southern coast of the Mediterranean Sea. In addition, dust storms arise when normally semiarid lands periodically become arid, undergo abnormally strong windy periods, or have their vegetation removed by humans or nature. These areas include sub-Saharan Africa, the U.S. Midwest, the northern coast of the Mediterranean, the steppe of central Asia, and all lands immediately adjacent to deserts.

Globally significant storms cover areas of several hundred to several thousand square miles and transport dust from one continent to another. Locally significant dust storms originate in overly cultivated agricultural fields, residential or commercial developments denuded of ground cover, major road construction sites, and any lands experiencing a temporary drought. Local storms are often confined to only a few square miles in area.

Locales with the highest frequency of dust storms are Mexico City and Kazakhstan in central Asia, with about 60 storms per year; western and northern China, with 30 storms each year; West Africa, with 20 storms; and Egypt, with 10 storms. Storms of the longest known duration occurred in the southwestern United States, with a storm of twenty-eight days in Amarillo, Texas, in April, 1935, and a storm of twenty-two days in the Texas Panhandle in March of 1936.

## PREVENTION AND PREPARATIONS

The number and intensity of dust storms and sandstorms are reduced through soil conservation practices, such as covering the soil with vegetation, reducing soil exposure on tilled land, creating wind barriers, installing buffer strips around exposed soils, and limiting the number and intensity of soil disturbing activities on vulnerable arid and semiarid soils. Vegetative cover slows the wind at ground level, protects soil particles from detachment, and traps blowing or floating soil particles, chemicals, and nutrients. Because the greatest wind erosion damage often occurs during seasons when no crops are growing or when natural vegetation is dormant, dead residues and standing stubble of the previous crop often remain in place until the next planting season. Planting grass or legume cover crops until the next planting season, or as part of a crop rotation cycle or no-till planting system, also reduces dust.

No-till and mulch-till planting systems reduce soil exposure to wind erosion. No-till systems leave the soil cover undisturbed before inserting crop seeds into the ground through a narrow slot in the soil. Mulch-till planting keeps a high percentage of the dead residues of previous crops on the surface when the new crop is planted. Row crops are planted at right angles to the prevailing winds to absorb wind energy and trap moving soil particles. Crops are planted in small fields to prevent avalanching caused by an increase in the amount of soil in particles transported by wind as the distance across bare soil increases.

Because wind breaks slow wind speeds at the surface of the soil, good wind barriers include tree plantings, cross-wind strips of perennial shrubs, and high grasses. The protected area is ten times the height of the barrier. Alley cropping is used in areas of sustained high wind; crops are planted between rows of larger, mature trees.

Strip farming reduces field width, thereby reducing wind erosion. Large fields are subdivided into narrow cultivated strips. Planting crops along the contour lines around hills is called contour strip cropping. Planting crops in strips across the top of predominant slopes is called field stripping. Crops are arranged so that a strip of hay or sod, such as grass, clover, alfalfa, or a close-growing small grain, such as wheat or oats, is alternated with a strip of cultivated row crop, such as tobacco, cotton, or corn. In areas of high wind, the greater the average wind velocity, the narrower the strips. Blown dust from the row-crop strip is trapped as it passes through the subsequent strip of hay or grain, thereby reducing dust. Contour strip cropping or field stripping can reduce soil erosion by 65 to 75 percent.

Limiting land-disturbing activities by humans on highly vulnerable arid and semiarid soils reduces the number and intensity of both dust storms and sandstorms. Deserts are especially vulnerable to impacts of animal herds and motor-vehicle traffic. Many fragile desert plants, shrubs, and trees are easily destroyed by animal or human activity, especially foraging and vehicle traffic. The surface of the desert consists of a thin layer of small and microscopic plants, microorganisms, and insects, whose combined activities produce a thin crust that limits the impact of wind on the surface of the desert. When this crust is broken by surface traffic, the underlying sands and minerals are vulnerable to wind erosion. Natural repair to the broken crust and natural revegetation processes may take decades or centuries.

## RESCUE AND RELIEF EFFORTS

Little can be done to protect humans, buildings, or crops from the impact of dry wind tornadoes or cyclones producing major dust storms or sandstorms, but soil conservation measures reduce the number and intensity of these storms. The effects of these storms on humans is partly ameliorated by remaining indoors, by wearing heavy clothing or remaining inside vehicles when outdoors, and by covering the nose and mouth to prevent the ingestion of dust, spores, and pollens.

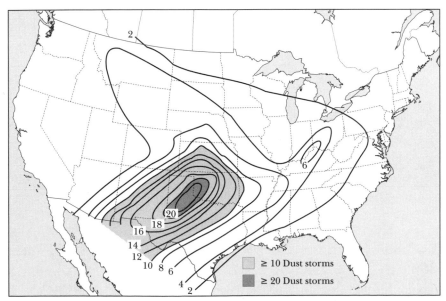

*The number of dust storms occurring in March, 1936, during the Dust Bowl years.*

## IMPACT

Sandstorms and dust storms have moved sufficient soil particles over the centuries to reshape continents; alter the distribution of plant and animal life; alternately heat and cool the earth; and silt rivers, lakes, and oceans. The volume of annual wind-blown dust is approximately equal to the volume of soil transported each year through water erosion. Approximately half a billion tons of dust is borne aloft each year, with more than half that dust deposited in the world's oceans.

The desertification processes associated with sandstorms and dust storms impacted the historic rise and fall of many civilizations, including the early Pueblo Indians of the American Southwest, the Harappan civilization of southwest Asia, the city-states of Arabia, and the caravan empires of sub-Saharan Africa. Dust storms on agricultural lands cause soil nutrient loss, reduce the moisture-retaining capacity of the soil, and concentrate salts and fertilizer acids in the soil, thereby reducing agricultural production. Efforts to replace lost topsoil with fertilizers have proven futile. Crop yields are reduced by up to 80 percent.

Sandstorms kill people and animals and damage, destroy, or bury roads, buildings, machinery, and agricultural fields. Many people and animals are killed each year by the force of the storms or by ingestion of wind-borne particles. In 1895, more than 20 percent of the cattle in eastern Colorado died of suffocation in a particularly intense dust storm.

Dust storms are a major source of air pollution and a major distribution vehicle for mold spores, pollens, and other harmful airborne particles. One pathogen causing "valley fever" or "desert rheumatism" kills approximately 120 people each year in the United States alone. Sandstorms and intense dust storms contribute to traffic accidents and disrupt mass-transportation systems. In many southwestern American states, dust storms are responsible for up to 20 percent of all traffic accident fatalities.

*Gordon Neal Diem*

## BIBLIOGRAPHY

Morales, Christer, ed. *Saharan Dust: Mobilization, Transport, Deposition.* Chichester, England: John Wiley & Sons, 1979. The editor presents numerous scientific papers and recommendations from a workshop held in Sweden sponsored by the Scientific Committee on Problems in the Environment.

Pewe, Troy L., ed. *Desert Dust: Origin, Characteristics, and Effect on Man.* Boulder, Colo.: Geological Society of America, 1981. This collection of scientific papers provides detail on the causes and effects of sandstorms and dust storms.

Stallings, Frank L. *Black Sunday: The Great Dust Storm of April 14, 1935.* Austin, Tex.: Eakin Press, 2001. A collection of newspaper reports and the eyewitness accounts of more than 100 people about this devastating dust storm.

Sundar, Christopher A., Donna V. Vulcan, and Ronald M. Welch. *Radiative Effects of Aerosols Generated from Biomass Burning, Dust Storms, and Forest Fires.* Washington, D.C.: National Aeronautics and Space Administration, 1996. This book discusses global heating and cooling from dust storms.

Tannehill, Ivan R. *Drought: Its Causes and Effects.* Princeton, N.J.: Princeton University Press, 1947. Discusses the effects of drought on dust storms.

U.S. Department of Agriculture. *Crop Residue Management to Reduce Erosion and Improve Soil Quality.* Conservation Research Reports 37-39. Washington, D.C.: Author, 1994-1995.

_____. *Soil Erosion by Wind.* Agriculture Information Bulletin Number 555. Washington, D.C.: Author, 1989. These public information booklets, as well as a variety of *Conservation Practice Job Sheets*, describe appropriate soil conservation measures to limit dust storms.

Worster, Donald. *Dust Bowl: The Southern Plains in the 1930's.* 25th anniversary ed. New York: Oxford University Press, 2004. Describes the dust storms of the southwestern United States.

# EARTHQUAKES

**FACTORS INVOLVED:** Geological forces, gravitational forces

**REGIONS AFFECTED:** Cities, coasts, deserts, forests, islands, mountains, plains, towns, valleys

## DEFINITION

Earthquakes often cause violent shaking that can persist for several minutes. This shaking can destroy buildings, bridges, and most other structures. It also can trigger landslides, tsunamis, volcanic eruptions, and other natural disasters.

## SCIENCE

Earthquakes are produced by sudden slips of large blocks of rock along fractures within the earth. This abrupt displacement generates waves that can travel vast distances and cause immense destruction when they reach the surface of the earth.

To get an idea of how this occurs, imagine a man trying to slide a very heavy crate across the floor. At first, it will not budge at all. He pushes harder and harder, until, quite suddenly, the crate slips across the floor a few inches before coming to rest again. This motion is called strike-slip motion and is thought to be the way in which most earthquakes occur. Next, imagine what would have happened if, instead of pushing directly on the crate, the man had instead pushed on a big spring, compressing it further as he pushed harder. When the crate suddenly slid across the floor, the spring would have expanded again, continuing to push the crate, even though the man was standing still. The energy stored in the spring is called elastic strain energy. Major earthquakes usually result from the accumulation of a great deal of elastic strain energy as plates move past each other with relative velocities of a few centimeters per year. After a number of decades, the accumulated elastic strain energy is sufficient to cause a sudden slip. With the crate example, the slip surface is between the bottom of the crate and the floor. Within the earth, it is a fracture in the rock called a fault.

Many faults are vertical fractures, which come to the surface of the

## MILESTONES

**May 29, 526:** The Antioch earthquake in Syria (now Turkey), estimated at magnitude 9.0, kills 250,000.

**January 23, 1556:** 830,000 people die in Shaanxi, China, the greatest death toll from an earthquake to date.

**November 1, 1755:** An earthquake during church services on All Saints' Day kills worshipers in Lisbon, Portugal, in stone cathedrals or in the accompanying tsunamis; as many as 50,000 perish.

**December 16, 1811; January 23 and February 7, 1812:** In the sparsely settled region of New Madrid, Missouri, the largest historic earthquakes in North America to date rearrange the Mississippi River and form Reelfoot Lake.

**January 9, 1857:** The San Andreas fault at Fort Tejon, California, in the northwest corner of Los Angeles County, ruptures dramatically. Trees snap off near the ground, landslides occur, and buildings collapse into rubble.

**April 17, 1889:** The first teleseism is recorded in Potsdam, Germany, of an earthquake on that date in Japan.

**April 18, 1906:** The San Andreas fault slips 20 feet near San Francisco. Much of the city is severely damaged by the earthquake, and a fire starts when cinders escape a damaged chimney, leveling the city.

**December 28, 1908:** The Messina earthquake kills 120,000 and destroys or severely damages numerous communities in Italy.

**1910:** American geologist H. F. Reid publishes a report on the 1906 San Francisco earthquake, outlining his theory of elastic rebound.

**September 1, 1923:** 143,000 people die as a result of the Great Kwanto Earthquake, centered in Sagami Bay, Japan.

**Early 1930's:** Charles Richter, working with Beno Gutenberg at the Seismological Laboratory of the California Institute of Technology, develops the Richter scale.

**1958:** H. Jeffreys and K. E. Bullen publish seismic travel time curves establishing the detailed, spherically symmetrical model of the earth.

**May 22, 1960:** A large earthquake, measuring 8.5, strikes off the coast of Chile, making the earth reverberate for several weeks. For the first time, scientists are able to determine many of the resonant modes of oscillation of the earth.

*continued*

**MILESTONES** *(continued)*

**March 27, 1964:** The Good Friday earthquake near Anchorage, Alaska, with a magnitude of 8.6, causes extensive damage near the southern coast of Alaska and generates tsunamis that damage vessels and marinas along the western coast of the United States.

**May 31, 1970:** The magnitude 7.7 Ancash earthquake in northern Peru leaves 70,000 dead, 140,000 injured, and 500,000 homeless.

**February 9, 1971:** In the first serious earthquake to strike a densely populated area in the United States since 1906, a moderate (magnitude 6.6) earthquake causes $1 billion in damage in Sylmar, California.

**February 4, 1976:** A slip over a 124-mile stretch of the Motagua fault in Guatemala kills 23,000.

**July 28, 1976:** The magnitude 8.0 Tangshan earthquake in northeastern China kills an estimated 250,000 people and seriously injures 160,000 more; almost the entire city of 1.1 million people is destroyed.

**May 18, 1980:** An earthquake occurs beneath Mount St. Helens, Washington, which causes a large landslide high on that mountain. This landslide exposes a pressurized magma chamber, which explodes with a north-directed lateral blast.

**September 19, 1985:** A magnitude 8.1 earthquake near Mexico City kills 10,000 people, injures 30,000, and causes billions of dollars worth of damage.

**December 7, 1988:** The Leninakan earthquake in Armenia leaves 60,000 dead, 15,000 injured, and 500,000 homeless; it destroys 450,000 buildings, including thousands of historical monuments, and causes $30 billion in damage.

**October 17, 1989:** An earthquake in the Santa Cruz Mountains, in the vicinity of Loma Prieta, California, kills 67 and produces more than $5 billion worth of damage in the San Francisco-Oakland area.

**January 17, 1994:** A moderate earthquake, with a magnitude of 6.7, strikes the northern edge of the Los Angeles basin near Northridge, California. There are 57 deaths, and damage is estimated at $20 billion.

**January 17, 1995:** The most costly natural disaster to date occurs when an earthquake strikes Kobe, Japan. The death toll exceeds 5,500, injuries require 37,000 people to seek medical attention, and damage is estimated at $50 billion.

**August 17, 1999:** More than 17,000 die when a magnitude 7.4 quake strikes İzmit, Turkey.

**December 26, 2003:** An earthquake in Bam, Iran, kills more than 26,000 and leaves 75,000 homeless.

**October 8, 2005:** A powerful earthquake rocks Kashmir in Pakistan. More than 90,000 are dead and about 106,000 are injured; 3.3 million people are made homeless, and the damage is estimated at $5 billion.

**May 26, 2006:** A 6.3 magnitude earthquake in Java, Indonesia, kills more than 6,000 people, injures nearly 40,000, and leaves 1.5 million homeless.

earth and are readily apparent from the offsets they produce in rivers, mountain ranges, and anthropogenic structures. The San Andreas fault in California is a well-known example. More often, earthquakes occur on faults that are not vertical but have a substantial slope to them. The quakes may occur along a segment of such a fault, which is buried deep beneath the surface of the earth. Often these faults can be followed up to the surface, using geological and geophysical methods, where their surface exposures can be mapped. Sometimes the faults do not extend to the surface; these are called hidden faults.

A portion of the energy released by slippage is transmitted away from the site in the form of elastic waves (waves that travel through a material because of its ability to recover from an instantaneous elastic deformation). Within the interior of the earth, there are two types of waves: P waves and S waves. A P wave is a sound wave, consisting of alternating regions of compressed and rarefied media. All materials—solids, liquids, and gases—transmit P waves. An S wave distorts the material through which it is trying to travel. If that material is capable of recovering from a distortion, the S wave will travel through it. Solids are defined as materials with this capability. As P waves and S waves reach the surface of the earth, they can generate surface waves there. These surface waves, which are also elastic waves, are considerably more complex, travel more slowly, and are usually much more damaging than P waves or S waves.

As elastic waves travel through different materials, they are filtered and transformed. Sometimes, particularly when traveling through mud or unconsolidated materials, the energy can be concentrated in waves with a period of a second or two. Many buildings resonate at such low frequencies, and the effect of a long series of these waves passing under such a building is like pushing someone on a swing: Each additional push is very small, but because the timing of the push is in harmony with the swinging, each push adds to the amount the swing moves. Because of this, regions far from an earthquake, if they are underlaid by mud, may experience much greater devastation than areas closer to the earthquake that are underlaid by bedrock.

Any major earthquake produces a series of elastic waves that can be detected just about anywhere on earth. From these waves scientists can determine the location and size of the earthquake. The location on the surface of the earth above the point where the earthquake is

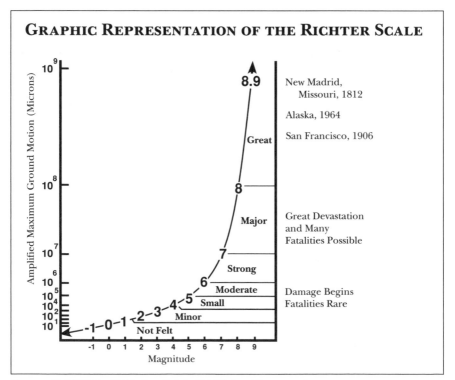

## GRAPHIC REPRESENTATION OF THE RICHTER SCALE

*Powerful earthquakes can topple entire buildings within seconds.* (National Oceanic and Atmospheric Administration)

thought to have happened is called the epicenter. Seismic data measure the size of an earthquake using some form of the Richter scale. Useful from a scientific perspective, such seismically determined sizes do not tell the whole story. If the epicenter is in an uninhabited area, even a large earthquake may cause no fatalities and produce little damage. In contrast, if the epicenter of a small earthquake is in a densely populated region characterized by thick accumulations of mud, death and destruction may be great. Another measure of earthquake size, the Modified Mercalli scale, calculates the intensity of shaking at the surface. Observations of damage and perceptions of witnesses are used to estimate this intensity.

In traveling from their source to the seismograph that records them, seismic waves propagate through regions of the earth about which little is known. Differences in composition, temperature, and other factors within a particular region of the earth may result in either early or late arrivals for waves moving through that region. Because the same region will be traversed by waves from many earthquakes, careful studies, compiling large sets of data acquired over decades of work, have been able to decipher much about the interior of the earth. Through the 1960's these different regions were represented as depth ranges. This produced a model for the earth in which properties varied as a series of spherical shells. As more sophisticated digital instruments came into use, lateral variations could be addressed. The computations required are similar to those in medicine in a computed tomography (CT or CAT) scan and form the basis for the field of seismic tomography.

## GEOGRAPHY

Earthquakes are not randomly distributed on earth: Most occur along tectonic plate boundaries. The surface of the earth is made up of a dozen or so tectonic plates, which are about 62 miles thick and persist with little deformation within them for hundreds of millions of years. Tectonic plates comprise the crust (either oceanic or continental crust) and a portion of the earth's mantle beneath it. The boundaries between them are named according to the relative motions between the two plates at that boundary. Plates diverge from each other along ridges (generally beneath the oceans, but occasionally running through a continent, such as the East African Rift Valley). Plates move past each other along transform faults, such as the San Andreas fault in California. They also converge, with one plate moving beneath the other, along subduction zones.

The forces driving these motions are among the most powerful on earth and have been moving the plates around for at least the last five hundred million years. Discovering and understanding this tectonic system was one of the principal achievements of the earth sciences during the latter half of the twentieth century.

Many geographic features are the result of interactions between the plates. Most subduction zones occur near coastlines, have a trench lying offshore, and have a string of volcanic mountains a little way in from the shore. This geography dominates the western coast of Central and South America. Often a chain of islands develops if the subduction zone involves two plates carrying oceanic crust. The Aleutian Islands off the coast of Alaska are a good example of this phenomenon. Most of the Pacific Ocean is surrounded by subduction zones, which are responsible for the earthquakes and volcanoes of the "Ring of Fire," a dramatic name given to this region before plate tectonics was understood. (One early theory held that the

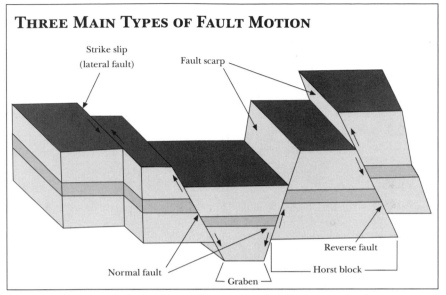

## THREE MAIN TYPES OF FAULT MOTION

Strike slip
(lateral fault)

Fault scarp

Reverse fault

Horst block

Normal fault

Graben

(Courtesy National Oceanic and Atmospheric Administration)

Moon had been ejected from the Pacific Ocean, and the Ring of Fire was the wound that remained in the earth.)

A plate carrying a continent subducting beneath another continental plate may create gigantic mountain ranges and immense uplifted regions such as the Himalayas. They were formed as the subcontinent of India drove into the southern edge of the Eurasian plate. In the process, wedges of crust were forced out to the side, forming some of the eastern portions of China and Indochina. The compression, occurring in a north-south direction, ejected these wedges to the east, much as a watermelon seed squeezed between the thumb and forefinger may be squirted across a table. Hence this process is called "watermelon-seed tectonics." Other places where it is thought to occur are Turkey and the Mojave Desert in California.

Although most earthquakes occur along plate boundaries, a few, including some very large ones, take place in plate interiors. The cause of these intraplate earthquakes is not well understood. It is generally believed, however, that future earthquakes will occur where earthquakes have occurred in the past, and these locations are considered to have substantial seismic risk. The very southeastern corner of Missouri, near the city of New Madrid, is one such area, having had a series of violent earthquakes in 1811 and 1812. Charleston, South Carolina, is another, as it was nearly destroyed by an earthquake in 1886.

### PREVENTION AND PREPARATIONS

Earthquakes are caused by the intermittent motion of tectonic plates past each other. Any attempt to stop the motion entirely is doomed to failure, as it only ensures greater motion at some later time. The only other way to prevent earthquakes is to increase their frequency, thereby avoiding a huge, damaging earthquake by inducing a large number of smaller, less harmful ones. Various scenarios have been proposed in which two sections of a fault are temporarily "locked" and the region between them is encouraged to slip, releasing the accumulated strain energy a little bit at a time. Because the risks involved in such an undertaking are great, and because the confidence in either locking or unlocking a section of the fault is small, such scenarios are rarely taken very seriously.

As prevention seems unlikely, preparation is of particular importance. Efforts here involve understanding the science, identifying places at particular risk for earthquakes (forecasting), and identifying and then observing precursory phenomena (which may lead to predicting impending earthquakes).

There are two premises on which forecasting is based: If there once was a damaging earthquake at some location, there is likely to be another one there at some time, and if that place recently had a big earthquake, it is unlikely that another one will occur there soon. Understanding faults, plate tectonics, and the earthquake process permits incorporation of these two premises into a concept of seismic gaps: Faults are identified in areas where damaging earthquakes have occurred in historic times. That portion of each fault which slipped during each historic earthquake is then mapped out. Segments that have had large strain-releasing earthquakes in the past, but not for the last thirty years or so, can then be picked out as the locations most likely to have damaging earthquakes in the near future. These seismic gaps represent places where there is a gap in the release of seismic energy and that are thus "due" for an earthquake. Although obviously useful, such forecasts are not specific enough for extensive preparations.

## COMPARISON OF MAGNITUDE AND INTENSITY

| *Richter Magnitude* | *Mercalli Intensity* | |
|---|---|---|
| 2 and less | I-II | Usually not felt by people |
| 3 | III | Felt indoors by some people |
| 4 | IV-V | Felt by most people |
| 5 | VI-VII | Felt by all; building damage |
| 6 | VII-VIII | People scared; moderate damage |
| 7 | IX-X | Major damage |
| 8 and up | XI-XII | Damage nearly total |

An earthquake prediction states a time, place, and magnitude for an expected earthquake. Scientists use a variety of precursors to give them clues about when and where future earthquakes will occur. Laboratory experiments during which rock samples are made to fracture and slip under controlled conditions have revealed some interesting phenomena. Just prior to failure, the volume of the sample being compressed actually increases. Sensitive microphones glued to the rock can detect a number of tiny noises inside the samples; tiny cracks within the sample grow longer and open wider. As they grow longer they fracture the rock just ahead of their tips, making the noises. As the cracks open wider they make the volume of the sample increase. When they grow sufficiently to interconnect, the rock fails. This behavior is called dilatancy and explains a number of precursory phenomena.

Ground deformation occurred prior to the Nigata, Japan, earthquake of 1964. Although dilatancy had not yet been discovered, the survey data revealed this deformation previously existed. Similarly, anomalous radon fluctuations were observed prior to earthquakes in the Garm District of Russia during the early 1960's. Dilatancy can explain these, too, as the opening cracks draw water in from surrounding regions at an enhanced rate, increasing the levels of radon in the springwater.

Dilatancy also affects seismic waves. The P wave velocity is affected by the amount of water in the growing cracks, whereas the S wave velocity is not. A drop in the ratio of the velocities of these two waves can indicate growing cracks. The length of time that this ratio remains depressed can indicate the size of the impending earthquake. The eventual rise in this velocity can indicate when the earthquake will occur. In 1971 this approach led to the first successful prediction of an earthquake, in the Adirondack Mountains of New York State.

Unfortunately, not all earthquakes are preceded by indications of dilatancy. If it does occur, however, it may provide a prediction of a major earthquake as much as a year or two in advance of the event. With that much warning, much could be done to reduce the number of people killed and injured by the earthquake. Most important, water levels in reservoirs behind dams could be lowered. Large meetings and conventions could be rescheduled. Emergency service personnel and volunteers could be trained, and people could be evacuated or schooled in earthquake survival.

## RESCUE AND RELIEF EFFORTS

Earthquakes damage and destroy buildings, infrastructure, and lines of communication. Because the crucial connections between the affected area and the outside world, often called lifelines, may be severed, rescue and relief operations are likely to depend on local resources. Setting up reserves of water, fuel, and generators is an obvious prudent step, which most communities in earthquake-prone areas take. Less apparent is the need to identify human resources, on a neighborhood scale, who can help in such a disaster. As an example, a person who was trained as an army cook might be invaluable in a neighborhood field kitchen.

As in any mass casualty incident, triage will be essential—and unpleasant. In triage, treatment is allocated to victims based on how severely they are hurt and how likely they are to survive if given treatment. Because resources are limited, some living, badly hurt victims will not be treated, effectively being left to die. The triage officer making these decisions must be medically trained yet cannot actively treat patients. Such unpleasant work requires considerable training and discipline.

Once treatment has begun, additional complications may be anticipated. Normal protocols often call for radio communications between Emergency Medical Service (EMS) personnel and medical doctors or hospital staff. After an earthquake this is likely to be impossible: Too many radios trying to transmit crowd the airwaves. Hospitals are likely to fill quickly. Ambulances may be used as first-aid stations, at least during the early stages of the rescue effort.

Fatalities are likely to be from head or chest injuries or from respiratory distress brought on by burial under debris. Those with compromised cardiovascular systems, caused by disease, age, or injuries, will be at greatest risk. Cultural and temporal variables can be important. A major earthquake during rush hour in Los Angeles might result in deaths and injuries from collisions on, and collapses of, the freeways. This could result in retired people being relatively spared. An earthquake at night in an economically depressed area in South America might kill most victims as their heavy adobe homes collapse on them. In this case, infants young enough to sleep next to their mothers are sometimes sheltered from falling debris and have a better chance of survival than the rest of their family members.

The extrication of victims from collapsed and damaged buildings after an earthquake presents some special problems. Big earthquakes are usually followed by a series of smaller earthquakes called aftershocks for days after the initial event. A large initial earthquake will have sizable aftershocks, some of which are capable of producing extensive damage to undamaged buildings. A major earthquake damages many buildings structurally, without causing their collapse. Weakened and then subjected to aftershocks, they represent death traps for rescue personnel. Great care must be taken to put as few of these people at risk as possible. Trained, organized groups—professional or volunteer—will most likely be more disciplined than the general population.

Plaintive cries for help, adrenaline coursing through the bloodstream, and the overwhelming sense of powerlessness engendered by a massive disaster can combine to put more people at risk. Debris may be pulled off a pile covering a whimpering child, who is scared but unhurt, and unwittingly added to another pile, burying a seriously hurt and unconscious individual.

As lifelines are restored, additional assets can be brought in to assist with extrication and medical services. To be effective, these need to be deployed where they are most needed, and priorities need to be established. Prior planning can anticipate many of the needs that will develop, but an overall command system must be in place to ensure that the right tools end up in the right places. Immediately after an earthquake, neighborhoods and localities need to be able to function as independent entities, but eventually the rescue operation needs to evolve into a well-coordinated regional effort.

## IMPACT

The impact of a devastating earthquake is profound, widespread, and long-lasting. Rescue efforts bring media attention, which in turn encourage assistance for the victims in the form of funds, clothes, and other materials. Sometimes the media portrays a disaster as an unfolding human interest story; much of the critically important work is less likely to make the news. Governments also often provide relief, but, more important, they restore the lifelines necessary for everyone's survival and the infrastructure required to return life to "normal." It is sobering to consider how much time may be needed to accomplish this. Electricity and phone service, taken for granted by most people, need wires and poles if they are to be delivered. After an earthquake in which landslides occur, many of those lines and poles are destroyed, as are many of the roads needed to bring in new lines and poles from outside the affected region. The roads that are in service are needed first to transport victims, rescue personnel, and equipment. Water and sewer distribution systems are other obvious high-priority systems to restore. Less apparent is the need for effective transportation if a modern metropolitan area is to remain viable. Elaborate networks of expressways, subways, rapid transit, trains, and buses are especially vulnerable to disruption by earthquakes and require enormous amounts of money and time to rebuild.

The financial resources necessary for recovery will not be available within the affected region, and they may not be immediately available within the country. As governments borrow money to accomplish the tasks immediately required, credit may tighten elsewhere, having serious consequences for the economy as a whole. For example, the San Francisco earthquake of 1906 is thought by many to have been an important contributing factor to the Panic of 1907.

The productivity and economic viability of the affected area are likely to remain depressed for a long time. Small companies, unable to afford a period of inactivity, may fail. Larger companies may transfer personnel and contracts to other localities. Industrial facilities may be so expensive to rebuild that other alternatives, such as relocating offshore, might become attractive. More significant, and much more difficult to predict, will be the long-term effect an earthquake has on the reputation of the area in which it occurs. Businesses dislike uncertainty. The extent and duration of earthquake-caused disruptions will be considered when companies evaluate the region in future decisions concerning location.

Earthquakes will also have an impact on how residents evaluate their own situation. Fear and the presence of danger will motivate some people to move away. For others, the quality of life will never entirely recover: Although people may remain in the area, concerns and worries about seismic risks will add stress to their lives. Such impacts may be very long-lasting.

A technologically advanced society is very fragile. Many systems are interdependent, and an entire economy depends on their working together. A serious earthquake interferes with this, killing and injuring some and inconveniencing and frightening nearly everyone. Perhaps the greatest impact of the next big earthquake will be the realization of this fact, suddenly thrust upon the population by events entirely beyond its control.

*Historic buildings were destroyed in the 2004 San Simeon quake in Paso Robles, California.* (FEMA)

## HISTORICAL OVERVIEW

Most cultures have oral histories describing earthquakes, and some have myths or legends attributing their cause to such sources as gods, catfish, or frogs. The Chinese history of earthquakes goes back at least to a device that could detect earthquakes, made by the Chinese scholar Chang Heng in about 132 C.E. However, the written record of a scientific approach to earthquakes, which is generally available to Western students, begins in the eighteenth century. A major earthquake occurred in Lisbon, Portugal, in 1755, which caused many scholars to begin thinking about earthquakes.

Scientific academies sponsored expeditions to Italy after several major earthquakes there. Investigators plotted damage to try to pinpoint where the events had occurred. In general they found concentric patterns, with the greatest damage in the center, but sometimes there were isolated pockets of intense damage far from the rest. This early work has been developed over the centuries, leading to the construction of maps showing what is now called the intensity of shaking, and using a scale, usually the Modified Mercalli scale, to try to quantify the event. Less successfully, the early investigators tried to plot the directions in which fallen pillars were aligned, in order to determine the directions in which the earth moved. Current knowledge suggests that the surface motions and building responses are far too complex for such an approach to have much value.

In 1872 a huge earthquake in Owens Valley, California, near the Nevada border, raised the Sierra Nevada as much as 23 feet (7 meters) along a fault. American geologist Grove Karl Gilbert, on observing the field evidence, concluded that the earthquake was the sudden release of accumulated elastic energy that had built up across the fault for a considerable period of time. When the frictional resistance along the fault was exceeded, an abrupt movement would occur, resulting in an earthquake. This was the first time the association of earthquakes with faults was recognized.

Additional information was sought on the frequency, timing, and duration of earthquakes, so scientists developed instruments. During the latter half of the eighteenth century, many different designs were used in the construction of many seismographs. Attention was directed at local events until 1889, when a recording made at Potsdam, Germany, showed a distinct earthquake, but no earthquakes had been felt in the vicinity. It turned out that an earthquake had occurred in Japan on that date, and that the seismic waves had traveled thousands of miles before being recorded in Germany. Waves that have traveled such distances are called teleseisms.

Because a great deal of theoretical work on the theory of elasticity had already been done, the understanding of how and why these waves traveled such great distances developed rapidly. Recognizing the value of the information these waves might provide to the study of the interior of the earth, scientists expended considerable efforts to refine, redesign, build, and deploy seismographs in laboratories throughout the world, particularly in the United States and Japan.

By 1906, British geologist Richard Dixon Oldham had established the existence of the earth's core, correctly interpreting the absence of certain waves at certain points on earth as being the result of a fluid interior. Also in 1906, a great earthquake and subsequent fire had devastated San Francisco; movement on the San Andreas fault was obvious. In some places the offset reached almost 20 feet (6 meters).

American geologist Harry Fielding Reid examined the field evidence and used several survey results to determine how the relative motion decreased with distance from the fault. His results quantified Gilbert's conclusions, let him estimate when the last important strain-relieving earthquake had taken place, and even let him guess when the next earthquake might occur along this segment of the fault. This has become known as the theory of elastic rebound.

By the early 1930's entire laboratories had been constructed to study earthquakes and their elastic waves. To permit workers to compare data, American scientist Charles Francis Richter, working with American seismologist Beno Gutenberg, suggested that they should all use a particular kind of seismograph, a logarithmic scale, and the same equations for how seismic wave amplitudes decreased with distance from their source. This was the basis for the Richter scale, which has evolved considerably but is still in use.

After World War II, the Cold War developed, with the Soviet Union and the United States building and testing nuclear warheads. To detect underground nuclear tests anywhere in the world, the United States deployed a network of sensitive seismographs that vastly increased both the quality and quantity of seismological data available to scientists all over the world. The same earthquake would now be recorded at dozens of locations, and details of the earth's interior were gradually revealed.

By 1958 the general model of the earth had been defined. By averaging the results from many earthquakes, recorded by many seismographs, scientists Sir Harold Jeffreys and Keith Edward Bullen compiled a graph of travel time curves. From these the seismic velocities within the earth could be determined as a function of depth. With additional constraints provided by other knowledge of the density distribution, reasonable estimates for the pressure, temperature, and composition of the earth were derived.

At the same time, geologists were shifting their attention to the ocean floor. By the 1960's a picture was emerging of a planet with an outer surface made up of a dozen or so plates that moved past each other, and sometimes over the tops of each other, at rates on the order of centimeters per year. This plate tectonic model provides the source of the deformation ultimately responsible for earthquakes. Movement of the plates past each other occurs in a spasmodic fashion, with elastic energy gradually building up until the strength of the material and the friction-resisting motion on a fault are overcome; then, a sudden displacement occurs, producing earthquakes.

When a gong or a cymbal is struck, vibrations occur at many different frequencies. The same thing can happen to the earth if it is struck by a large enough earthquake. This happened in 1960, when an earthquake off the coast of Chile made the earth resonate for several weeks. Scientists detected these very low frequencies, which have periods of about an hour, using instruments called strain meters. These data further refined our understanding of the earth.

With advances in electronics, communications, and computers, a new generation of digital seismographs was developed and deployed. New mathematical developments such as the Fourier transform permitted scientists to interpret the data these seismographs obtained. It became possible to examine how seismic velocities varied from place to place at the same depth. These studies, called seismic tomography, revealed that the internal structure of the earth was more complex than just a series of spherical shells with different seismic properties.

*Otto H. Muller*

**BIBLIOGRAPHY**

Bolt, Bruce A. *Earthquakes.* 5th ed. New York: W. H. Freeman, 2006. In a manner suitable for a beginning student, this popular book presents the knowledge and wisdom of a man who studied earthquakes for decades. While technical details are generally not developed at length, the author's familiarity with all types of seismological information is apparent.

Brumbaugh, David S. *Earthquakes, Science, and Society.* Upper Saddle River, N.J.: Prentice Hall, 1999. This book covers earthquakes and their impact on society with a thorough, yet easily understood, approach. It explains the physics underlying earthquakes and seismology with unusual clarity. Seismic tomography, seismic refraction, and internal reflections are treated well.

Coch, Nicholas K. "Earthquake Hazards." In *Geohazards: Natural and Human.* Englewood Cliffs, N.J.: Prentice Hall, 1995. A good treatment of the subject at an introductory level. Generally restricted to earthquakes within the United States, but it also includes good discussions of tsunamis.

Heppenheimer, T. A. *The Coming Quake: Science and Trembling on the California Earthquake Frontier.* New York: Times Books, 1988. This very readable book describes the study of earthquakes from a human perspective. The author narrates a history of scientific developments, giving details of the people involved and their emotional involvement in their work.

Keller, Edward A., and Nicholas Pinter. *Active Tectonics: Earthquakes, Uplift, and Landscape.* 2d ed. Upper Saddle River, N.J.: Prentice Hall, 2002. Looking at earthquakes from the perspective of how they alter the landscape, this book provides some uncommon insights. Although it requires little in the way of background knowledge from its readers, it manages to develop considerable understanding of fairly complex technical material. Little attention is paid to the impact of earthquake disasters on society.

Kimball, Virginia. *Earthquake Ready.* Rev. ed. Malibu, Calif.: Roundtable, 1992. This book details much of what can be done to prepare for and survive an earthquake. Its technical adviser was Kate Hutton, a seismologist at the California Institute of Technology in Pasadena, California.

Lundgren, Lawrence W. "Earthquake Hazards." In *Environmental Ge-*

*ology*. 2d ed. Upper Saddle River, N.J.: Prentice Hall, 1999. Includes case studies of five earthquakes that occurred between 1975 and 1995.

Zeilinga de Boer, Jelle, and Donald Theodore Sanders. *Earthquakes in Human History: The Far-Reaching Effects of Seismic Disruptions*. Princeton, N.J.: Princeton University Press, 2005. Describes how earthquakes are produced and analyzes their effects on societies and cultures across history.

# EL NIÑO

**FACTORS INVOLVED:** Geography, rain, temperature, weather conditions

**REGIONS AFFECTED:** All

## DEFINITION

El Niño is a recurring weather phenomenon involving large-scale alterations in sea surface temperatures, air pressure, and precipitation patterns in the Pacific Ocean. It can cause severe storms and droughts in the bordering continents and has effects worldwide.

## SCIENCE

The Spanish words *El Niño* (the boy) allude to the infant Christ. It is the traditional term used by Peruvian fishermen to refer to a slight warming of the ocean during the Christmas season. Scientists borrowed the name and reapplied it to abnormal, irregularly recurring fluctuations in sea surface temperature, air pressure, wind strength, and precipitation in the equatorial Pacific Ocean. These conditions are part of a weather phenomenon that scientists call the El Niño-Southern Oscillation (ENSO). El Niño conditions can last up to two years.

Under normal conditions westward-blowing trade winds push water in a broad band along the equator toward Indonesia and northern Australia. A bulge of water builds up that is about 1.5 feet higher than the surface of the eastern Pacific. The western Pacific is also warmer, as much as 46 degrees Fahrenheit (8 degrees Celsius), and the thermocline, the border between warm water and cold water, is much deeper. The air above this vast pool of warm water is moist, and evaporation is rapid. As a result, clouds form and rain falls abundantly. The average air pressure is low. Meanwhile, in the eastern Pacific, off the South American northern coast, the sea surface is cold as water wells up from the depths. Evaporation is slow, and there is little cloud formation or rain. The air pressure is high.

Sometimes the trade winds weaken. Scientists do not fully understand why this happens, although weather patterns to the north and south are known to influence the change. The trade winds can no

*El Niño storms in 1998 caused the Rio Nido mudslides in Northern California.* (FEMA)

longer hold back the bulge of warm water in the western Pacific. It flows eastward, generally within 5 degrees of latitude north and south of the equator. As the water bulge flows into the central Pacific, two sets of huge subsurface waves, Kelvin waves moving east and Rossby waves moving west, are created. They move slowly. The Kelvin waves take as long as two and a half months to cross the ocean to South America, and the Rossby waves reach the western Pacific boundary after six to ten months. As they spread, the Kelvin waves deepen the shallow central and eastern thermoclines as much as 98 feet (30 meters) and help propel the band of warm water, while the Rossby waves raise the deep western thermocline slightly.

An El Niño begins when the long finger of warm water extends to South America, raising the average surface temperature there. Scientists gauge the severity of an El Niño by the amount of temperature rise. A moderate El Niño involves an increase of 36 to 37 degrees Fahrenheit (2 to 3 degrees Celsius) above the normal summer and autumn temperatures for the Southern Hemisphere, a strong El Niño has a 37 to 41 degrees Fahrenheit (3 to 5 degrees Celsius) increase, and a severe El Niño can warm the sea surface nearly 46 degrees Fahrenheit (8 degrees Celsius).

The effects of the warm water are relatively rapid and dramatic. The warm layer blocks the normal upwelling of cold water near Peru and Ecuador, diverting it southward. The increased surface temperature accelerates evaporation. The coastal air turns more humid, and as it rises, the water vapor injects tremendous thermal energy into the atmosphere. As clouds form from the vapor, winds are generated that push the clouds inland in large storms. The storms bring downpours to regions that are normally desert. There is a rise in the sea level because of the warm water, which is less dense; that rise, together with high waves from the storms battering the coast, causes beaches to disappear in some areas and pile up in others. A huge low-pressure system settles in the central Pacific, centered approximately on Tahiti.

In the Australia-Indonesia region, conditions are nearly the reverse. The air pressure becomes abnormally high—in fact, this large-scale variation from low to high air pressure makes up the Southern Oscillation part of ENSO. Drought strikes areas that normally receive substantial rainfall. Sea levels fall, sometimes exposing coral reefs. There are further abnormal weather conditions in more distant regions, which scientists call teleconnections to El Niño.

When the Kelvin waves hit the South American coast and the Rossby waves reach the westernmost Pacific, they rebound. The western thermocline is deepened, and the eastern thermocline rises. This action begins the reversal of El Niño effects. The warm water retreats westward, pushed back by strengthening trade winds. Eventually, normal weather patterns resume.

If these oscillations came regularly, El Niños would simply be the extreme of a pattern. However, the period is not regular. For at least the last five thousand years, scientists believe, an El Niño occurred every two to ten years. Sometimes a decade, or even several decades, passes without one. Some, but not all, events are separated by abnormally cold weather in the eastern Pacific, a phenomenon known as La Niña, anti-El Niño, or El Viejo.

## GEOGRAPHY

El Niños profoundly influence weather patterns in the Pacific Ocean. In addition to increasing rainfall along the northwestern South

American seaboard, the warm water can increase the number of Pacific Ocean hurricanes, which can strike Central and North America and the Pacific islands. Above-normal water temperatures also have been recorded along the California coast of North America. Accordingly, there is more precipitation, causing coastal flooding and piling up large snowpacks in the Sierra Nevada. The Pacific Northwest, southern Alaska, the north coast of China, Korea, and Japan have above-average winter air temperatures. Australia and the maritime area of Indonesia and Southeast Asia suffer coastal and inland drought as rainfall is sparse throughout the western equatorial Pacific.

Teleconnections disrupt normal weather patterns throughout much of the Southern Hemisphere. Sections of the eastern Amazon River basin experience drought, and the monsoons in northern India may be short or fail entirely. Low rainfall occurs in southeastern Africa and drought in Sahelian Africa, particularly Ethiopia. There are also indications that El Niños affect Atlantic Ocean weather patterns. Northern Europe can be unusually cold, while across the Atlantic mild conditions prevail along the eastern seaboard of the United States, and the American Southeast has a wet winter. During the Atlantic hurricane season, fewer and weaker hurricanes arise.

### PREVENTION AND PREPARATIONS
No El Niños are identical because external weather forces cause variations in the development, duration, and severity of each. Moreover, El Niños do not recur regularly. Predicting them is therefore difficult. Since the late 1950's, however, intensive basic scientific research has identified the dynamics of the phenomena, and technological developments have made prediction and tracking of El Niños ever more reliable, allowing potentially affected areas to prepare for harsh weather.

Weather stations in the western and eastern Pacific look for changes in air pressure and signs of declining precipitation. The Tropical Atmosphere-Ocean (TAO) array comprises hundreds of buoys; most monitor water temperature and atmospheric conditions, but some also measure the depth of the thermocline. Weather satellites can use infrared imaging and laser range-finding to follow the path of expanding warm waters and to gauge sea surface level. Data from all such sources is fed into computers with special software that compares the information with past El Niños and fits it into empirically derived formulas in order to model the potential development of a new event.

While computer modeling is not foolproof, it is accurate enough that Pacific-bordering nations make preparations based upon the forecasts. Disaster relief agencies, such as the United States Federal Emergency Management Administration (FEMA), stockpile food, medicines, and sanitation and construction supplies in anticipation of floods and hurricanes. Some governments, as well as the World Meteorological Organization, maintain Web sites with the latest information on El Niños so citizens can make preparations of their own. Governments of countries in potential drought areas have staved off disaster by encouraging farmers to plant drought-resistant crops or those that mature before the El Niño season. Moving people away from canyons and low-lying lands that are subject to flooding can sometimes save lives.

## RESCUE AND RELIEF EFFORTS

El Niños do not directly threaten life and property. Instead, the storms that they spawn do the damage. The chief danger comes from flash floods in deserts, such as those in coastal Peru and Ecuador, flooding from rain-swollen rivers, and high winds from tropical storms. Since it is difficult to predict exactly where one of these conditions will occur, emergency workers usually respond only after a crisis develops. Their efforts follow the pattern for all flooding and windstorms: Move residents out of the area of danger and institute searches for those swept away by flash floods or caught in collapsed buildings.

Because flooding can be sudden, serious, and widespread, sometimes appearing simultaneously in widely separate locales, a substantial danger exists to public health from polluted drinking water. This is particularly true in areas that lack sewer systems, but even sophisticated city sewers can overflow. In such cases, water-borne diseases, such as cholera and typhoid, may wreak far greater harm to the populace than flooding or winds. Rescue workers must therefore provide clean water and treat outbreaks as they appear.

**IMPACT**

Because an El Niño prevents nutrient-rich cold water from rising near the coast of South America, fish must change their feeding grounds. Important commercial species, such as the anchoveta, seek cooler water to the south. This is a boon to Chilean fishers, but the fisheries of Peru and Ecuador are drastically reduced. Fishing boats make few, small catches, and the crews suffer economically, as do industries dependent upon them, such as fishmeal production. Seabirds that feed on the fish also suffer; large-scale die-offs have been recorded. Similar alterations in fishing patterns off the coasts of Central and North America occur, forcing fishers to travel farther for their catches and causing starvation among birds and seals.

Severe storms can decimate crops and kill livestock in the eastern Pacific nations, while drought does the same in Australia and the western Pacific. In Indonesia, dry forests often ignite and burn out of control, lifting smoke into the atmosphere and destroying property. The economic damage of a severe El Niño can easily exceed $1 billion on the West Coast of the United States alone, and many times that amount worldwide. The death toll from windstorms, flooding and attendant disease outbreaks, and drought-caused famine may reach into the thousands, principally in South America. Scientists suspect that global warming may make future El Niños more powerful, raising the potential for yet greater destructiveness.

*Roger Smith*

**BIBLIOGRAPHY**

Allan, Rob, Janette Lindesay, and David Parker. *El Niño Southern Oscillation and Climatic Variability.* Collingwood, Australia: CSIRO, 1997. Offers a scholarly introduction to the history of El Niño studies, the oceanic-atmospheric forces behind the phenomenon, and forecasting methods, followed by hundreds of color graphs displaying data on conditions during El Niños from 1871 to 1994.

Arnold, Caroline. *El Niño: Stormy Weather for People and Wildlife.* New York: Clarion, 1998. Intended for young readers, a richly illustrated explanation of the mechanics of El Niño, its effects, and forecasting methods. A clear introduction for general readers who are science-shy.

Babkina, A. M., ed. *El Niño: Overview and Bibliography.* Hauppauge,

N.Y.: Nova Science, 2003. Analyzes this weather pattern, including stronger events such as the El Nino of 1982-1983. Provides a detailed overview, as well as comprehensive title, author, and subject indexes.

D'Aleo, Joseph S. *The Oryx Resource Guide to El Niño and La Niña.* Westport, Conn.: Oryx Press, 2002. Chronicles the basic causes and effects of El Niño and La Niña, including their historical, meteorological, ecological, and economic impacts.

Fagan, Brian. *Floods, Famines, and Emperors: El Niño and the Fate of Civilization.* New York: Basic Books, 1999. Following a popular explanation of El Niño, Fagan examines evidence of its influence on ancient civilizations, concluding with an overview of the 1982-1983 and 1997-1998 episodes.

Glantz, Michael H. *Currents of Change: El Niño's Impact on Climate and Society.* New York: Cambridge University Press, 1996. Glantz, an environmental scientist, outlines the natural causes of El Niños for nonscientists and discusses the phenomenon's effects on society at length.

Lyons, Walter A. *The Handy Weather Answer Book.* Detroit: Visible Ink Press, 1997. Explains the fundamental science of weather systems and describes forecasting and the instruments used to gather meteorological data. A chapter address El Niños and climate change. The question-and-answer text is simple and clear, accompanied by illustrations.

Nash, J. Madeleine. *El Niño: Unlocking the Secrets of the Master Weather-Maker.* New York: Warner Books, 2002. Nash describes how generations of scientists and explorers helped unravel the mystery of the El Niño weather phenomenon.

Philander, S. George. *Is the Temperature Rising? The Uncertain Science of Global Warming.* Princeton, N.J.: Princeton University Press, 1998. Intended for college students, an enjoyable survey of the science behind climatic phenomena, with a lucid chapter on ENSO.

_____. *Our Affair with El Niño: How We Transformed an Enchanting Peruvian Current into a Global Climate Hazard.* Princeton, N.J.: Princeton University Press, 2004. Philander discusses the scientific, political, economic, and cultural developments that shaped the perception of the El Niño current.

# EPIDEMICS

FACTORS INVOLVED: Animals, human activity,
microorganisms, plants, temperature, weather
conditions
REGIONS AFFECTED: Cities, forests, islands, towns

## DEFINITION

An epidemic is the spreading of an infectious disease over a wide
range of a human population that historically leads to a dramatic loss
of life. Preventive measures, which include aggressive sanitation procedures, have reduced the impact of epidemics on human life, but
new threats have emerged.

## SCIENCE

Contagious or communicable diseases are those transmitted from one
organism to another. Living microorganisms, also known as parasites,
such as bacteria, fungi, or viruses, may invade or attach themselves to a
host organism and replicate, thus creating infectious diseases. A disease that affects a large human population is called an epidemic.

In a disease situation the host organism serves as the environment
where the parasite thrives. With many diseases, such as syphilis, the
parasite remains present throughout the lifetime of the host unless it
is destroyed by treatment. Generally, the parasite appears to have a
degree of specificity with regard to the host. Thus, microorganisms
adapted to plant hosts are rarely capable of attacking an animal host
and vice versa. However, a given parasite may attack different types of
animal hosts, including both vertebrates and invertebrates.

Many times the parasite emigrates from one host to another by
means of an insect carrier or other vector. In other cases the parasites
may spend one part of their life in an intermediate host. This may enhance or decrease the harmful effect the parasite will have on the
host, as the intermediate host may or may not interact constructively
with the parasite. As a result geographic or seasonal differences in
the disease outbreak are very likely to occur.

Occasionally, diseases are spread among rodents by an intermediate host, such as fleas. The rodent-flea-rodent sequence is called

enzootic, meaning the infection is present in an animal community at all times but manifests itself only in a small fraction of instances. However, once the environmental conditions are favorable the condition becomes epizootic, and a large number of animals become infected at the same time. As the rodent population is reduced by death, fleas from the dead animals fail to find other host rodents and begin infecting other animals that are present in the immediate area, including humans. The overall infestation is slow at the beginning but quickly explodes, with a devastating number of victims. The human involvement in this progression is therefore more coincidental than programmed.

Most pathogenic parasites adapt comfortably to their hosts and do not survive the conditions outside the host's tissues. Exceptions to this case are those microorganisms whose lives involve a resistant-spore stage. Such examples include the *Coccidioides* fungus, which is responsible for desert fever and the anthrax bacillus that affects cows, sheep, goats, and even humans. An animal disease that can also be transferred to humans is called zoonosis.

Epidemiology is the medical field that studies the distribution of disease among human populations, as well as the factors responsible for this distribution. Contrary to most other medical branches, however, epidemiology is concerned more with groups of people rather than with the patients themselves. As a result, the field relies heavily on statistical patterns and historical trends. Its development arose as a result of the great epidemics of the last few centuries that led to an immeasurable loss of human lives. Scientists at the time began looking into the identification of the high risk associated with certain diseases in an attempt to establish preventive measures. Epidemiological studies are classified as descriptive or analytic. In descriptive epidemiology, scientists survey the nature of the population affected by the disorder in question. Data on factors such as ethnicity, age, sex, geographic description, occupation, and time trends are closely monitored and recorded. The most common measures of disease are mortality, which is the number of yearly deaths per 1,000 of population at risk; the incidence, which is defined as the number of new cases yearly per 100,000 of population at risk; and prevalence, which is the number of existing cases at a given time per 100 of population at risk.

In analytic epidemiology, a careful analysis of the collected data

# MILESTONES

**11th century B.C.E.:** Biblical passage Samuel I tells of the Philistine plague, a pestilence outbreak that occurred after the capture of the Ark of the Covenant.

**7th century B.C.E.:** Assyrian pestilence slays 185,000 Assyrians, forcing King Sennacherib to retreat from Judah without capturing Jerusalem.

**451 B.C.E.:** The Roman pestilence, an unidentified disease but probably anthrax, kills a large portion of the slave population and some in the citizenry and prevents the Aequians of Latium from attacking Rome.

**430 B.C.E.:** The mysterious Plague of Athens early in the Peloponnesian War against Sparta results in about 30,000 dead.

**387 B.C.E.:** According the records of Livy, a series of 11 epidemics strikes Rome through the end of the republic.

**250-243 B.C.E.:** "Hunpox," or perhaps smallpox, strikes China.

**48 B.C.E.:** Epidemic, flood, and famine occur in China.

**542-543 C.E.:** Plague of Justinian is the first pandemic of bubonic plague that devastates Africa, Asia Minor, and Europe. The first year the plague kills 300,000 in Constantinople; the infection resurfaces repeatedly over the next half century.

**585-587:** The Japanese smallpox epidemic, probably the country's first documented episode of the disease, infects peasants and nobility alike. Because it occurs after the acceptance of Buddhism, it is believed to be a punishment from the Shinto gods and results in burning of temples and attacks on Buddhist nuns and priests.

**1320-1352:** Europe is stricken by the Black Death (bubonic plague), claiming over 40 million lives.

**1347-1380:** The Black Death kills an estimated 25 million in Asia. A reported two-thirds of the population in China succumbs.

**1494-1495:** French army syphilis epidemic strikes in Naples and is considered the first appearance of this venereal infection in Europe.

**1507:** Hispaniola smallpox is the first recorded epidemic in the New World, representing the first wave of diseases that eventually depopulate America of most of its native inhabitants. In the next two centuries, the population plunges by an estimated 80 percent.

**1520-1521:** About 2 to 5 million die in the Aztec Empire when they contract smallpox during the Spanish conquest and colonization of Mexico.

**1878:** The Great Yellow Fever Epidemic results in over 100,000 cases and 20,000 deaths, particularly in Memphis, Tennessee.

**1892-1894:** A cholera pandemic leaves millions dead but confirms the theory that the disease is caused by bacteria in contaminated water.

**1900-1915:** "Typhoid Mary" Mallon, a cook, spreads typhoid fever to more than 50 people, causing at least 3 deaths.

**1916:** The Great Polio Epidemic affects 26 states, particularly New York, prompting quarantines and resulting in 27,000 reported cases and at least 7,000 deaths.

**1918-1920:** The Great Flu Pandemic sweeps the globe, killing 30 to 40 million, perhaps the largest single biological event in human history.

**1976:** 221 American Legion veterans contract a mysterious type of pneumonia at a hotel in Philadelphia, and 29 of them die; the media names the illness "Legionnaires' disease."

**1976:** An Ebola virus epidemic in Zaire kills 280 people and proves one of the deadliest diseases of the late twentieth century.

**1981:** U.S. epidemic reported by U.S. Centers for Disease Control in June and given the name acquired immunodeficiency syndrome (AIDS). In some regions of Africa the infection touches 90 percent of the population and poses a constant pandemic threat.

**1995:** An outbreak of Ebola virus in Kitwit, Zaire, leaves 245 dead.

**1999:** 7 die in an epidemic of encephalitis in New England and New York.

**2002:** A virulent atypical pneumonia, dubbed severe acute respiratory syndrome (SARS), spreads quickly through China and then internationally, infecting at least 8,422 victims and causing 916 known deaths.

is made in an attempt to draw conclusions. For instance, in the prospective-cohort study, members of a population are observed over a long period of time, and their health status is evaluated. The analytic studies can be either observational or experimental. In observational studies, the researcher does not alter the behavior or exposure of the study subjects but instead monitors them in order to learn whether those exposed to different factors differ in disease rates. On the other hand, in experimental studies the scientist alters the behavior, exposure, or treatment of people to determine the result of intervention on the disease. The weighted data are often statistically analyzed using t-tests, analysis of variance, and multiple logistic regression.

An epidemic that takes place over a large geographical area is known as a pandemic. Its rise and decline is mainly affected by the ability of the infectious invading agent to transfer the disease to the susceptible individual host. Interestingly enough, the population of infected individuals that survives the parasite usually acquires a type of immunity. This immunity diminishes the epidemic and prevents it from reoccurring within a certain time period in the same geographic area. As a result the invading parasite is unable to reproduce itself in this immunity-equipped host population. This may be the reason that areas that have exhibited the Ebola epidemic for several months with a death rate of almost 95 percent suddenly display a suppressed outbreak.

Within a certain time frame, however, the host's susceptibility to the invader may be reproduced due to several factors. These include the removal of the immune generation by death, the deterioration of the individual immunity by external conditions, and the birth of offspring who do not have the ability to naturally resist the disease.

In some cases, such as syphilis, the disease severity appears to be less now than a few centuries ago. One theory suggests that the ability of the parasite to infect as many hosts as possible has produced a negative effect on the parasite itself. Eliminating all hosts steadfastly will lead to the extinction of the parasite itself. Therefore, once the adaptation of the parasite to the host has become close, the tendency for the disease outbreak appears less severe. Ecological studies suggest, however, that it is incorrect to assume that the host-parasite antagonism will reduce in intensity and that the continuous fight for dominance remains in full force.

## GEOGRAPHY
Epidemics can take place anywhere on earth as long as the conditions allow it. Historically these conditions favor an isolated environment with animal or insect carriers, unsanitary conditions, and large human

# TYPES OF VIRAL INFECTION

| Family | | Conditions |
|---|---|---|
| Adenoviruses | | Respiratory and eye infections |
| Arenaviruses | | Lassa fever |
| Coronaviruses | | Common cold |
| Herpesviruses | | Cold sores, genital herpes, chickenpox, herpes zoster (shingles), glandular fever, congenital abnormalities (cytomegalovirus) |
| Orthomyxoviruses | | Influenza |
| Papovaviruses | | Warts |
| Paramyxoviruses | | Mumps, measles, rubella |
| Picornaviruses | | Poliomyelitis, viral hepatitis types A and B, respiratory infections, myocarditis |
| Poxviruses | | Cowpox, smallpox (eradicated), molluscum contagiosum |
| Retroviruses | | AIDS, degenerative brain diseases, possibly various kinds of cancer |
| Rhabdoviruses | | Rabies |
| Togaviruses | | Yellow fever, dengue, encephalitis |

populations. The infectious disease can be spread easily to other areas and have an equally strong impact there. Rodents have long served as one of the primary factors in spreading diseases to people, especially if the human population is contained. The tsutsugamushi disease (also known as scrub typhus) is transmitted by the bite of a rat mite.

One of the first epidemics in history that involved infected rats occurred at the beginning of the Peloponnesian War in Greece (431-404 B.C.E.), in which the rats were transferred by ships. The Athenians, who were the dominant naval force in the conflict, were besieged by the Spartan army inside Athens. The infected rats were brought into the city unintentionally via ships that were transporting food from Egypt. The ensuing Plague of Athens led to the decline of the Pericles regime and tilted the scales of the war toward the Spartan army.

The historically devastating bubonic plague in Europe occurred in the fourteenth century, almost two centuries after the so-called Black Death originated in Mesopotamia. The mass spreading of rats is greatly attributed by many historians to the onset of the Crusades and led to an estimated 25 million lives lost in Europe alone. France was particularly affected (1348-1350), with many cities losing about one-third of their populations. Nothing appeared to check the disease in populations without immunity: neither bonfires to disinfect air, nor demonstrations of penitence, nor persecutions of Jews and Gypsies. Oceangoing ships also appear to have been responsible for the epidemic in China during the end of the nineteenth century.

It is believed by many scholars that the origins of venereal syphilis were in America, since historical accounts of the outbreak first appeared in Europe after Christopher Columbus's return trip from the New World at the end of the fifteenth century. Moreover, skeletal remains of pre-Columbian American Indians indicate the presence of the *Treponema pallidum* spirochete, which is responsible for the disease. Among the victims of that disease were England's king Henry VIII and several members of the Italian Borgia family in the middle of the sixteenth century.

## PREVENTION AND PREPARATIONS

There seems to be a variable degree of natural susceptibility to a specific disease among different people. This occurs because the outcome of the interaction of parasite and host is variable in each individual case. As a result individuals who have low resistance quickly show symptoms of the disease and easily display the infection. On the other hand, people with strong resistance do not show the symptoms, and the infection is not recognizable.

Most diseases seem to be preventable unless they are idiopathic (particular to the individual), such as inherited metabolic defects. Diseases that are caused by environmental factors may be avoided by eliminating or greatly reducing the effectiveness of the factors responsible. The various epidemics in Europe, such as the Black Death and the London plague, had much less impact on the upper classes. More affluent groups that had sufficient land or wages that would allow for the replacement of tools and isolation from the infected areas suffered much less. On the other hand, the poor, who had very few possessions and a lack of sanitation and pure water, were forced to live under miserable conditions that allowed diseases to thrive.

Transmission of infection may be avoided by preventing contact between the susceptible host and the parasite. Historically, the easiest application of this principle has been quarantine, which in several cases had very limited success. It is nearly impossible to prevent diseases from spreading across borders because of airborne factors, such as mosquitoes infected with malaria and flies carrying the plague. Rocky Mountain spotted fever, which is believed to have originated in the northwestern part of the United States but spread to Mexico, South America, and Africa, is transmitted to humans via tick bites and is native to many rodents.

Syphilis would not have been so devastating in Europe if prostitutes did not spread the disease to their patrons. The consequences would not have been as severe if mercury treatment, the most popular method of combating syphilis at the time, was given to prostitutes. However, the expense, together with the social belief that such women were not worth the treatment, prohibited the remedy.

The last two cases of the plague in European urban areas were in Marseilles, France (1720), and Messina, Italy (1740), which were not as destructive as previous plagues because of more elaborate and organized methods of quarantine. The same was true during the last months of the Great Plague of London (1665). Some historians give credit for the containment of epidemics to the isolation of lepers, many of whom modern scientists believe were carrying communicable diseases other than leprosy. Another way to prevent the spread of disease is to exterminate animals that may carry the infectious factors, which has taken place as late as the 1990's, in the case of bovine spongiform encephalopathy, commonly called mad cow disease.

The spreading of plagues is greatly confined by controlling rat populations, particularly those on ships, and by preventing rodents from landing at uninfected ports. One plague bacillus can infect as many as 80 rodents, giving rise to the sylvatic plague. Using sprays to eliminate mosquitoes reduces outbreaks of malaria, which occur especially in swampy areas. Louse-borne typhus may be regulated in humans by strong disinfecting methods. Typhus has become virtually nonexistent in industrialized societies through the extermination of lice and fleas, while typhoid fever has been eliminated by the use of sanitized water. Examples of this involve the chlorination of water in swimming pools and municipal water sources, as well as pasteurization of milk. Despite the fact that plague epidemics have come under control in recent centuries, there still exist many foci of infection.

The explosive development of medical technology after World War II led to the synthesis and administration of significant medica-

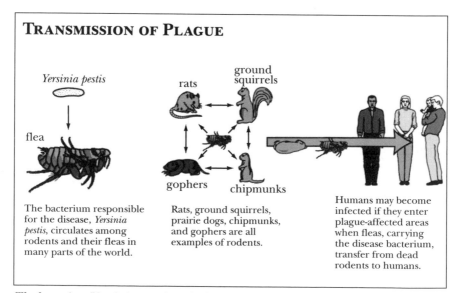

**TRANSMISSION OF PLAGUE**

*Yersinia pestis*

flea

rats

ground squirrels

gophers chipmunks

The bacterium responsible for the disease, *Yersinia pestis*, circulates among rodents and their fleas in many parts of the world.

Rats, ground squirrels, prairie dogs, chipmunks, and gophers are all examples of rodents.

Humans may become infected if they enter plague-affected areas when fleas, carrying the disease bacterium, transfer from dead rodents to humans.

*The bacterium* Yersinia pestis, *which causes plague, follows a path from fleas to rodents to humans.*

tions, such as antibiotics and vaccines, which led to the decisive control of epidemics. Developing an artificial immunity, such as through vaccination, is extremely effective because the infecting agent cannot inhabit the organism after the virus has been administered to it. This was demonstrated with the diphtheria, smallpox, and poliomyelitis (polio) vaccines that were designed for children after World War II. The polio vaccine against infantile paralysis is a combination of the killed virus, which is injected, and the attenuated or weakened virus, which is given orally.

In the early 1980's the acquired immunodeficiency syndrome (AIDS) epidemic appeared. During this decade many thousands, possibly millions, of people died all over the world. Although quarantine is generally not possible in the society of industrialized countries, other measures of prevention are lessening the disease's spread. The use of prophylactics during sexual contact, extensive screening of blood transfusions, and education about the impact of the virus all seem to have had a positive effect on the number of people affected. To a much lesser degree the various forms of hepatitis have claimed a large number of victims. Although not as much in the public eye as AIDS, the disease is communicable, and municipal health departments have tried to control its spread by monitoring the sanitation conditions of restaurants.

### RESCUE AND RELIEF EFFORTS
Throughout history, epidemics have been controlled by the destruction of the organisms responsible. The fact that the Great Plague of London never reappeared is attributed, according to some scholars, to the great fire that burned the city in September, 1666. In the eighteenth century, bodies were often buried with caustic bases. The pioneering work of English scientist Joseph Lister in the nineteenth century introduced doctors to antiseptics, and detergents were used more frequently.

The various laboratory procedures that were developed in the twentieth century provided first the detection of the disease and then the prescribed routes for cure. Thus, the eradication of syphilis started with the development of the serological test for syphilis (STS), which detects syphilis reagin and the treponemal antibody, two antibodies formed by the organism once the bacteria have invaded it. Penicillin and other antibiotics helped curb the number of syphilis victims. American doctor Jonas Salk's polio vaccine in the 1950's gave all children the chance to walk without crutches. The wide availability of quinine has saved millions of people from malaria. A vaccine against the plague is currently available and is being used in areas where the epidemic continues to flourish.

The World Health Organization (WHO) was set up in 1948 to increase the international effort toward improved health conditions, particularly in poor areas of Africa, Asia, and South America. The WHO was the successor of the Health Organization of the League of Nations, established in 1923, and the Office International d'Hygiene Publique, created in 1907. Unlike the other two organizations, whose duties included quarantine measures, drug standardization, and epidemic control, WHO undertakes the task of promoting the highest possible conditions for universal health to all populations. Its responsibilities include the revising and updating of health regulations, support of research services, and the dissemination of information that concerns any potential pestilent-disease outbreak. The organization also collaborates and shares information with all member countries on the latest developments in nutrition research, updated vaccinations, drug addiction, cancer research, hazards of nuclear radiation, and efforts to curb the spread of AIDS.

Much credit has been given to the WHO for its mass campaign against infectious diseases, which led to the control of a large number of epidemics. As a result, smallpox has been eradicated, cholera and the plague have been practically eliminated, and most other diseases have been substantially reduced. Intensive programs that have provided pure water, antibiotics, pesticides, primary health care facilities, and clean sanitation systems to underdeveloped countries helped to reduce infant mortality and increase the average life span in these places.

During the late 1980's and throughout the 1990's a concentrated effort was coordinated by the WHO enlisting the governments of its member countries in the war against AIDS. Data collection, education campaigns, promotions encouraging safe sex, continuous research, health-care providers, and infection control were employed to overcome dangerous and unsanitary practices in the underdeveloped world.

It should also be noted that many of the countries that are vulnerable to natural disasters, such as floods, mudslides, earthquakes, tornadoes, and typhoons, face the menacing problem of refugees and homeless people after these events. The lack of sanitary conditions and an efficient way to remove the dead, a reduced number of medical supplies and personnel, and poverty increase the casualty count in many disasters. The WHO has been helped in these situations by other international relief organizations, such as the Red Cross and the Peace Corps, together with the voluntary contributions of other countries.

## IMPACT

Epidemics have played a role in checking the human population. The Great Plague of London claimed more than 75,000 of a total population of 460,000 and forced the king and his court to flee to the countryside for more than eight months, while the Parliament kept a short session at Oxford. The outbreak in Canton and Hong Kong left almost 100,000 dead. Severe epidemics of poliomyelitis have been reported in many parts of the world, especially during the twentieth century. About 300,000 cases were recorded in the United States alone during the 1942-1953 period. Western Europe, and especially Germany, Belgium, and Denmark, as well as Japan, Korea, Singapore, and the Philippines, also suffered many casualties in the early 1950's.

When the carriers of the epidemic are rodents, the economic damage to the afflicted area is also immense. Norway rats, black rats, and the house mouse had devastating effects as they devoured crops of wheat, sugar beets, and potatoes in Germany at the end of the World War I, Russia in 1932-1935, and especially France in 1790-1935, where at least 20 mouse plagues have been reported.

Epidemiological studies and comparisons have shown that the twentieth century was pivotal in transforming the patterns of frequent death from disease to the lowest in human history. Infant and child mortality were reduced dramatically, cases of famine and epidemic were lessened, and modern science shifted many of its efforts to degenerative diseases that affect the elderly. Many countries still faced epidemics of relatively minor proportions in areas where civil strife occurred, especially Somalia, Rwanda, the Sudan, even into the 1990's. The aftermath of the hurricanes in Bangladesh and the Caribbean in that decade proved that epidemics were not fully eliminated from society.

During the twentieth century, the epidemiologic transition of the human race shifted. Until the early part of that century the pattern of mortality and disease afflicted infants and children as well as younger adults and was related to bacteriological epidemics. In contrast, by the late twentieth century, with the exception of AIDS and occasional outbreaks of epidemics in underdeveloped countries, most diseases were human-made and degenerative, such as the ones attributed to drug use, smoking, and drinking. As a result the average life span increased sharply, by almost twenty-five years after the early 1960's. This holds true for industrialized countries; however, the pattern is only slowly changing in developing countries, which have not had the same socioeconomic development as industrialized countries. Nevertheless, the twentieth century decline in mortality in developing countries was significantly more rapid than that of the nineteenth century in countries now classified as industrialized.

## HISTORICAL OVERVIEW

Epidemic diseases are the greatest destructive force in human history. Epidemics have killed millions across continents and even more so influenced cultural, economic, and political institutions. Great empires, powerful armies, and a host of human endeavors have crumbled under the weight of disease and, likewise, factored in subsequent societal changes. Epidemics are contagious diseases that spread rapidly and extensively through a community, region, or country. When they sweep across the globe they are referred to as pandemics. Prior to the introduction of vaccination and antibiotics, viral and bacterial infections posed a constant and often widespread threat to human existence.

The history of epidemics dates from the earliest written records, an influence upon human life throughout time. In Western culture an epidemic is often referred to as a pestilence, which is symbolized in the Bible's book of Revelation as one of the three great enemies of humanity, along with famine and war. Characterized as the Horsemen of the Apocalypse, these three serve as a convoy for a fourth rider, Death.

Peoples throughout ages, regions, and religions explained illness and death as divine judgment for the sins of humanity, psychologically interlacing poor health with their own moral depravity. Illness was punishment; cast from the hands of God, disease tortured individuals and often entire populations with more than the hardships of sickness. Modern medical science, together with the social sciences, has since revealed secular connections between social disorder and the spread of contagious infections. Still, many cultures maintain the belief that sickness and death are a form of divine retribution. However, medical theory also has ancient roots.

Healers and medical practitioners speculated on the origins of disease and epidemics throughout recorded history. The Greeks developed a more formalized framework for understanding the causes of illness and periodic epidemics, rejecting the idea of divine retribution. Hippocrates (c. 460-370 B.C.E.) is considered the "father of medicine" and the most prominent physician of the ancient world. His name is associated with the high ideals of medical practice. The *Corpus Hippocraticum*, a collection of nearly sixty treatises written by his students following his death, established the foundation of medical knowledge, especially relating to endemic and epidemic diseases. The most notable treatise, *Airs, Waters, and Places*, discusses the links between the environment and disease. It states that some diseases maintain a constant presence in a population and are referred to as "endemic." Other diseases flare infrequently but with deadly force; these are termed "epidemics." We still employ these terms today.

Less enduring were early notions of the body, which, according to Hippocratic doctrine, consisted of four humors: blood, phlegm, yellow bile, and black bile. Good health meant keeping the humors in balance through proper diet, temperament, and correction of bodily deficiencies. Disease occurred when the humoral balance was upset, and epidemics resulted from excesses in the natural environment. In the latter, changing seasons and atmospheric conditions corresponded to the prevalence of vast instances of contagious diseases. Thus, drastic changes that upset the natural environment produced widespread sickness in humans. The ideal for human health was to live a balanced and unstressed life within a harmonic environment. Hippocratic doctrine related epidemics as a natural force in nature without understanding the role of microorganisms.

It was only within the last one hundred years that science expanded upon the Hippocratic doctrine to understand the mechanics of disease, how it spreads, and how it may be prevented or cured. The outbreak of an epidemic is dependent upon a variety of factors, some of which are seemingly unrelated to the actual spread of contagious infections. Among the important factors to consider in the formation of an epidemic are the general health of a population; living conditions, including hygiene and sanitation practices; immunity to a particular disease; access to medical treatment; community public health responses; and environmental conditions. Less obvious factors favoring the spread of disease may include economic disarray; the introduction of new people or products, especially after a period of isolation; a massive disruption resulting from war or natural disasters, such as earthquakes, famines, and floods; or an explosion in insect or rodent populations. Thus, epidemics are often dependent on a variety of factors that may work independently or in tandem to cause widespread destruction.

Historical references to epidemics are found in a variety of ancient texts. *The Gilgamesh Epic* (2000 B.C.E.) mentions the impact of natural disasters, floods in particular, and affirms the destructive force of the god of pestilence. The ancient writings illustrate how disease can have far more extensive effects than simply reducing populations. Histories of the great civilizations in Babylon, China, and Egypt document a host of diseases and widespread sickness. Many of these, such as bubonic plague, diphtheria, smallpox, and typhus, have paralleled human existence into the modern world. Other population-decimating diseases are difficult to define clearly given the lack of precise descriptions. For example, the last plague of Egypt, recounted in Exodus, offers little scientific evidence for identification of a specific disease other than that it killed the firstborn children.

Similarly, the Plague of Athens in 430 B.C.E., which struck during the Peloponnesian War between Athens and Sparta, not only influenced the outcome of an important historic event but also produced a turning point in world history. Athenians were infected by an epidemic that killed 25 percent of the population. Thucydides, the Greek historian and witness to the plague and war, described the ailment as causing "violent sensations of heat in the head," sneezing and hoarseness, unquenchable thirst, and death in seven to ten days. He also described the collapse of morality within the city where without the "fear of gods or law of men there was none to restrain them."

The plague, a disease without clear identification, in this case lengthened the war and thereby facilitated the eventual downfall of the Athenian Empire.

The Roman Empire also experienced several epidemics with significant consequences. Malaria may have been endemic in the Mediterranean region during much of antiquity and produced major problems in the Roman Empire from 100 B.C.E. The vastness of the empire, which extended from the African Sahara to Scotland and from the Caspian Sea to Spain, meant that infections from the hinterland found easy transportation to vulnerable populations. For example, the Plague of Antonius attacked the Empire between 164 and 189 C.E. and produced a ghastly mortality rate. Galen, the famous Roman physician, described victims with high fevers, throat inflammation, diarrhea, skin eruptions after a week of illness, and then death. Medical scholars maintain that this may have been one of the first smallpox epidemics in Western history. The disease may have started in Mongolia and moved eastward into the Germanic tribes, with whom the Romans were at war.

Of historical importance, the Antonius plague helped stimulate the acceptance and spread of Christianity within the Empire. Christianity provided hope for believers in miraculous cures, resurrection, and eternal salvation. In addition, the teachings of Christ, which stressed care for the sick, fit perfectly into an era marked by widespread illnesses. The establishment of charitable hospitals for the sick and indigent became a foundation of the faith. During the fourth century, a woman named Fabiola founded the first such hospital in Rome and institutionalized through medical care the religion's tenets, which have lasted into the twenty-first century. The epidemic in this instance promoted a religion that beforehand was of little significance.

Powerful epidemics not only devastated populations but also shattered the authority of governments, religions, and economic systems. The Black Death of the fourteenth century offers the best example of the destructive force of epidemics or, in this case, pandemics, because the affliction spread from Central Asia to East Asia and west to Europe. Fleas served as the vector, or agent that carries a pathogen, from rats to humans. In this manner, the causative bacillus *Pasteurella pestis* or *Yersinia pestis* spread through the movement of rats along caravan routes and accompanied the Mongol invasions in Central Asia.

The regions suffered massive devastation. In Europe the bubonic plague swept urban and rural communities in huge waves, claiming perhaps 50 percent of the population. The loss of life fractured the feudal economic and social order, splintered control of the Roman Catholic Church's dominance, and helped usher in a new political order. The plague continued as a serious threat to Europeans into the eighteenth century. In other parts of the world, especially Asia, the plague flared, frequently with enormous loss of life and institutional destruction.

In 1911 an epidemic of bubonic plague swept the Manchurian region of northern China. The death toll, perhaps 60 percent of the population, could have been much worse had modern public health initiatives not held the disease in check. Chinese people traditionally believed that heaven sends a natural disaster as a sign of the end of an empire. The decaying Qing Dynasty, the last imperial dynasty in China's history, collapsed under the combined weight of social disruption and the force of the epidemic.

In the twentieth century, epidemics were checked by the development of antibiotics, widespread inoculations, and international public health measures. Still, the so-called Spanish Flu pandemic of 1918, arguably the greatest single biological event in human history, killed 30-40 million people worldwide, 600,000 in the United States alone. In the modern age, where an infected person can travel the globe in a few hours, a potential exists for natural disasters of giant proportions. Thus, government health organizations, such as the United States Public Health Service and the World Health Organization continually monitor disease and varying social and environmental conditions to prevent the outbreak of epidemics.

In November, 2002, many thought that these fears had been realized with the spread of a virulent atypical pneumonia, dubbed severe acute respiratory syndrome (SARS), through China and then internationally. At least 8,422 people were infected, and 916 known deaths occurred before the epidemic ended the following July. Subsequent concerns have been centered on the threat posed by avian influenza, often termed "bird flu," which sometimes affects humans and could mutate into a strain transmitted between people.

*Soraya Ghayourmanesh*
*Nicholas Casner*

**BIBLIOGRAPHY**

Bollet, Alfred J. *Plagues and Poxes: The Impact of Human History on Epidemic Disease.* New York: Demos, 2004. Focuses on specific diseases and their historical effect. Intended for general readers.

Ernester, Virginia L. "Epidemiology." In *McGraw-Hill Encyclopedia of Science and Technology.* 8th ed. New York: McGraw-Hill, 1997. This article discusses epidemiology and its branches, including descriptive and analytic approaches, with emphasis on observational and experimental studies.

Farrell, Jeanette. *Invisible Enemies: Stories of Infectious Diseases.* 2d ed. New York: Farrar, Straus and Giroux, 2005. Intended for young people. Explores humankind's struggle against dangerous diseases.

Karlen, Arno. *Man and Microbes: Disease and Plagues in History and Modern Times.* New York: Putnam, 1995. Describes the history of communicable diseases, such as cholera, leprosy, AIDS, viral encephalitis, lethal Ebola viruses, and streptococcal infections.

Lampton, Christopher F. *Epidemic.* Brookfield, Wis.: Millbrook Press, 1992. This text, designed for young adults, discusses how epidemics begin and spread and what can be done to prevent them. Emphasis is on the Black Death and AIDS.

McNeill, William Hardy. *Plagues and Peoples.* Garden City, N.Y.: Doubleday, 1998. Topics include the impact of the Mongol Empire on transoceanic exchanges and the ecological impact of Mediterranean science after 1700.

Ranger, Terence, and Paul Slack, eds. *Epidemics and Ideas: Essays in the Historical Perception of Pestilence.* New York: Cambridge University Press, 1997. This book views medicine and disease as conceived by different civilizations, including those of classical Athens, the Dark Ages, Hawaii, and India.

Thomas, Gordon. *Anatomy of an Epidemic.* Garden City, N.Y.: Doubleday, 1982. Analysis and causes of epidemics are thoroughly investigated by the author.

Watts, Sheldon J. *Epidemics and History: Disease, Power, and Imperialism.* New Haven, Conn.: Yale University Press, 1998. This book discusses the human response to plagues in Europe and the Middle East from 1347-1844, with special chapters on leprosy, smallpox, syphilis, cholera, and yellow fever.

# Explosions

**FACTORS INVOLVED:** Chemical reactions, human activity
**REGIONS AFFECTED:** Cities, towns

## DEFINITION

The detonation of pipes or storage tanks containing fuel and grain dust in silos occurs with little warning and often in densely populated areas, so that the explosions have devastating, although localized, effects on life and property.

## SCIENCE

For an explosion to occur, three conditions must exist. First, a fuel must be present in sufficiently concentrated form. Industrial society is awash with volatile materials—the hydrocarbons of petroleum and natural gas used for power, volatile chemicals for processing and fabrication, and the residue of manufacturing and agriculture. Second, there must be an ignition source. Third, oxygen must be present, and it is, except under special conditions, everywhere humans live.

When a fuel and an oxygen-bearing agent, or oxidant, react to produce heat, light, and fire, they are combusting. Explosions are fast combustion. More precisely, an explosion is combustion that expands so quickly that the fuel volume (and its container, if there is one) cannot shed energy rapidly enough to remain stable. The energy from the chemical reactions spreads into surrounding space. This runaway reaction, or self-acceleration, produces two types of explosions. If the rate is slower than the speed of sound, the reaction spreads outward as burning materials ignite the materials next to them. The process is called deflagration, and explosives that deflagrate are known as low explosives. If the rate is faster than the speed of sound, a shock wave progressively combusts materials by compressing them. This process is called detonation and occurs in high explosives.

Ignition starts an explosion. All materials have some minimum temperature, called a flash point, at which a combustible mixture of air and vapor exists, and increasing the pressure on the materials may lower this point. Beyond the flash point, the fuel awaits only an igni-

## MILESTONES

**June 3, 1816:** The steamboat *Washington* explodes on the Ohio River.

**May, 1817:** The steamboat *Constitution* explodes on the Mississippi River.

**April 27, 1865:** 1,500 die in the explosion of the steamboat *Sultana* on the Mississippi River.

**September 8, 1880:** A mine explosion at the Seaham Colliery in Sunderland, England, kills 164.

**April 28, 1914:** An explosion in the Eccles Mine in West Virginia leaves 181 dead.

**December 6, 1917:** Munitions ships in Halifax, Nova Scotia, harbor explode and burn; 2,000 die.

**May 6, 1937:** The German zeppelin *Hindenburg* explodes into a massive fireball as it tries to land in Lakehurst, New Jersey, killing 36.

**July 17, 1944:** Two ammunition ships in Port Chicago, California, explode, killing 300.

**March 25, 1947:** A mine explosion in Centralia, Illinois, kills 111.

**April 16, 1947:** The French vessel *Grandcamp* explodes in Texas City, Texas, killing 581.

**April 25-26, 1986:** 32 are killed when a nuclear reactor at Chernobyl, Russia, explodes.

**July 6, 1988:** The explosion of Piper Alpha oil rig in the North Sea kills 167.

**June 8, 1998:** A Kansas grain elevator explodes, killing 6.

**April 22, 2004:** In Ryongchon, North Korea, a train carrying flammable cargo explodes at the railway station, killing 54 people and injuring 1,249.

tion source—electric spark, sharp blow, static electricity, or friction—to start the explosion. Some materials, in fact, combust spontaneously if they are sufficiently hot, as is the case, for instance, with oil-soaked rags. Most often the fuels are liquid, but many gases will also explode when the vapor forms a sufficiently dense cloud. Fuels that explode when ignited by a nonexplosive source are known as primary explosives. Additionally, some explosions occur when pressurized equipment, such as steam boilers, rupture, although these explosions are seldom catastrophic on their own.

The most common and easily obtainable commercial explosives in the United States are mixtures of ammonium nitrate (also used as fertilizer) and fuel oil mixtures (ANFOs), accounting for 95 percent of commercial applications. Unfortunately, late in the twentieth century ANFOs also became weapons in the form of car bombs used by terrorists.

Dust constitutes a special, important category of explosive materials. About 80 percent of industrial dusts are explosive, as is all the dust produced by milling and storing grain. All that is necessary for an explosion, in addition to an ignition source, is that the dust be dry, concentrated, mixed with air, and in a confined space. Under these conditions, dust that is only the thickness of a coin is explosive.

The power of commercial explosives is usually measured on a scale comparing them to trinitrotoluene (TNT), where TNT equals 100. Most primary explosives have a rating of about 50. The aluminum nitrate in ANFOs on its own, for instance, has a rating of 57, which rises considerably in the presence of fuel oil. Almost universally, however, the power of an accidental explosion is expressed as equivalent to tons of TNT.

After ignition, a shock wave continues beyond the initial flash point into the surrounding environment and gives the explosion its power to shatter and crush, or brisance. Following the shock wave is a region of vacuum, followed in turn by high pressure—a pair of effects called backlash. The shock wave and backlash together may produce subtle but serious damage. The shock wave can knock walls and supports out of place, and then the backlash can move them back into place, but in dangerously weakened condition. The damage is difficult to detect. Heat (often in the form of fire) also spreads out from the explosion, extending its impact with secondary detonations and deflagrations, while flying debris and ground vibrations worsen the damage.

### GEOGRAPHY

Explosions are phenomena of industrial civilization—especially its energy production. About 80 percent of explosions in the United States take place in industrial plants. Because most industry is located near metropolitan areas, explosions are most likely to occur in cities. Naturally, facilities making or transporting commercial or military explosives run a high risk of accidental explosions, but petroleum refineries; storage tanks for natural gas; and liquefied petroleum gas, propane, and gasoline are also at risk and are more likely to occupy the outskirts of a city. Moreover, terrorists usually target heavily populated areas, especially those associated with a symbol of power or wealth, such as military headquarters or corporate offices.

Towns likewise suffer explosions from fuel processing and storage. In addition, agricultural communities in grain-producing regions store the grain in large silos. If the grain dust is ignited, the silos explode with spectacular, deadly violence.

The arteries of communication between inhabited areas also see explosions. Tanker trucks on highways and tanker cars on railways may explode if they rupture during a wreck, and leaks in pipelines conveying natural gas and petroleum products can also lead to explosions. Human-caused explosions in wilderness areas are rare, usually the by-product of an airplane crash or military accident.

## PREVENTION AND PREPARATIONS

Preventing accidental industrial or residential explosions first requires that the three minimum conditions for an explosion do not exist. Fuels must be used, stored, and moved at conditions well below their flash points, and ignition sources, especially sparks from machinery, must be eliminated. In some cases, oxygen levels can be lowered.

Additionally, the design of fuel-handling buildings and equipment can ward off accidents or reduce their effects. Reinforcing buildings, locating hazardous equipment in the center of rooms, installing water systems to douse flames, venting rooms to the outside environment, and installing grating rather than solid decks all can serve to contain, suppress, or dispel an explosion's destructive force. Locating critical structures, such as storage tanks and processing plants, far from one another prevents secondary explosions. Automatic shutdown sensors on pipelines and temperature sensors in ovens, boilers, and processing machinery can eliminate the conditions for an explosion.

Government agencies, insurance companies, public utilities, and private contractors offer risk analysis of existing structures and equipment and may recommend safety improvements. Experts point out, however, that technology alone cannot prevent accidents. Human error accounts for about 60 percent of accidental explosions. Proper training in handling and storing materials is therefore essential, both for workers on the job and people at home. Especially important is knowing how to avoid an accidental ignition.

Because explosive materials are usually highly toxic, preventive measures must also safeguard pollution of the environment. Fuels—in gas, liquid, or solid form—ejected from an explosion can poison wildlife and even lead to further explosions. For this reason, thorough cleanup of a disaster site is important.

## RESCUE AND RELIEF EFFORTS

Immediately following a disastrous explosion, rescue workers have three paramount tasks: stopping fires, ensuring the injured are located and receive adequate medical care, and evacuating anyone who is threatened by the explosion's aftermath. All three tasks involve substantial risks.

An explosion of petroleum products or a natural gas leak often leaves some of the fuel unignited. This can form pools or, if it is a gas, collect in sewers or low-lying areas. Fires started by the initial detonation may then ignite the leftover fuel after rescuers have entered the disaster zone, placing them in peril. Likewise, buildings damaged in the explosion may look safe but then suddenly collapse as rescue workers search for survivors. Digging survivors from building rubble poses similar hazards and must be conducted with utmost care. Debris, disturbed by digging, may suddenly settle or shift, killing those trapped below and injuring rescuers.

Most industrial plants and surrounding cities maintain evacuation plans for disasters. The plans prescribe the areas to be cleared of residents in an emergency; who is to perform the evacuation; and places to set up emergency medical facilities, temporary lodging, and kitchens. Rescue officials allow residents back into the area only after thorough inspection shows that all fires have been put out and buildings are safe.

For small explosions, local police and firefighters conduct the rescue work, while medical personnel in area facilities take care of the injured. In large disasters, police, firefighters, and medical personnel from surrounding areas may be called. In the United States, state police, the National Guard, and federal armed forces, all coordinated by state or federal agencies, may become involved.

## IMPACT

While uncommon, explosions cause great damage, and do so spectacularly. Between January of 1995 and July of 1997, for instance, 39 industrial explosions occurred, causing an average of almost $1.5 million in damage each. In 1998, the 18 grain-dust explosions alone cost about $30 million and killed 7 people. ANFOs have caused some of the worst disasters in American history. In 1947, a fire broke out in the *Grandcamp,* a cargo ship docked near the Monsanto Chemical Company factory in Texas City. The crew could not extinguish it, and 2,500 tons of ammonium nitrate exploded in its hold, also igniting the same cargo in a nearby ship. The factory was destroyed, as well as two-thirds of the buildings in Texas City. More than 500 people died. ANFOs also appeal to terrorists because they are cheap and relatively easy to obtain. In 1995, a truck full of ANFOs tore apart the Alfred P. Murrah Federal Building in Oklahoma City, killing 169 people.

Because of industrial accidents, state and federal legislators enacted regulations designed to minimize the danger of explosions and, should one occur, to safeguard life and property. The building codes, procedures, and technological measures that implement the regulations increase immediate production costs to industry but, by reducing the number of accidents, save money in the long run.

Likewise, to guard against terrorist bombs, increased control of explosive materials, security in public buildings and airports, and surveillance costs taxpayers billions of dollars. Measures to protect against accidental or terrorist explosions, critics maintain, make society ever more dependent upon technology and security forces, and to some degree affect individual liberty.

## HISTORICAL OVERVIEW

Explosions occur when there is a pressure differential on either side of a barrier or when inherently unstable chemicals ignite. A few explosions are entirely a result of natural situations. This is the case with volcanoes, a portion of whose cone may explode upon eruption, as was the case when Mount St. Helens erupted on May 18, 1980, but most are the consequence of human-made structures. The startling increase in human ability to create artificial structures since the onset of the Industrial Revolution is responsible for most of the memorable explosions in history.

Among the earliest explosions that caused a significant loss of life were those occurring in mines, especially coal mines, where large accumulations of coal gas could arise. When most coal mining was at or near the surface, this was not a problem, but as mines were sunk deeper into the earth, as happened in the nineteenth century, the risk of explosion increased. Explosions in British coal mines killed 1.2 miners for every 1,000 employed between 1850 and 1870. However, the introduction of new machinery and government regulation dramatically reduced the number of accidents and fatalities in British mines in the twentieth century.

Coal mining in the United States expanded less quickly than in Great Britain because the United States had ample wood fuel for a longer period of time. However, from the middle of the nineteenth century, coal production grew rapidly, especially for industrial uses. Between 1900 and the U.S. entrance into World War I in 1917, there were 14 mine disasters in the United States in which more than 100 people died. One of the worst mining disasters in U.S. history occurred in March, 1947, in Centralia, Illinois, when 111 miners were killed. In the United States, the shift to other fuels in the years after World War II, as well as the shift away from shaft mining to open-face mining, dramatically reduced the risk in coal mining. Coal mining in underdeveloped countries is highly labor intensive, and when explosions occur the loss of life is substantial. An explosion at the Chasnala coal mine in India on December 27, 1975, killed 431 miners.

Among the most spectacular explosions occurring in the United States in the early years of the nineteenth century were those on steamboats, especially those plying the midwestern rivers. The first major steamboat disaster on the midwestern river system occurred in 1816, when the *Washington* blew up on a trip between Wheeling, West Virginia, and Marietta, Ohio. The second occurred in May, 1817, when the *Constitution* blew up on the lower Mississippi River. Most steamboat explosions were attributed at the time to the preference for high-pressure steam engines on these rivers, but the fascination of the public with the speed of travel they provided (compared to horse-drawn land transportation) led to much overcrowding on the steamboats, partly accounting for the high number of casualties when explosions occurred. In 1848, the U.S. Commissioner of Patents estimated that 110 lives had been lost annually to steamboat explosions since 1830.

After the introduction of regulation of steamboats by the federal government in 1852, the number of explosions dropped somewhat. Still, a catastrophic explosion occurred in April of 1865, when the *Sultana* blew up near Memphis, Tennessee, taking the lives of 1,500 people. This was the worst steamboat explosion in U.S. history. After that, as railroads replaced steamboats, casualties dropped dramatically.

The increase in the use of military explosives from the middle of the nineteenth century onward led to many explosions of munitions. The most spectacular munitions explosion occurred during World War I, when two munitions ships collided in the harbor of Halifax, Nova Scotia, Canada; the resulting explosion and fire killed about 2,000 people. A similar event in July, 1944, in Port Chicago, California, killed more than 300. In 1947, an explosion of a Norwegian vessel carrying nitrate outside Brest, France, killed 20 people and injured 500. An explosion at a naval torpedo and mine factory in Cadiz, Spain, also in 1947, killed 300 to 500 people. The same year, on April 16, a French vessel exploded in Texas City, Texas, killing 581.

The oil and gas industry has also experienced some major explosions. One of the most deadly was an explosion on the Piper Alpha oil rig in the North Sea, July 6, 1988; 167 people died. In September of 1998 an explosion at a gas plant in Australia killed only 2 persons but shut down the plant and cut off gas supplies to the entire state of Victoria for more than a week.

Although casualties have generally been few because few workers are involved, periodic explosions occur in grain elevators. On June 8, 1998, a Kansas grain elevator exploded, killing 6 workers trapped in a small tunnel.

The most fearsome explosion of the twentieth century was the meltdown at the Russian atomic-energy plant at Chernobyl on April 25-26, 1986. Several explosions blew off the steel cover on the reactor, permitting the release of large amounts of radioactive material into the atmosphere. Prevailing winds carried this radioactive material over much of Eastern Europe. The entire reactor was shut down after the accident; 32 people were killed in the explosion.

*Roger Smith*
*Nancy M. Gordon*

**BIBLIOGRAPHY**

Bodurtha, Frank. *Industrial Explosion Prevention and Protection.* New York: McGraw-Hill, 1980. For readers sophisticated in science, this book offers a technical discussion of how industrial products— mainly gases—can ignite and how to prevent accidents.

Brown, G. I. *The Big Bang: A History of Explosives.* Gloucestershire, England: Sutton, 1998. Brown summarizes the history of explosives and their use, from gunpowder to nuclear bombs.

Cleary, Margot Keam. *Great Disasters of the Twentieth Century.* New York: Gallery Books, 1990. A somewhat grisly picture book (mostly black-and-white photographs) of natural and human-caused disasters, accompanied by descriptive text.

Crowl, Daniel A. *Understanding Explosions.* New York: Center for Chemical Process Safety of the American Institute of Chemical Engineers, 2003. Explains the many different types of explosions and offers practical methods to prevent them from occurring.

Davis, Lee. *Man-Made Catastrophes: From the Burning of Rome to the Lockerbie Crash.* New York: Facts On File, 1993. Brief descriptions of various types of disasters illustrating, according to the author, how human folly and carelessness wreak havoc.

*Fires and Explosives.* Vol. 7 in *The Associated Press Library of Disasters.* Danbury, Conn.: Grolier Educational, 1998. Drawn from the story and photograph files of the Associated Press, this volume, written for young readers, tells about famous explosions worldwide.

Rossotti, Hazel. *Fire.* Oxford: Oxford University Press, 1993. A compellingly written history of fire and explosives that explains the basic science and discusses types of disasters, as well as practical uses.

# FAMINES

**FACTORS INVOLVED:** Geography, human activity, rain,
   temperature, weather conditions
**REGIONS AFFECTED:** All

## DEFINITION
Famines recur periodically in many parts of the world, most devastatingly in heavily populated arid and semiarid regions that rely on rainfall for the production of food. Famines are less deadly in modern times because of transportation improvements and international relief capacities.

## SCIENCE
The most common cause of famine is drought, although other weather conditions can cause famine conditions by inhibiting production of food. Severe cold late into a planting season, for instance, can reduce harvests substantially, as can excessive rains during the planting, growing, and harvesting seasons. Excessive rain tends to stimulate the growth of molds and blights, which can severely damage food crops. The Irish potato famine of 1845-1849 is an example of this kind of phenomenon. More often than not, however, weather-induced famines are a function of lack of precipitation, whether in the form of snow or rain, in nonirrigated areas that rely on seasonal precipitation for cultivation.

Research has shown that regional and global weather patterns are responsible for cyclical periods of drought in many parts of the world. The El Niño and La Niña phenomena, for instance, are known to affect weather patterns throughout the world. When the Pacific Ocean heats up, as it does in fairly regular cycles along the equator several hundred miles off the western coast of South America, moisture evaporates into the atmosphere and surges to the east in the Northern Hemisphere, bringing moisture-laden storms in its wake. Moisture in the Southern Hemisphere tends to head away from South America. In 1997, flooding related to El Niño struck as far away as the horn of Africa, where unseasonably heavy rains caused considerable damage in Somalia. El Niño periods are fol-

## MILESTONES

**c. 3500 B.C.E.:** The first known references of famine are recorded in Egypt.

**436 B.C.E.:** Thousands of Romans prefer drowning in the Tiber to starvation.**917-918 C.E.:** Famine strikes northern India as uncounted thousands die.

**1064-1072:** Egypt faces starvation as the Nile fails to flood for seven consecutive years.

**1200-1202:** A severe famine across Egypt kills more than 100,000; widespread cannibalism is reported.

**1235:** An estimated 20,000 inhabitants of London die of starvation.

**1315-1317:** Central Europe, struck by excessive rains, experiences crop failures and famine.

**1320-1352:** Europe is stricken by the bubonic plague, which induces famine, claiming more than 40 million lives.

**1333-1337:** Famine strikes China, and millions die of starvation.

**1557:** Severe cold and excessive rain causes famine in the Volga region of Russia.

**1769:** Drought-induced famine kills millions in the Bengal region of India.

**1845-1849:** Ireland's potato famine leads to death of over 1 million and the emigration of more than 1 million Irish.

**1876-1878:** Drought strikes India, leaving about 5 million dead.

**1876-1879:** China experiences a drought that leaves 10 million or more dead.

**1921-1922:** Famine strikes the Soviet Union, which pleads for international aid; Western assistance saves millions, but several million die.

**1932-1934:** Communist collectivization schemes in the Soviet Union precipitate famine; an estimated 5 million die.

**1959-1962:** As many as 30 million die in Communist China as a result of the Great Leap Forward famine.

**1967-1969:** The Biafran civil war in Nigeria leads to death of 1.5 million Biafrans because of starvation.

**1968-1974:** The Sahel drought leads to famine; international aid limits deaths to about a half million.

> **1975-1979:** Khmer Rouge policies of genocide provoke famine in Cambodia; more than 1 million die of starvation.
>
> **1984-1985:** Drought in Ethiopia, the Sahel, and southern Africa endangers more than 20 million Africans, but extensive international aid helps to mitigate the suffering.
>
> **1992-1994:** Civil war sparks famine in Somalia, where hundreds of thousands die before international efforts restore food supplies.

lowed by La Niña. The waters of the equatorial Pacific cool down, and, where once moisture-laden storms coursed across the land, sunbaked days follow.

Although drought is a natural phenomenon that lies beyond the control of human science and policy, the activities of human beings combine with natural conditions to worsen droughts. For instance, deforestation reduces the capacity of foliage and land to absorb water, which leads to silting of rivers. The wind and water erosion brought about by deforestation deplete topsoil needed for cultivation. The loss of land for agriculture inhibits growth of the food supply, placing populations at risk, especially during prolonged droughts. Similarly, when land is overcultivated or overgrazed, it becomes less productive. In Bangladesh, where extensive deforestation has occurred, especially in the Himalayas, large-scale death occurs because of both floods and drought, whereas in the Philippines, where deforestation has been less extensive, mortality is not nearly as great, although the frequency of monsoons is about the same for both countries.

Apart from patterns of cultivation and deforestation, which are human-made contributing factors to drought, other human-made factors sometimes operating alone or in concert with drought conditions can cause famine. International and civil wars, for example, can inhibit production of food. A prolonged war can wreak havoc on agricultural production, inducing a largely human-made famine. Government policies that increase food prices can cause localized famine in regions where people have too little money to buy food. Governmental export of food crops is known to have caused famines by reducing domestic food resources.

## GEOGRAPHY

Almost any part of the globe can be subject to famine, but some areas are more prone than others. Famines rarely occur, despite periodic drought, in the Western Hemisphere. Centuries ago, the populations of North and South America were predominantly nomadic. When faced with localized drought, nomads responded by migration. When widespread and prolonged drought occurred in the American Southwest, the thriving Anasazi people eventually migrated elsewhere. Generally, peoples in the Americas relied on a variety of crops, some fairly resistant to drought, for food. Moreover, the Americas were sparsely populated, so that widespread famine was less likely. Many areas were well watered, and rivers rising from mountain ranges provided water resources to the widely scattered populations, even in arid regions.

Historically, the continents most susceptible to drought include Europe, Asia, and Africa, where larger concentrations of population often subsisted on arid or semiarid lands more prone to drought. With larger populations, overcultivation of land and deforestation are more common, and these regions became even more susceptible to drought. Several consecutive years of poor rains could provoke widespread and devastating famine. Today, Europe, though still liable to drought, rarely experiences famine. Owing to its highly developed economies with agriculturally diverse production and extensive transportation capacities, famine has been eliminated as a major concern in Europe. Asia and Africa, however, remain highly susceptible to both drought and famine. Asia is heavily populated, and successive years of drought can severely limit food production. North Korea in the late 1990's experienced severe drought and famine. Africa, though less heavily populated than Asia, has seen dramatic population growth for several decades, and in semiarid zones, such as the Sahel region, overcultivation and overgrazing has placed extensive areas of land into highly fragile, drought-prone zones. Coupled with this, Africa, like parts of Asia, has experienced widespread political instability and civil war, which have exacerbated drought-related conditions and contributed to famine.

## PREVENTION AND PREPARATIONS

Although it is not yet possible for humans to prevent drought or to manipulate weather conditions that lead to drought, it is possible to predict droughts, to prepare for them, and to prevent famine. Because famine is normally a function of prolonged drought, there is usually plenty of warning before famines begin. The same satellite technology that allows meteorologists to predict weather can be used to prepare long-term forecasts. Remote-sensing satellite imagery can document the progress of deforestation and predict crop production.

Social science also comes to humanity's aid. When drought has existed for a year, farmers and livestock owners tend to sell off herds in order to buy food. Similarly, the next year's seed may be consumed in the first year of a drought by farmers who then sell livestock for the purchase of more seed. Yet another year of drought can put producers at immediate risk of starvation.

Migration patterns also suggest where the effects of drought are being felt most acutely. By paying close attention to these indicators, governments and international agencies are in a good position to know when famine is likely to make an appearance. If a country is further troubled by civil wars or regional violence, then famine is likely to be more acute and possibly highly localized.

Given the well-documented factors that contribute to famine and the attention the international community has given to early warning in the past several decades, there is no reason for famine to break out unannounced. Predicting the localities of famine is one thing, however, and taking steps to prepare for a famine is quite another. Often, local governments or neighboring governments are reluctant to ask for food and other emergency supplies for fear of precipitating population movements that might be forestalled with good rains. Sometimes, governments are quite willing to overlook famine conditions in areas of their countries controlled by opposition rebel groups. In addition, well-meaning international food aid can actually depress prices for homegrown foods, thereby giving local farmers even less incentive to produce much beyond their subsistence needs. While governments take the primary responsibility for prevention of famine, international agencies have been established within the United Nations system to monitor famine emergencies. The United Nations Disaster Relief Organization did so until the early 1990's, and it was succeeded by the U.N. Department for Humanitarian Affairs and later by the U.N. Office for the Coordination of Humanitarian Affairs (UNOCHA), which coordinates a variety of intergovernmental, governmental, and nongovernmental agencies dedicated to provision of disaster aid. There is increasing awareness, however, that all such measures are highly remedial and that the most significant factor in preventing famine is the broader development of national economies.

## RESCUE AND RELIEF EFFORTS

The existence of U.N. organizations for the prevention and mitigation of humanitarian disasters such as famine, when coupled with the phenomenal growth of private humanitarian agencies and the resources of wealthier donor nations, has substantially reduced mortality in modern droughts and famines. In the latter half of the twentieth century, despite the fact that global population more than doubled, mortality during famines rarely exceeded a few hundred thousand, whereas in previous decades and centuries famine often claimed millions of lives. This decline in famine-related deaths is due in large part to the global nature of modern communication and transportation systems, wider public awareness of famine emergencies, the existence of agencies dedicated to the prevention of famine, and to the emergence of disaster mitigation agencies within and among governments.

Within the U.N. system, apart from UNOCHA, the United Nations High Commissioner for Refugees (UNHCR) often provides assistance to people who have fled persecution and natural disasters such as drought and famine. The United Nations Children's Fund (UNICEF) is also very active in famine situations, providing food and medical attention to children who are victims of famine; the United Nations Development Program (UNDP) is similarly involved in famine detection and prevention programs. The World Food Program (WFP) provides food aid to areas experiencing food deficits, and a private agency, the International Committee of the Red Cross (ICRC) often provides relief in famine areas, especially those where civil war is a factor.

Nongovernmental organizations such as Oxford Committee for Famine Relief (Oxfam), Cooperative for American Relief to Everywhere (CARE), Catholic Relief Services, World Vision, Save the Children, and countless other agencies are heavily engaged in the provision of both long-term development and humanitarian aid. The U.S. government's Office of Foreign Disaster Assistance (OFDA) and its parent organization, the U.S. Agency for International Development, are engaged in the provision of emergency famine aid and prolonged development assistance. Likewise, the U.S. Department of States Bureau for Population, Refugees, and Migration provides emergency assistance to populations in distress. Most governments have similar kinds of agencies to provide managerial capacity for response to famine emergencies. Sometimes the military establishments of countries are in a position to bring their logistical capabilities to bear when famines rage out of control and demand immediate and extensive food delivery. With a truly global famine mitigation system now in existence, there is little reason, other than political neglect, for famine to cause extensive starvation and death.

## IMPACT

Famines affect more people than any other form of disaster. Although fewer people die from famine today than in previous centuries, it is still not unusual for a famine in a very poor country or in a country experiencing civil war to affect millions and kill hundreds of thousands. Famines can wipe out whole villages and destroy regions. The impact of prolonged famines and civil discontent is felt much more strongly in poor countries than in wealthy ones, where capacities and infrastructure to respond to localized drought is far more developed. Famine kills people in poor countries, not rich ones, which leads most scholars to conclude that long-term economic development is the single most effective way to prevent famine and mitigate its effects.

## HISTORICAL OVERVIEW

Famine has occurred with great regularity and deadliness throughout history. Even in ancient times, it was greatly feared. Along with death, war, and pestilence, famine is portrayed in the Bible as one of the Four Horsemen of the Apocalypse in the New Testament book of Revelation, where the rider on the black horse carries scales to indicate the scarcity of grain and the need for it to be carefully weighed. References to famine are also frequently found in the Old Testament. Genesis describes famine as reasons for Abraham, Isaac, and

Jacob at different times to migrate from Canaan to Egypt, and the story of Jacob's son, Joseph, indicates that famine had also struck Egypt. Ancient Egyptian records and art indicate that famine was a noteworthy reality of the land along the Nile. It is common even today, when famines attain great magnitude, to speak of a famine of "biblical proportions."

Famines occur when a widespread shortage of food causes malnutrition, starvation, and death. Famines are commonly associated with civil wars and conflicts in which food supplies are interrupted, as well as with prolonged droughts that limit food production. A population facing famine and malnutrition is often highly susceptible to disease. Thus, the biblical association of famine with war, pestilence, and death is based on empirical reality. The historical record testifies to this association.

The earliest known reference to famine was in Egypt around 3500 B.C.E. Egypt is situated in a very arid zone, and it depends on the regular flow of the Nile and the seasonal flooding that permits regular planting and harvesting, which in turn depends upon monsoonal rains in the highlands of East Africa. When the rains fail, so does the regular flow of the Nile, thus threatening agriculture. Parts of China, India, the great steppes of Russia, and the Sahel region of Africa are likewise prone to periodic droughts, and thus to famine. Even areas that are normally well watered can be subject to occasional drought, however, and they may put local populations at risk of famine. A traditional means of coping with localized drought and famine is migration to areas where food is more plentiful. This, in turn, has provoked conflict among migrants, however.

The consistently largest and most frequent famines have occurred in China and India, countries that have always had very large populations. Areas with large populations that rely heavily on monsoonal rains for agricultural production are particularly vulnerable to large-scale famine when several successive years of drought occur. The most devastating famines in modern times have occurred in China. As many as 13 million people perished in the great famine of 1876-1879, during which people sold their children or resorted to cannibalism. During about the same time span, an estimated 5 million people died in India from famine, as drought affected much of Asia. In the twentieth century, famine related to Communist China's Great

Leap Forward occurred between 1959 and 1962, when it is estimated by some that as many as 30 million died. The largest death toll owing to famine in history occurred during the Black Death of 1320-1352, in which over 40 million are estimated to have perished either from disease or from starvation resulting from disrupted agriculture.

While drought is a major cause of famine, sometimes too much rain can lead to famine by interrupting harvests or destroying crops. This was the case in Europe from 1315 to 1317; bad weather in Ireland from 1845 to 1847 contributed to the blight of the potato crop, the death of 1 million Irish, and the migration of more than 1 million. The Great Irish Famine was also a function of British economic policy, because wheat exports continued from Ireland to Great Britain during the potato famine, and little was done to divert such food stocks to the starving.

Famine rarely occurs in modern times in wealthy, industrialized countries. Rather, it tends to be associated with poverty in the Third World, where subsistence farming is still the means of livelihood for millions. Thus, Africa and Asia still experience much famine, which is also a result of their being prone to political instability and civil war. Diverse food sources and less extensive population in much of South America and the Western Hemisphere generally prevent these regions from being prone to famine. Moreover, the emergence of international assistance agencies and foreign food aid have mitigated famine emergencies even in the more drought-prone areas of Africa and Asia in modern times, thus substantially reducing mortality.

*Robert F. Gorman*

**BIBLIOGRAPHY**

Aptekar, Lewis. *Environmental Disasters in Global Perspective.* New York: G. K. Hall, 1994. This is a trim and useful volume concerning the definition of natural disasters and their prevention and mitigation.

Cuny, Frederick C. *Famine, Conflict and Response: A Basic Guide.* West Hartford, Conn.: Kumarian Press, 1999. Cuny, a noted humanitarian relief worker who disappeared in Chechnya in 1995, offers long-term solutions to famine by identifying its causes and promoting the efficient use of resources during a crisis.

Curtis, Donald, Michael Hubbard, and Andrew Shepherd. *Preventing*

*Famine: Policies and Prospects for Africa.* London: Routledge, 1988. An anthology of case studies, this book draws largely from African settings concerning the early detection and prevention of famine.

Field, John Osgood, ed. *The Challenge of Famine: Recent Experience, Lessons Learned.* West Hartford, Conn.: Kumarian Press, 1993. This is a fine collection of critiques of famine responses in several African cases.

Varnis, Stephen. *Reluctant Aid or Aiding the Reluctant: U.S. Food Aid Policy and Ethiopian Famine Relief.* New Brunswick, N.J.: Transaction, 1990. This volume combines balance and careful documentation of the political obstacles preventing timely famine relief.

Von Braun, Joachim, Tesfaye Teklu, and Patrick Webb. *Famine in Africa: Causes, Responses, and Prevention.* Baltimore: Johns Hopkins University Press, 1999. Presents the results of field work and other research from various regions. Explains the factors that cause famines and assesses efforts to mitigate and prevent them.

# FIRES

**FACTORS INVOLVED:** Chemical reactions, geography, human activity, weather conditions, wind
**REGIONS AFFECTED:** All

## DEFINITION

Fires occur throughout the world as a result of many causes. They can inflict devastating damage to natural environments, cities, and buildings, causing billions of dollars in damage. Large fires may be accompanied by many deaths and injuries to people and animals.

## SCIENCE

Fire occurs through the process of combustion. Combustion is an exothermic, self-sustaining, chemical reaction usually involving the oxidation of a fuel by oxygen in the atmosphere. Emission of heat, light, and mechanical energy, such as sound, usually occurs. An exothermic reaction is one in which the new substances produced have less energy than the original substances. This means that there is energy in various forms produced in the reaction. In fires, the energy is released primarily as heat and light.

A fuel is a material that will burn. In most environments, carbon is a constituent element. Many typical fuels must undergo a process called pyrolysis before they will burn. Wood, for example, exists in many buildings in the form of furniture and framing to support the walls and roof. In its normal condition, wood does not burn. It must be broken down through the application of heat into its constituent elements before it can be oxidized. This is the process of pyrolysis.

Oxidation is a chemical reaction in which an oxidizing agent and a reducing agent combine to form a product with less energy than the original materials. The oxygen is usually obtained from the air. The fuel is the reducing agent. For the process to begin, a source of heat must be applied to the fuel. This heat is needed to raise the temperature of the material to its ignition point, or the lowest temperature at which it will burn. Ignition can occur from a variety of natural and human sources. Electric wires or appliances can come in contact with combustible materials, raising their temperature. Natural sources such as

## MILESTONES

**64 C.E.:** Much of the city burns during the Great Fire of Rome.

**March, 1657:** The Meireki Fire destroys Edo (now Tokyo), Japan, killing more than 100,000 people.

**1666:** In the Great Fire of London, about 436 acres of the city burn, eliminating the Great Plague.

**1679:** Fire burns portions of the city of Boston.

**1788:** New Orleans burns.

**1812:** Moscow is set on fire by troops of Napoleon I.

**1814:** Washington, D.C. is burned by occupying British troops.

**1842:** Most of the city of Hamburg, Germany, burns, leaving 100 dead.

**May 4, 1850:** Fire burns large portions of the city of San Francisco.

**May 3-4, 1851:** San Francisco again experiences large fires; 30 die.

**December 24, 1851:** The Library of Congress is burned.

**October 8, 1871:** The Great Peshtigo Fire affects a large area in northern Wisconsin; 1,200 are killed, and 2 billion trees are burned.

**October 8-10, 1871:** The Great Chicago Fire leaves 250 dead and causes $200 million in damage.

**November 9-10, 1872:** The Great Boston Fire kills 13, destroys 776 buildings, and causes $75 million in damage.

**April 18-19, 1906:** A fire follows the magnitude 8.3 earthquake in San Francisco.

**November 13, 1909:** A fire breaks out in the Cherry Mine in Illinois, trapping and killing 259 miners.

**1910:** Wildfires rage throughout the U.S. West in the most destructive fire year in U.S. history to date.

**March 25, 1911:** The Triangle Shirtwaist Factory fire occurs in New York City; 145 employees, mostly young girls, die.

**November 28, 1942:** The Cocoanut Grove nightclub burns in Boston, killing 491.

**July, 1943:** Hamburg, Germany, is destroyed, mostly by fires caused by incendiary bombing; 60,000-100,000 are killed.

**1945:** A large section of Oregon forest ignites in the third in a series of wildfires known as the Tillamook burn.

**February 13, 1945:** 25,000 die in the firebombing of Dresden.

**March 9, 1945:** Incendiary bombs destroy 25 percent of Tokyo.

**November 21, 1980:** A fire in the MGM Grand Hotel in Las Vegas kills 84.

**Summer, 1988:** Fires affect some 1.2 million acres in Yellowstone National Park and other western forests.

**September, 3, 1991:** A chicken-processing plant in North Carolina burns, killing 25 workers.

**October 19-21, 1991:** Wildfires burn much of Oakland Hills, California; 25 die.

**April 19, 1993:** A cult compound in Waco, Texas, is destroyed by fire.

**July 4-10, 1994:** A Glenwood Springs, Colorado, forest fire kills 14 firefighters.

**April 15, 1997:** A fire at a tent city outside Mecca, Saudi Arabia, costs 300 lives.

**January-March, 1998:** Large forest fires burn in Indonesia, sickening thousands; 234 die in a Garuda Indonesia plane crash caused by poor visibility from smoke.

**October 21-November 4, 2003:** Warm winds fuel at least 12 wildfires that burn simultaneously across Southern California; 22 die, 80,000 are displaced, and 3,500 homes are destroyed.

lightning can start wildfires. People can deliberately start fires using an accelerant; arson is responsible for many fires throughout the world.

Three factors are necessary for a fire to begin. They are illustrated as the fire triangle of heat, fuel, and oxygen. A fire with these three elements will be a glowing fire. For self-sustaining combustion to occur, a fourth factor, a chain reaction, must be added to the original three factors. This converts the fire triangle to a fire tetrahedral, or four-sided pyramid. A chain reaction occurs when the heat produced by the fire is enough not only to burn the fuel but also to preheat the next segment of fuel so that the fire can grow. As long as the rate of heat production is greater than the rate at which heat is dissipated to the surroundings, more fuel can be ignited and the fire will spread. When the heat produced by the fire is dissipated to the surroundings, the fire will gradually decay.

A fire will continue until the available fuel is consumed, the available oxygen is used, the flames are extinguished by cooling, or the number of excited molecules is reduced. Fire extinguishment and prevention strategies are aimed at breaking or removing one leg of the fire triangle or tetrahedral.

In most fires, either the action of a person or an act of nature, such as a lightning strike or earthquake, are required to bring the factors together for a fire to start. The act of a person may be deliberate, as in the case of arson; accidental, as in the case of someone falling asleep in bed with a lighted cigarette; or an act of omission, such as a building not being constructed in a safe manner.

There are two basic kinds of fires. A fuel-controlled fire is one that has an adequate amount of oxygen but has limited contact with fuel. A ventilation-controlled fire has access to adequate amounts of fuel but has limited contact with oxygen. The National Fire Protection Agency (NFPA) has classified four types of fires. Type A fires involve ordinary combustibles such as wood, paper, cloth, or fiber; they can be extinguished with water or foam. Type B fires involve flammable liquids, such as hot grease, paints, thinners, gasoline, oil, or other liquid fuels; they can be extinguished with a chemical foam or carbon dioxide. Type C fires, electrical fires, can be extinguished with a nonconducting extinguishing agent such as carbon dioxide or a dry chemical. Type D fires involve flammable metals, such as magnesium or sodium alloys, and they can be put out by smothering with a dry powder with a sodium chloride or graphite base.

Four basic mechanisms of heat transfer are involved in fires. Convection is heat transfer within a fluid. In most fires, this occurs within the air. As a fluid is heated, its molecules become less dense and rise. Air at normal density will move into the area of heat, replacing the less dense air that has risen. As this air is heated, it will also rise. This explains the natural movement of fire gases and smoke from lower areas to higher ones. Conduction is heat transfer between two bodies in direct contact with each other. Heat can be transferred through the molecules in a wall by conduction.

A combination of convection and conduction occurs between a solid and a fluid at their boundary. Radiant heat transfer involves heat transfer by electromagnetic waves across distances. A surface, such as a wall, that has been heated by a fire can transfer radiant heat across the room to heat another wall surface or a person's skin even if there is no direct contact. This process occurs in the same way that the heat energy from the sun is transferred to the earth across millions of miles of space. The fourth form of heat transfer involved in fires is latent heat transfer. Latent heat is the heat that is involved in the change of state of a substance. In a fire, water used as an extinguishing agent will be converted to steam, absorbing large quantities of heat energy as it changes from a liquid to a gas.

A conflagration is a fire that spreads over some distance, often a portion of a city or a town. A large group fire spreads from building to building within a complex of buildings. The number of conflagrations and large group fires were substantially reduced in the twentieth century. This decrease is attributed to building codes that require fire-resistant construction of the exterior walls and roofs of buildings in cities, modern fire-department capabilities to extinguish fires, adequate urban water systems that have large quantities of water available for fire extinguishment, and limits on openings between buildings that are located close to one another.

Three main types of conflagrations have occurred since 1950. The first are urban/wild land interface fires. An urban/wild land interface is the area where an urban or suburban area adjoins the natural or undeveloped environment. Fires may start in the wild land and be driven by strong winds and available combustibles into residential or urban areas over a large fire front that cannot be extinguished. The Oakland Hills fire of 1991 is an example of this type of fire. These fires were the most prevalent type of conflagration in the 1990's.

Conflagrations also occur in "congested combustible districts." These fires are typical of urban conflagrations before the 1900's, when the need for streets wide enough for automobiles changed the character of cities around the world. The congested combustible district is one with narrow streets lined with continuous buildings. The Great Boston Fire of 1872 is an example of this type of fire.

Third, conflagrations can be driven by strong winds among houses with wood shingles or other flammable roofing materials. These fires often occur in the southwestern United States. Last, large group fires often occur in old manufacturing districts, where the buildings are abandoned or are poorly maintained. The fire in Chelsea, Massachusetts, in 1908 is an example of this type of fire.

## GEOGRAPHY

Fires occur in all geographic regions of the world. Air as a source of oxygen is available in all environments that support human habitation. Fuels are also present in every environment. The trees and grasses in natural environments will become fuels for wildfires; the furnishings in homes, the materials used in the construction of many buildings, and the clothes people wear are all potential fuels in the presence of heat.

Most fires occur outdoors. These are often called wildfires or brushfires. Fires can occur in forests, grasslands, and farms (crop fires). Wildfires can be started either by an act of nature, such as a lightning strike, or by human actions. Many wildfires are started by accident or by carelessness. Examples of this include leaving a campfire unattended or discarding smoking materials through the window of a car into a natural area.

Trash fires, or the burning of debris in land clearings, can also spread beyond the point of origin. Forest management personnel often direct controlled burns in natural areas to burn underbrush, consume fallen limbs and dead plants, and rejuvenate the forest ecosystem. This practice is thought to reduce the hazard of wildfires because a large amount of fuel is consumed in a controlled manner. There are dangers, however, as in the May, 2000, fire in Los Alamos, New Mexico, in which a controlled burn grew into a major conflagration and destroyed hundreds of homes.

Most deaths and injuries from fire occur in homes and garages. Historically, there have also been large numbers of deaths and injuries in public buildings, such as theaters, assembly buildings, schools, hospitals, stores, offices, hotels, boardinghouses, dormitories, and other community facilities. Modern building codes and construction practices have reduced the number and severity of these fires.

The industrial environment poses many serious fire hazards. Industry includes storage, manufacturing, defense, utility, and other large-scale operations. The presence of large amounts of potential fuel or volatile materials such as solvents in an industrial plant in a large open building constitute a potential fire threat.

Fires may also occur in structures that are not buildings, such as bridges, tunnels, vacant buildings, and buildings under construction. While much public fear and awareness of fire is centered on large fires in public buildings, most people who are killed in fires in the United States die in their homes or cars. Approximately 80 percent of fire deaths and 70 percent of fire injuries occur in homes and cars.

The mobile environment is composed of trains, automobiles, airplanes, and other transportation vehicles. Many people die or are injured from fires that occur after vehicles crash or are otherwise involved in accidents. However, it is important to note that only one-sixth the number of people die in vehicle fires as die in home fires each year.

The dangers of fire to people and property are omnipresent. Therefore, strategies for design, fire protection, and fire prevention must reach everywhere. Significant progress appears to have been made in reducing fires that result in multiple deaths and large property losses.

## PREVENTION AND PREPARATIONS

Fires can be prevented by attacking each leg of the fire triangle or tetrahedral. Sources of heat, particularly open flames, must be isolated from fuels. This can be accomplished in several ways. Rooms that contain sources of heat, such as boiler rooms, mechanical plants, and shops, are usually built with fire-resistant enclosures to contain or compartmentalize the building. Electric wires and electrical appliances must be adequately insulated so the heat produced cannot escape to building materials or furnishings.

Fuels must be limited in wild lands and buildings. Controlled burns, described earlier, provide a method of decreasing fuels in the natural environment. Buildings can be constructed of and furnished with materials that are noncombustible. The amount of fuel in a building is often expressed as the amount of combustible materials by weight compared to an equivalent amount of wood. This is known as a fuel load. Products used in homes and commercial buildings can be redesigned to reduce their fire risk.

Most fires are the result of either careless or deliberate human behavior. Therefore, educating people about fire risks and appropriate fire-prevention strategies is an essential element in fire prevention. Educating the general public could potentially have the greatest impact on reducing the number and severity of fires, but it is perhaps the most difficult strategy to implement. Fire-protection authorities believe that to modify the behavior of the American public with regard to fires requires more than a brief exposure to fire-safety education. The NFPA has produced the "Learn Not to Burn" curriculum material for use in schools across the United States, which consists of a series of exercises with which teachers may teach children of the dangers of fire, fire-prevention strategies, and methods of protecting themselves and their families in the event of a fire. The NFPA reported that in the 1990's only a small percentage of schools actually used this material, however.

The NFPA and many municipal fire departments regularly conduct community meetings and demonstrations of fire protection and prevention techniques, distribute brochures and educational kits, and conduct open houses during Fire Prevention Week activities. These efforts have been aimed at emphasizing actions to prevent fires and appropriate behaviors during fires.

Preparation for fires and protection during a fire can take several forms. Preparing for a fire consists of maintaining buildings to have limited fuels and heat sources. Fuels should be stored in protected areas, and electrical systems and other potential sources of heat must be properly maintained. Access to volatile substances should be limited. A fire-detection system, such as smoke detectors with audible and visible alarms that notify building occupants during the earliest stages of a fire, is an essential preparation component. If the detection system is attached to an automatic suppression configuration, such as a sprinkler system, the fire can be extinguished before it moves beyond the area of origin, reducing its threat to people and property. Providing fire extinguishers, standpipe systems, and other opportunities for manual fire suppression in buildings is also necessary. The fire-detection, alarm, sprinkler, and standpipe systems are called active fire protection systems.

Maintaining a fire department with adequate personnel and equipment is necessary if fires do start and are not suppressed by automatic equipment. A community emergency notification system, such as the 911 telephone line, is required to contact the fire department quickly to ensure that personnel can arrive at the scene with enough time to suppress a fire and rescue people.

Buildings are required to be designed to confine fires to the area of origin by a series of fire and smoke barriers that subdivide a building into a series of compartments. The use of fire- and smoke-resistant walls to confine fire spread is called a passive fire protection method. Other passive fire protection strategies include limiting the use of materials that contribute to fire growth and limiting the size of buildings based on the relative combustibility of their construction systems and contents.

Providing safe ways for people to leave a burning building is an essential method of fire protection. The path from a point inside a building to safety outside the building is called the means of egress. The means of egress consists of three components. The exit access is the unprotected path from any point in a building to an exit. This distance is limited in all buildings so people can move quickly to an exit. An exit is a fire-resistant, smoke-resistant enclosure that leads one from an exit access to the exit discharge, the opening that takes one from an exit to the safety of the "public way." An exit may be a fire stairway in a tall building, a horizontal corridor, or doors that lead directly out of a building in a small, one-story structure. The number and size of exits are determined by how many people will use the building.

It is essential that the exits do not become overly congested during fire evacuations. Fire exits must be illuminated with lights connected to an emergency power source so that when the normal electric service in a building is interrupted during a fire, people can still find the exits in smoke-filled corridors. In very large buildings or in structures such as hospitals, where people cannot be moved out of the building, places of refuge are provided. A place of refuge is an area in a building that is protected from fire and smoke where people can move to await rescue. Conducting fire drills in homes, schools, workplaces, and other buildings is essential so people know how to react in the event of a fire. Many large buildings have voice systems for someone to provide evacuation instructions to occupants through loudspeakers on each floor.

## RESCUE AND RELIEF EFFORTS

Three hazards are posed by fire: smoke inhalation, burns, and building collapse or explosion. Some of the gases present in a fire, such as carbon monoxide, hydrogen cyanide, and carbon dioxide, are narcotics or materials that cause pain or loss of consciousness. Particles and

*Firefighters monitor a wildfire carefully in order to predict its path and distribute resources wisely.* (FEMA)

other gases can cause irritations of the pulmonary system or eyes, ears, and nose. Other gases, such as hydrogen chloride, are toxic in the quantities created during a fire. The combined effects of breathing these gases is called smoke inhalation. It is treated by removing people to a safe environment with clean air and administering oxygen.

Injuries and death in fires are primarily caused by the effects of smoke inhalation. Smoke consists of airborne solid and liquid particulates and gases that result from pyrolysis and combustion. The combustion process is never fully complete, so there are also a number of unburned fuel particles and gases in the smoke as well. Many of the particles are about the same size as the wavelength of visible light. Light is scattered by the smoke particles, making vision very difficult in smoke-filled rooms.

Heat is another major product of the combustion process. Typical building fires exceed temperatures of 1,000 to 1,500 degrees Fahrenheit. Human beings cannot survive temperatures of this magnitude.

The skin will receive second-degree burns when exposed to temperatures of 212 degrees Fahrenheit for fifteen seconds. People will go into shock as a result of exposure to heat, irritants, and oxygen deficiency experienced even at the periphery of fires. This condition can lead to elevated heart rates that can bring on heart attacks.

Burns are classified as first, second, and third degree depending upon the damage done to the skin. First-degree burns are characterized by redness, pain, and sometimes a swelling of the outermost layers of the skin. Second-degree burns usually penetrate deeper into the skin than first-degree burns. Fluids accumulate beneath the skin, forming blisters. The skin becomes moist and pink. Third-degree burns result in dry, charred skin that exposes the layers beneath. Third-degree burns are life-threatening and require special treatment.

People can also be injured or die in fires as a result of collapse of burning buildings and explosions. In some fires in large buildings there have been reports of panicked behavior contributing to fire deaths. The NFPA defines panic as a sudden and excessive feeling of alarm or fear, usually affecting a number of people, which is vaguely apprehended, originates in some real or supposed danger, and leads to competitive, fear-induced flight in which people might trample others in an attempt to flee. Fire investigators state that this type of panic does not occur in many fires.

It is often very difficult for fire rescue workers to remove people trapped in a building. In tall buildings, people must be evacuated by ladders or helicopters to areas of safety, where initial medical evaluation and treatment can occur. Rescue workers require special fire-resistant clothing and self-contained breathing apparatus to move into a fire scene to remove people without injuring themselves in the process. Fire-department personnel and emergency medical technicians are specially trained to remove people from fires and provide initial first aid. For those suffering from severe smoke inhalation or third-degree burns, special treatment is required. Many hospitals in large metropolitan areas have special burn centers to treat severe injuries. There have been incidents reported in which people have walked away from a fire scene only to die within a few days as a result of exposure to toxic gases.

Fire department personnel stay at a fire scene until the combustion process has stopped. In a large fire, smoldering can continue under a top layer of ash for some time after the fire has been apparently extinguished, only to restart at a later time when a wind blows some of the ash into contact with a new fuel.

## IMPACT

The short-term effects of fire include damage to and destruction of property, including both buildings and natural lands; injury and death of people and animals; and a loss of homes or workplaces, which can have a lasting impact on a community. In the United States there are over 2.4 million reported fires each year. Many estimate that the actual number of fires is much greater than this. There are more than 6,000 deaths and 30,000 injuries each year from fires, resulting in over $5.5 billion in fire losses. While there was a decrease in fire deaths in the 1970's and 1980's, attributed to requirements for the installation of smoke detectors in residences, the rates remained relatively constant after that time. The fire death rates in the United States and Canada are almost twice those of other developed countries. Fire remains the second most prevalent cause of accidental death in homes. It is the primary cause of death among children and young adults. Most of the 6,000 fire deaths in the United States each year occur in two segments of the population: the very young and the elderly.

## HISTORICAL OVERVIEW

Throughout the history of civilization, humans and fire have been intimately intertwined. Mastery of fire provided a boon to prehistoric humans, and they used it to shape their environment. Primitive peoples used fire to "drive the game," that is, to force wild game into a small area of concentration, where the kill was much easier. As long as humans remained hunter-gatherers, use of fire was central to survival. Indeed, it has been suggested that the growing ability of such people to control the wild game population led to the extinction of many species.

When humankind converted from hunting to agriculture, fire was equally essential, for domestic fire was needed to convert the harvested grains into edible food for humans. The use of fire was at the heart of the growth in technology as well, for the manipulation of raw materials nearly always depended on fire: Pottery needed to be baked to make it usable as containers, and metals needed to be heated at ever higher temperatures to make the fluid metal that could be transformed into usable items.

Fire is a tricky tool and requires proper management. All too often, fire escapes from the control of the humans wielding it and creates devastation. A vast number of escaped fires were certainly never recorded: Little is known of the fire usages of Mesoamericans prior to the arrival of Europeans at the end of the fifteenth century, although there is archaeological evidence of their use of fire, probably in religious ceremonies. They also used it to manufacture jewelry from the gold they found in the mountains.

One of the earliest recorded instances of uncontrolled fire was the fire that burned much of the city of Rome during the reign of the Emperor Nero, in 64 C.E. Part of Nero's unsavory reputation comes from the story that he amused himself while the city burned and destroyed the homes of hundreds of thousands of its citizens: "Nero fiddled while Rome burned."

Countless unrecorded fires must have taken place during the collapse of the ancient civilization of Rome. At the time, wood was the universal building material, especially for domestic use, and many homes must have burned down when a cooking fire raged out of control. Occasionally such escaped domestic fires had their uses, notably when a large portion of the city of London burned in 1666: The city's population had just been decimated by an epidemic of bubonic plague, carried by rats. When the houses burned down in the Great Fire of London, the rats burned with them, and the plague was ended.

It is known that the indigenous peoples in America used fire extensively, both to heat their dwellings and, particularly, to modify the environment. They used fire to clear the underbrush in the eastern United States, where otherwise forest cover dominated the landscape. Fire enabled them to rid a small portion of land of trees that they had girdled and of the brush that grew up when the trees died, leaving them a clearing where they could plant the corn, beans, and squash that formed an important part of their diet. They also burned the land to eliminate underbrush within the forest, making travel through it, as well as hunting, easier. These practices were adopted by the European settlers who, in any case, brought with them a tradition of the use of fire for land management.

Fire also shaped the environment without intervention by humans. In the parts of America where rainfall is scarce, lightning often strikes, especially during the summer. The grasslands of the Great Plains are believed to be largely the product of frequent widespread fires that burned over the land often enough to prevent trees from developing. As more American Indians were concentrated on the Great Plains, fire was used by them to manage the great herds of buffalo that grazed there. It was only as the Europeans began to establish settlements on the Great Plains that efforts were made to contain the grass fires.

Meanwhile, fire had become an important tool in warfare. In ancient times, barricades were generally made of wood, and many attempts were made to burn them by tossing burning brands into the area under siege. The development of what came to be known as Greek fire—material that would burst into flame on contact—made possible a more potent use of fire in sieges. In addition, it became the practice of conquering armies to set fire to urban centers they conquered. Napoleon I's army burned Moscow in 1812, and Washington, D.C., was burned by the British in 1814. In World War II, fire started by aerial bombardment became an important tool. Many fires were begun in London from 1940 through 1945 as a result of German bombardment. The Allies retaliated by setting fire to both Hamburg, in 1943, and Dresden, in 1945. That same year, incendiary bombs rained down on Tokyo, burning large portions of the city.

As urban concentrations grew, the risk of fire grew with them. Portions of the city of Boston burned as early as 1679. In 1788, the city of New Orleans burned, as did the city of Hamburg in 1842. In 1850 and again in 1851, the city of San Francisco burned. Chicago burned in 1871, allegedly when Mrs. O'Leary's cow kicked over a kerosene lantern. In 1894, a part of the grounds and structures of the World Columbian Exposition in Chicago burned. Much of San Francisco burned again following the devastating earthquake of 1906.

A number of fires in individual buildings became major disasters. Perhaps the most infamous was the Triangle Shirtwaist Factory fire, in 1911, when 145 trapped workers died. On November 28, 1942, the Cocoanut Grove nightclub in Boston burned, causing 491 deaths. The MGM Grand Hotel in Las Vegas burned in 1980, and 84 people died. A

*A helicopter douses a forest fire with water, one of many methods of combating the spread of flames.* (FEMA)

chicken-processing plant in North Carolina burned on September 3, 1991, killing 25 workers. Eighty-six people died in 1993, following an extended siege by federal agents at a cult compound in Waco, Texas. In 2003, 100 people were killed when pyrotechnics ignited sound-proofing foam at a club in Rhode Island during a concert.

Although the number of victims of building fires in the United States has declined, a number of such disasters continued to occur abroad in which the death toll exceeded 100. In 1960, a mental hospital in Guatemala City caught on fire, and 225 died. A movie theater in Syria burned the same year, with a loss of 152 persons. The following year, a circus caught fire in Brazil, killing more than 300. In 1971 and 1972, fires in a hotel and nightclub in South Korea and Japan, respectively, each claimed more than 100 victims, as did a department store fire in Japan in 1973.

Large congregations of people are particularly at risk. In 1975 a fire in a tent city in Saudi Arabia resulted in the loss of 138 individuals; 300 pilgrims to Mecca lost their lives in a similar fire in 1997. In 1977, 164 people were killed in Kentucky when a nightclub burned, as did 100 people attending a Great White concert in Rhode Island in 2003 when pyrotechnics ignited soundproofing foam. A fire at a nursing home in Jamaica resulted in the deaths of 157. In 1994, a fire in a toy factory in Thailand killed 213 people, and the same year a theater in China burned, with some 300 losing their lives.

Besides localized fires in buildings, wildfires have been consistent causes of disaster, even though the loss of life has been much less dramatic. The most famous of these was the fire in Peshtigo, Wisconsin, in 1871, when at least 1,200 died. Large forest fires burned the same year in Minnesota and Michigan. In 1881 large portions of the northern half of the lower peninsula of Michigan were engulfed in forest fires. In 1894 fires broke out again in the northern, forested sections of Michigan, Wisconsin, and Minnesota, reappearing in 1908. All these fires were a product of the heavy logging that had taken place in the last thirty years of the nineteenth century and the first decade of the twentieth. By 1910 the north woods of the Great Lakes states were logged out, and the problem was transferred to the heavily timbered regions to the west.

In 1910, wildfires raged throughout the West and the Midwest; more than 6 million acres of national forestland burned, destroying large acreages of privately owned forestland as well. That year was the worst year in history of losses to forest fires, though it was to be rivaled by the years 1945, 1988, and 1996.

In the dry regions of the United States, as well as elsewhere in the world, forest and brushfires are common in drought years. Nearly every year there are brushfires in California and in the arid Southwest, where the brush accumulations grow rapidly. The spread of settlement into these regions has heightened the risk of disaster, and there is some evidence that arson plays a part. Aerial surveillance has helped to reduce the risk to individuals, and local and national agencies have developed new tools for fighting such conflagrations. Even so, tragedies sometimes occur: In July of 1994, 14 firefighters lost their lives in Glenwood Springs, Colorado, when a sudden wind gust moved a forest fire uphill at a rate of more than 100 feet per second.

The huge forest fires that burned in and around Yellowstone National Park in 1988 attracted the attention of the world through television broadcasts. The United States Forest Service, which had for more than fifty years followed a policy of fire suppression, from the massive burns of 1910 until the late 1970's, had then changed its policy. It had become clear that, at least in the West, fire suppression, associated with the popular icon, Smokey Bear, had the effect of allowing large quantities of tinder to build up in the forest. Once a fire got started, the large amounts of fuel made it easy for the fire to expand into a major disaster. Thus the forest service had taken a "let burn" policy, allowing fires that did not threaten people to burn, hoping to keep down the accumulation of brush. However, in 1988 the fires got away from the officials in control, and the public was outraged when more than 1 million acres burned around Yellowstone, America's most-visited national park.

Huge forest fires in Alaska the same year drove the total of burned acreage to more than 3.5 million, and federal officials were forced to revise their fire policy. There was, after 1988, a greater use of what is called controlled burning, deliberately set fires that are confined to a limited area, designed to eliminate the buildup of combustible materials before they create massive conflagrations.

Forest fires will continue to be a problem, especially wherever drought conditions exist. In 1998, drought conditions in Indonesia led to extensive wildfires, some of them escaped fires that had been set by cultivators to open up new areas for farming. The smoke and haze from these fires spread all over Southeast Asia. In 1996, 6 million acres of U.S. forestland burned, the worst fire year since 1951, when the last of the four wildfires in Oregon known collectively as the Tillamook burn took a heavy toll.

One of the worst fire seasons in history occurred in 2000. As many as eighty forest fires were burning at a time in thirteen states in the western United States. Dry summer thunderstorms ignited vegetation that had not seen rain in months. Fires were responsible for more than 6.5 million acres burned, and firefighters were recruited from as far away as Hawaii, New Zealand, and Australia. In California, more than 70,000 acres of the Sequoia National Forest burned, along with 25,000 acres in Idaho and 20,000 in Nevada. Montana experienced its worst fire season in over fifty years, with 8 deaths from fire by August. The federal government allotted $590 million in emergency funds to combat the conflagrations. Because there had been few fires—and little rain—in these areas in previous years, there was much "fuel" for the fires in the undergrowth and vegetation.

In the fall of 2003, Southern California experienced at least 12 wildfires that burned simultaneously from Los Angeles to San Diego. Fueled by dry conditions and the warm winds called Santa Anas, the fires killed 22 people and displaced 80,000 more, destroying 3,500 homes. This Fire Siege of 2003 tested local fire departments to the limit and again highlighted the danger of urban/wild lands interface. As earth's climate warms and drought conditions occur more frequently, more large fires are a probability.

*Gary W. Siebein*
*Nancy M. Gordon*

## BIBLIOGRAPHY

Branigan, Francis. *Building Construction for the Fire Service.* Quincy, Mass.: National Fire Protection Association, 1992. This book is a primer on fire safety in buildings, written from the perspective of firefighters.

Cote, Arthur, ed. *Fire Protection Handbook.* 19th ed. Quincy, Mass.: National Fire Protection Association, 2003. This handbook by the leading fire-safety association in the world contains detailed chapters on every aspect of fire prevention and control by leaders in the field. It is updated continually and is the definitive work in the area.

Cote, Arthur, and Percy Bugbee. *Principles of Fire Protection.* Quincy, Mass.: National Fire Protection Association, 1995. This book by two noted fire researchers presents a concise summary of fire principles and fire-protection strategies.

Cottrell, William H., Jr. *The Book of Fire.* 2d ed. Missoula, Mont.: Mountain Press, 2004. Intended for students and general readers. Explains how heat, ignition, and flame can progress to a wildfire.

Lathrop, James K., ed. *Life Safety Code Handbook.* 5th ed. Quincy, Mass.: National Fire Protection Association, 1991. This is an illustrated annotated guide to the rules and regulations governing life safety in buildings. It includes many illustrations on how to design safety features in buildings.

Lyons, Paul Robert. *Fire in America!* Boston: National Fire Protection Association, 1976. This book presents the history of fires in cities, buildings, and vehicles from ancient times to modern times, in a readable and illustrated format.

Tebeau, Mark. *Eating Smoke: Fire in Urban America, 1800-1950.* Baltimore: Johns Hopkins University Press, 2003. Shows how the changing practices of firefighters and fire insurers helped to shape American cities and urban life.

# FLOODS

**FACTORS INVOLVED:** Geography, human activity, plants, rain, snow, temperature, weather conditions

**REGIONS AFFECTED:** Cities, forests, islands, mountains, plains, rivers, towns, valleys

## DEFINITION

Floods occur when streams or rivers overflow their banks and inundate the adjacent floodplain. They have caused enormous destruction of property and loss of life ever since human societies settled in large numbers along river valleys.

## SCIENCE

Floods are difficult to define. This is partly because there are no natural breaks in nature and partly because flood thresholds are selected based on human criteria, which can vary. A flood is commonly defined as the result of a river overflowing its banks and spreading out over the bordering floodplain. The scientific definition is based on discharge, which is the volume of water moving past a given point in the stream channel per unit of time (cubic feet per second).

Two aspects that are instrumental in flood occurrence are the amount of surface runoff and the uniformity of runoff from different parts of the watershed (a region that drains to a body of water). If the response and travel times are uniform, then the flow is less likely to result in a flood. Conversely, watersheds that have soils and bedrock with higher infiltration rates are prone to flooding. Flood magnitude depends on the intensity, duration, and areal extent of precipitation in conjunction with the condition of the land. If the soils in the watershed have been saturated due to antecedent precipitation, the flooding potential is much greater. For example, the unusual occurrence of Hurricanes Connie and Diane in 1955 striking so close together in time resulted in substantial flooding along the Delaware River in New Jersey and Pennsylvania because the ground was already saturated from the first storm.

Floods are caused by climatological conditions and part-climatological factors. Climatological conditions include heavy rain from tropical storms and hurricanes, severe thunderstorms, midlatitude cyclones and frontal passages, and rapid snow and ice melt. Part-climatological factors consist of tides and storm surges in coastal areas. Other factors that may cause floods are ice- and logjam breakups, earthquakes, landslides, and dam failures.

Flood-intensifying conditions include fixed basin characteristics, such as area, shape, slope, aspect (north- or south-facing), and elevation; and variable basin characteristics, including water-storage capacity and transmissibility in the soil and bedrock, soil infiltration rates, and extent of wetlands and lakes. Channel characteristics, such as length, slope, roughness, and shape, also may intensify floods, as may the human effects of river regulation: conjunctive use of groundwater, interbasin transfers, wastewater release, water diversion and irrigation, urbanization and increases in impervious cover, deforestation and reforestation, levees, and land drainage.

Because floods are capable of such extensive damage, knowledge of the magnitude and frequency of these events would be very useful. Accordingly, hydrologists use statistical methodology to obtain estimates of the probability that a flood of a certain size will occur in a given year. The estimates are based on historical stream-flow records, and special graph paper is used. The peak discharge for each year of record is plotted on the vertical Y-axis, which is scaled arithmetically. The horizontal X-axis on the bottom is scaled in probability terms, which provides the percent probability that a given discharge will be equaled or exceeded.

The plotting position for each annual peak flow is calculated using a special equation. A straight line is drawn through the array of data points on the graph, which then becomes a flood-frequency graph for a location (gauging station) on a particular river. The horizontal X-axis at the top of the graph provides the return period in years (or recurrence interval), which is the inverse value of the probability percentage on the bottom X-axis. Thus, a discharge associated with a value of 5 percent means that this discharge is expected to be equaled or exceeded in five out of one hundred years. In this example of a 5 percent probability value, the return period is twenty years, implying that on the average, this particular discharge is estimated to be equaled or exceeded once every twenty years. This frequency estimate can also be called the twenty-year-flood.

## MILESTONES

**1228:** Flooding in Holland results in at least 100,000 deaths.

**1333:** The Arno River floods Venice, with a level of up to 14 feet (4.2 meters).

**1642:** More than 300,000 people die in China from flooding.

**1887:** The Yellow River floods, covering over 50,000 square miles of the North China Plain. Over 900,000 people die from the floodwaters and an additional 2 to 4 million die afterward due to flood-related causes.

**1889:** A dam bursts upstream from Johnstown, Pennsylvania, and the floodwaters kill over 2,200 people.

**1911:** The Yangtze River in China floods, killing more than 100,000 people.

**1927:** Extensive flooding of the Mississippi River results in 313 deaths.

**March 12, 1928:** The St. Francis Dam collapses in Southern California, leading to about 450 deaths.

**1938:** Chinese soldiers are ordered to destroy the levees of the Yellow River in order to create a flood to stop the advance of Japanese troops. It works, but at a terrible cost to the Chinese people; more than 1 million die.

**1939:** Flooding of the Yellow River kills over 200,000 people.

**1947:** Honshū Island, Japan, is hit by floods that kill more than 1,900 people.

**February 1, 1953:** A massive flood in the North Sea kills 1,853 in the Netherlands, Great Britain, and Belgium.

**November 1, 1959:** More than 2,000 people die in floods in western Mexico.

**October 10, 1960:** Bangladesh floods kill a total of 6,000 people.

**October 31, 1960:** Floods kill 4,000 in Bangladesh.

**November 3-4, 1966:** Flooding in Florence, Italy, destroys many works of art.

**January 24-March 21, 1967:** Flooding in eastern Brazil takes 1,250 lives.

**July 21-August 15, 1968:** Flooding in Gujarat State in India results in 1,000 deaths.

**October 7, 1968:** Floods in northeastern India claim 780 lives.

**June 9, 1972:** Heavy rainfall over Rapid City, South Dakota, causes an upstream dam to fail and release floodwaters, and 238 people lose their lives.

**July 31, 1976:** A flash flood rushes down Big Thompson Canyon, Colorado, sweeping 139 people to their deaths.

**July, 1981:** Over 1,300 people die in the flooding of Sichuan, Hubei Province, China.

**June-August, 1993:** Largest recorded floods of the Mississippi River occur; 52 people die, over $18 billion in damage is inflicted, and more than 20 million acres are flooded.

**February-March, 2000:** Severe flooding in Mozambique, caused by five weeks of rain followed by Cyclone Eline, kills 800 people and 20,000 cattle.

Note that the flood estimate is stated in probability terms. This has confused some people, who believe that if a twenty-year-flood event occurred, then the next flood of that magnitude will not occur again for another twenty years. This is incorrect, as two twenty-year-floods can occur in the same year, even though the probability is low. A fifty-year-flood and hundred-year-flood have a probability of being equaled or exceeded of only 2 and 1 percent, respectively.

The longer the historical record of floods, the more confidence may be taken in the estimated flood frequencies. However, the historical period of record for many bodies of water of fifty or even seventy-five years is considerably shorter than the total time the water has been flowing. In addition, many watersheds have been extensively changed by urbanization, farming activities, logging, and mining to such an extent that previous discharges may not be in accord with current conditions. Also, climatic change, particularly near large metropolitan areas, may have been great enough to make quantifiable changes in discharge. Thus, forecasts that are based on past flows may not be suitable for estimating future flows.

Flash floods differ from long-duration floods of large streams in that they begin very quickly and last only a short time. They often occur with torrential thunderstorm rains of 8 to 12 inches in a twenty-four-hour period over hilly watersheds that have steep ground and channel slopes. Three climatological situations are associated with flash floods. One is a hurricane that occurs over a landmass, which happens often in the eastern United States. The second situation occurs when moist tropical air is brought into a slow-moving or stationary weather front, which is common in the central and eastern United States. The third occurs in the mountainous western states, as typified by the flash floods caused by winter storms in California.

The hydrologic effects of urbanization on flooding potential are substantial. Roofs, driveways, sidewalks, roads, and parking lots greatly increase the amount of impervious cover in the watershed. For example, it is estimated that residential subdivisions with lot sizes of 6,000 square feet (0.14 acres) and 15,000 square feet (0.34 acres) have impervious areas of 80 and 25 percent, respectively. Commercial and industrial zones have impervious areas of 60 to 95 percent. A typical suburban shopping center with its large expanse of parking area has about 90 percent impervious cover.

As the impervious cover increases, infiltration is reduced and overland flow is increased. Consequently, the frequency and flood peak heights are increased during large storms. Another change related to urbanization is the installation of storm sewers, which route storm runoff from paved areas directly to streams. This short-circuiting of the hydrologic cycle reduces the travel time to the stream channel, reduces the lag time between the precipitation event and the ensuing runoff, and increases the height of the flood peak. In essence, an increasing volume of water is sent to the stream channel in a shorter period of time.

## GEOGRAPHY

Floods are one of the most common and damaging of natural hazards. They can occur anywhere in the world but are most prevalent in valleys in humid regions when bodies of water overflow their banks. The water that cannot be accommodated within the stream channel flows out over the floodplain—a low, flat area on one or both sides of the channel. Floodplains have attracted human settlement for thousands of years, as witnessed by the ancient civilizations that developed along the Nile River in Egypt, the Yangtze and Yellow Rivers of China, and the Tigris and Euphrates Rivers in Mesopotamia (now Iraq). More people are living in river valleys than ever before, and the number is increasing. About 7 percent of the United States consists of floodplains that are subject to inundation by a hundred-year-flood. Most of the largest cities of the nation are part of this 7 percent. Even as flood damages increase, development in the floodplain has been growing by about 2 percent a year.

Large areas of the floodplain not only are inundated but also are subjected to rapidly moving water, which has enormous capacity to move objects such as cars, buildings, and bridges. If the flood is large enough, the water will inundate even stream terraces, which are older floodplains that are higher than the stream. For example, Hurricane Agnes in 1972 caused the Susquehanna River to rise nearly 16 feet above flood stage, inundating the downtown portion of Harrisburg, Pennsylvania, which was built on a terrace.

Floods can also be devastating in semiarid areas where sparsely vegetated slopes offer little resistance to large volumes of overland flow generated by a storm event. For example, the winter storms in January, 1969, in Southern California and the consequent flooding resulted in 100 deaths. Floods also occur in coastal and estuarine environments. A winter storm in 1953 resulted in severe coastal flooding in eastern England and northwestern Europe (particularly the Netherlands), causing the deaths of almost 2,000 people, the destruction of 40,000 homes, and the loss of thousands of cattle. Bangladesh is particularly vulnerable to coastal flooding. Most of the population of over 115 million in an area about the size of New York State live in the downstream floodplain of the Brahmaputra and Ganges Rivers. In addition, its location at the head of the Bay of Bengal only accentuates the storm surges that frequently occur in this area from tropical storms. For example, coastal storm surges killed 225,000 people in 1970 in Bangladesh.

## PREVENTION AND PREPARATIONS

Societies have made many attempts over the years to prevent floods, most of which involve some form of structural control. For example, the Flood Control Acts of 1928 and 1936 assigned the U.S. Army Corps of Engineers the responsibility of building reservoirs, levees, channels, and stream diversions along the Mississippi and its major tributaries. As a result of this legislation, 76 reservoirs and 2,200 miles of levees in the Upper Mississippi River basin alone were built by the

*The Mississippi River floods Cape Girardeau, Missouri, in 1927.* (National Oceanic and Atmospheric Administration)

Army after the late 1930's. State and local governments constructed an additional 5,800 miles of levees in the same watershed. The U.S. Natural Resources Conservation Service (formerly the Soil Conservation Service) built over 3,000 reservoirs on the smaller tributaries in the basin. All these very expensive efforts on the Mississippi and similar efforts on other watersheds still did not prevent the disastrous floods in 1993 on the Mississippi and in 1997 on the Red River in North Dakota and Minnesota.

Flood-abatement measures can be divided into structural and nonstructural approaches. The structural approach involves the application of engineering techniques that attempt either to hold back runoff in the watershed or to change the lower reaches of the river, where inundation of the floodplain is most probable. The nonstructural approach is best illustrated by zoning regulations.

One form of a structural measure is to treat watershed slopes by planting trees or other types of vegetative cover so as to increase infiltration, which thereby decreases the amount of overland flow. This measure, when combined with the building of storage dams in the valley bottoms, can substantially reduce the flood peaks and increase the lag time between the storm event and the runoff downstream.

Another very common type of structural measure is to build artificial levees (or dikes) along the channel. They are usually built of earth, may be broad enough to contain an automobile trail, and should be high enough to contain a flood. During high water on the Mississippi at New Orleans, it is possible to see ships sailing above when standing at the foot of the levee.

Starting in 1879 with the Mississippi River Commission, a large system of levees was constructed in the hope of containing all floods. This levee system has been expanded and improved so that it totals over 2,500 miles in length and is as high as 30 feet in some places. One problem with the levees is that the river channel aggrades or builds up over time so that it is higher than the bordering floodplain. If the levees fail, the water in the channel will rush into the floodplain, which is at a lower elevation, and create a disastrous flood. For example, the Yellow River in China in 1887 flooded an area of 50,000 square miles (nearly the size of England), which resulted in the direct deaths of nearly 1 million people and the indirect deaths of millions more by the famine that followed.

Another structural measure that has been tried by the Army Corps of Engineers on the Mississippi is to cut channels (also known as cutoffs) across the wide meander loops, which shortens the river length. This reduction in length increases the river slope, which correspondingly increases the average velocity of the water. As velocity increases, more water can move through the channel, and the flood peak can be reduced. Although the technique was initially successful, the river responded by developing new meanders, which only increased the length.

Where feasible, selected portions of the floodplain may be established as temporary basins that will be deliberately flooded in order to reduce the flood peak in the main channel. A related structural measure, which is used in the delta region of the Lower Mississippi, is to use floodways that divert water from the channel directly to the ocean. For example, the Bonne Carre floodway upstream of New Orleans is designed to divert excess water to Lake Pontchartrain, which is adjoined to the Gulf of Mexico.

As an alternative to structural flood abatement measures that involve engineering solutions, the nonstructural approach is to view floods and the damages they cause as natural events that will continue in the future even after expensive and elaborate engineering structures have been built. Levees that were designed for a hundred-year-flood will fail if a flood of greater magnitude, say a two-hundred-year-flood, occurs. The real problem is the ongoing urban, commercial, and industrial development in the floodplain. Consequently, the nonstructural measure that has received increasing attention is floodplain zoning, which restricts development in flood-prone areas. This type of planning allows some agricultural activity and recreation in the floodplain as these types of land use call for occasional flooding. Under this form of zoning, permanent structures such as houses, schools, businesses, and industries would not be permitted in the flood-prone portions of the floodplain.

One of the major nonstructural techniques that has developed over the years in the United States to reduce flood losses is flood insurance. The notion of an insurance program that provides money for flood losses appeared to be reasonable because the pooling of risks, collection of annual premiums, and payments of claims to those property owners who suffer losses was similar to other types of insurance programs, such as fire insurance.

The first attempts to begin a federal flood insurance program began after flooding of the Kansas and Missouri Rivers in 1951. Legislation was introduced over the years and finally resulted in the National Flood Insurance Act of 1968. This act created the National Flood Insurance Program, which is administered through the Federal Emergency Management Agency (FEMA). The objectives of the program are to have nationwide flood insurance available to all communities that have potential for flooding, try to keep future development away from flood-prone areas, assist local and state governments in proper floodplain use, and make additional studies of flood hazards. One of the useful outcomes of the program has been the preparation of maps showing the approximate delineation of the area that would be covered by the hundred-year-flood. These maps are made available to all floodplain communities and provide essential information to realtors and mortgage-lending institutions. The flood insurance program is meant to be self-supporting.

There is some controversy about flood insurance, however. For example, although one of the intents of the program is to assist people who cannot buy insurance at private market rates, the effect has been to encourage building on the floodplain because people feel that the government will help them no matter what happens. Some people would even like to move their homes and commercial facilities to higher land in another location, but property owners can only collect for damages if they rebuild in the same flood-prone location. If these criticisms are correct, this policy of rebuilding on the floodplain will only perpetuate the problem.

As distinct from an earthquake, which occurs without warning, major storms and the associated possibility of flooding can be learned of in advance. Satellites and specially equipped reconnaissance airplanes can track storms over the ocean that may be heading for land and provide early warning of potentially heavy rainfall and storm surges. The River and Flood Forecasting Service of the U.S. National Weather Service maintains eighty-five offices at various locations along the major rivers of the nation. These offices issue flood forecasts to the communities within their region. The flood warnings are disseminated to local governmental agencies, who may then close roads and bridges and recommend evacuation of flood-prone areas. Parts of coastal Florida have evacuation routing directions on highway signs.

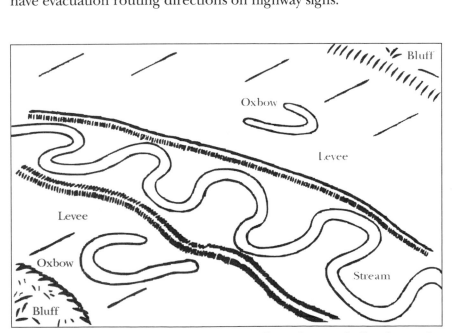

*Levees are structures designed to contain stream flow, oxbows are bodies of water that were detached from the stream, and bluffs are the boundaries of a floodplain.*

## RESCUE AND RELIEF EFFORTS

The U.S. Army Corps of Engineers has been actively involved in flood control efforts since 1824, and much more so after 1890. This involvement in flood fighting was broadened in 1955, when Congress authorized them under Public Law 84-99 to engage in preparation and emergency response to floods. The Corps became responsible for implementing precautionary measures when there was an imminent threat of potentially serious flooding, providing any necessary emergency assistance during floods so as to prevent loss of life and property damage, providing immediate postflood assistance, and rehabilitating any flood-control structures that were damaged.

In order to respond quickly and provide assistance under emergency conditions, the Corps established emergency-response plans in conjunction with training of personnel for emergency response and recovery activities. These plans are tested by conducting exercises with state and local governments and other federal agencies, such as FEMA. When flooding is imminent or has already occurred, the Corps has the authority to provide state and local governments with technical assistance, supplies and materials, and equipment. Emergency construction—which includes stream obstruction removal; temporary levee construction; and the strengthening, repairing, and increasing of the height of existing levees—may also be included. Sandbagging levees to protect buildings during a flood constitutes 90 percent of the emergency assistance. For example, about 500,000 sandbags were used during the 1986 flood near Tulsa, Oklahoma.

As soon as the flood subsides, the Corps is authorized to remove debris that blocks critical water supply intakes, sewer outfalls, and key rail and road arteries. Restoration of public services and facilities is also provided.

The nonengineering relief efforts are handled by other agencies. Foremost among them is the American Red Cross, which started in 1905 to establish shelters for the homeless and arrange for meals for flood victims and rescue workers. Other civic and religious organizations join in the rescue effort with food, clothing, miscellaneous household goods, and money. These organizations can also assist in cleanup and rebuilding operations.

*Debris can be the dangerous aspect of a flood. Timber clogs the Kansas River in Kansas City following the spring floods of 1903.* (National Oceanic and Atmospheric Administration)

## IMPACT

Among the natural hazards in the world, floods rank first in the number of fatalities. An estimated 40 percent of all the fatalities that occur from natural hazards are attributed to flooding. People are attracted to river valleys for water supply; navigation; arable, level land; and waste disposal—yet these are the same lands that are the most susceptible to floods. Flood damages tend to be more in terms of property loss and less in fatalities in industrialized societies because the latter have the technology for better monitoring, storm and flood warnings, and evacuation procedures. In contrast, developing countries, particularly those with high population densities, suffer greater loss of life, because prevention and relief efforts are less well organized. The estimated distribution of fatalities and property losses from flooding is 5 and 75 percent in developed countries, respectively, as compared to 95 and 25 percent in developing countries, respectively.

These differences can be illustrated by the Great Mississippi River Flood of 1993 and several historical floods in China. Unusually heavy rain in the Upper Mississippi River basin in the late spring and early summer of 1993 was the immediate cause of the flood. For many locations, monthly rainfall totals were the highest ever measured in over a century. Levees failed and allowed enormous volumes of water to spread out over the floodplain, inundating an area of over 15,000 square miles (nearly the size of Switzerland). An estimated 70,000 people were driven from their homes, 52 lives were lost, and the property damage topped $18 billion. Historical records for floods in the densely populated floodplain of the Yellow River in China estimate an astonishing 900,000 and 3.7 million deaths in 1887 and 1931, respectively—a sad world record.

Obviously, water is the key element in flood damage. The water overflowing the stream channels inundates land that has buildings, equipment, crops, roads and rails, and lines of communication that were not intended to operate underwater. In addition, the high velocity of floodwaters has extra capacity to carry sediment and debris, such as parts of buildings, which damage other structures in its path and are later dumped at some inconvenient location.

The most dramatic damage from floods is loss of human life. Other forms of damage include loss of livestock in rural areas; destruction of crops, buildings, transport facilities, and stored materials, such as seed, fertilizer, and foodstuffs; and soil erosion by the rapidly moving water. Even the coffins in cemeteries may be scoured out and destroyed, as was the case in the Great Mississippi River Flood of 1993.

### HISTORICAL OVERVIEW

Flooding of rivers and coastal areas has been a natural phenomenon ever since Earth cooled sufficiently for water to accumulate on its surface. Floods are important in numerous geological processes, such as erosion of the continents, transport of sediments, and the formation of many fluvial and coastal landforms. There are a number of causes of flooding in historic times. The most common cause is an excess of precipitation in a drainage basin, which then leads to rivers overflowing their banks and inundating the surrounding areas. In general, rivers flood about every one to two years. This type of flooding may be very local, in the case of flash flooding, or it may be more widespread, as when large-scale storms dump great quantities of rain over extended areas for long periods of time. A second common reason for flooding is the movement of typhoons or hurricanes into coastal areas, which often causes severe coastal flooding. Flooding may also be caused by the collapse of human-made structures, such as dams or levees. Finally, there are a few examples of flooding caused directly by humans as an act of war or terrorism.

Perhaps the most spectacular example of large-scale flooding occurred during the Pleistocene epoch (the Ice Age) in eastern Washington and Idaho, when an ice dam in western Montana broke and released a torrent of floodwaters. The floodwaters raced across eastern Washington at velocities of 98 feet (30 meters) per second and scoured much of the area down to bedrock. The discharge of the floodwaters was estimated at about 179 million cubic yards (13.7 million cubic meters) per second, and the total water released in this catastrophic flood is estimated to be approximately 81.7 million cubic yards (25,000 cubic meters), an amount about equal to five times the water held in Lake Erie. The flood may have lasted as long as eleven days. Many other ice-dam collapses probably resulted in similar, if less catastrophic, floods during the ice ages, but the record of the eastern Washington flood is the best preserved.

When humans began to live in towns and cities, they commonly chose sites along rivers. The rivers provided water, transportation, and food, and the floodplains had fertile soils. Civilizations arose along the Tigris (western Asia), Euphrates (western Asia), Nile (eastern Africa), and Yellow (northern China) Rivers. Each of these civilizations depended directly or indirectly on the flooding of these rivers. The yearly floods brought nutrients to the floodplains, which became the early agricultural bases for these civilizations. As populations grew after the agricultural revolution began, more and more people moved into areas that were inundated periodically by floods. Floods are the most widespread of the natural hazards, and, because of the extensive development in the floodplains, floods are the most commonly experienced natural disaster. For centuries, floods were seen as necessary but completely uncontrollable acts of nature.

However, this view changed when people realized that some floods might be controlled by constructing levees and dams. Chinese engineers have tried to control the flooding of the Yellow River for over 2,500 years. Levees have been built along this river to control the river during high water flow, but the program requires constant expansion and maintenance. The Yellow River is the muddiest river in the world, and it continually deposits sediment in its channel, thus raising the level of the river water. This aggradation of the channel bed requires that even higher levees be constructed. The levees do control moderate flooding events but have frequently broken during higher flow levels.

The Yellow River has broken through its levees 1,593 times since the year 1800. Each levee breach causes a flood, many of which have been catastrophic. In 1887 more than 900,000 people lost their lives as the Yellow River flooded, and an additional 2 to 4 million people died later as the result of the flooding. The Yellow River flooded again in 1921, 1931, 1938, and 1939. Millions of Chinese have died during the flooding of this river known as "China's Sorrow." The 1938 flood was created by the Chinese army as it dynamited the levees in order to cause a flood southward to stop the advancing Japanese troops. The strategy worked, but at a great cost. Over 1 million Chinese people died in this human-made flood, and many more suffered for years afterward due to hunger and disease caused by the inundation of the agricultural areas.

The Yellow River has not been the only danger in China. Flooding of the Yangtze River in China has also caused extensive damage and great loss of life. In India, the Ganges and Brahmaputra Rivers annually flood because of the enormous amount of rain and snowfall in the Himalayas, which are the source area for these rivers. Monsoon conditions add to the flooding during most years, and rivers commonly inundate large regions along the lower stretches of these rivers. Yearly flooding of the lowlands in Bangladesh is often compounded by coastal flooding caused by oceanic storms moving inland. In October of 1960, two separate floods killed 6,000 people and 4,000 people, respectively. In August of 1968 more than 1,000 people perished in a flood in the Gujarat State, India, and this was followed by another deadly flood three months later in northeastern India, which resulted in the death of 780 people.

Owing to the enormous population growth in Asia and the relatively low level of flood control in many parts of the region, damage and death from flooding in this area have historically been great. It is estimated that in the twenty-year period between 1947 and 1967 more than 154,000 people were killed by floods in Asia.

Flooding in Europe has also caused damage, suffering, and loss of life. Records indicate that a flood in Holland in 1228 killed an estimated 100,000 residents. On November 4, 1333, Florence experienced one of its greatest floods when the Arno River overflowed its banks and inundated the city to a depth of 14 feet (4.2 meters). In 1966, Florence was once again flooded by the Arno River, but to the even greater depth of 22 feet. In total, 24 people perished in the flood. This flood also damaged priceless paintings, sculptures, tapestries, books, and maps.

On October 9, 1963, Italy suffered a devastating flood caused by the overtopping of a high arch dam in Vaiont. The flood was caused by an enormous rockslide that rushed into the reservoir behind the dam. The rock debris filled the reservoir and displaced the water toward the dam in waves as high as 230 feet (70 meters). The water flowed over the dam (which was not destroyed) and down the river valley at great speeds. A total of 1,800 people died. In the period from 1947 to 1967, floods took 10,540 lives in Europe (excluding the Soviet Union).

Flooding has also been extensive in the United States. One of the great tragedies in the late nineteenth century was caused by the collapse of the dam above Johnstown, Pennsylvania. In the western part of the country another dam collapse occurred in 1928, when the St. Francis Dam in Southern California ruptured, sending a flood downstream. More than 450 people in the Santa Paula area died from this flood.

Regional flooding of the Missouri-Mississippi drainage basin has long caused problems for the midwestern part of the country. Flooding of the lower stretches of the Mississippi River in the late 1800's caused engineers to design extensive levee systems to hold back the floodwaters. In 1927 the river rose to its then-historic high water level, causing extensive damage in the southern states. The river breached its levees in 225 locations, and 313 people lost their lives. The Mississippi again flooded in 1943 and 1944.

In 1972, Hurricane Agnes moved onshore and northward through the eastern part of the country, dumping enormous quantities of rain in the region and causing extensive flooding east of the Appalachian Mountains from North Carolina to New York State. A total of 113 people lost their lives in these floods. Estimated damages were in excess of $3 billion, the largest flood disaster in United States history at that time. Also in 1972, the devastating Rapid City, South Dakota, flood occurred. A tremendous thunderstorm broke over the area, dumping up to 15 inches (38 centimeters) of rain in less than six hours. The upstream dam was overtopped, and the river inundated the floodplain and much of Rapid City. The death total was 238, and damages exceeded $160 million.

The following year, the Mississippi River flooded extensively again, resulting in over $1.155 billion in damage. However, the extensive flood-control measures and early evacuation kept the death toll to a low level. In 1976, a thunderstorm dropped over 7.5 inches (19 centimeters) of rain in four hours over Big Thompson Canyon in Colorado. The flash flood that resulted killed 139 people. Only a few days earlier the Teton Dam in Idaho had collapsed, killing 11 people.

The largest flood of the Mississippi River in the 133 years of record keeping occurred in 1993. High-water marks were recorded at St. Louis, and the river broke through or overtopped 1,083 levees in the upper part of the basin. More than 20 million acres were flooded, and damages exceeded $18 billion. At least 52 people died in the floods.

*Robert M. Hordon*
*Jay R. Yett*

**BIBLIOGRAPHY**

Beyer, Jacqueline L. "Human Response to Floods." In *Perspectives on Water*, edited by David H. Spiedel, Lon C. Ruedisili, and Allen F. Agnew. New York: Oxford University Press, 1988. This is a well-written chapter that focuses on flooding and how societies respond to its danger.

Dunne, Thomas, and Luna B. Leopold. *Water in Environmental Planning*. New York: W. H. Freeman, 1978. This is a classic book that contains several very useful chapters on runoff processes, flood hazard calculations, and human adjustments to floods.

Dzurik, Andrew A. *Water Resources Planning*. 2d ed. New York: Rowman & Littlefield, 1996. In addition to other material on planning issues in water resources, this book contains a good chapter on floodplain management.

Hornberger, George M., Jeffrey P. Raffensberger, Patricia L. Wilberg, and Keith N. Eshleman. *Elements of Physical Hydrology*. Baltimore:

Johns Hopkins University Press, 1998. Contains a chapter that provides a technical discussion on streams and floods from an engineering perspective.

Jones, J. A. A. *Global Hydrology*. Essex, England: Longman, 1997. A well-documented book on hydrology and environmental management, including a chapter on floods and magnitude-frequency relationships.

Martini, I. Peter, Victor R. Baker, and Guillermina Garzón, eds. *Flood and Megaflood Processes and Deposits: Recent and Ancient Examples*. Malden, Mass.: Blackwell Science, 2002. Promotes an understanding of large floods and their impact.

Myers, Mary Fran, and Gilbert F. White. "The Challenge of the Mississippi Floods." In *Environmental Management*, edited by Lewis Owen and Tim Unwin. Malden, Mass.: Blackwell, 1997. This chapter provides a readable account of the issues involved in the destructive 1993 Mississippi floods.

O'Connor, Jim E., and John E. Costa. *The World's Largest Floods, Past and Present: Their Causes and Magnitudes*. Reston, Va.: U.S. Geological Survey, 2004. A circular from the U.S. Geological Survey. Includes bibliographical references. Also available online at http://pubs.usgs.gov/circ/2004/circ1254.

Strahler, Alan, and Arthur Strahler. *Introducing Physical Geography*. 4th ed. Hoboken, N.J.: John Wiley & Sons, 2006. One of the better standard college books that has useful text and illustrations on runoff processes and floods.

White, Gilbert F. *Choice of Adjustment to Floods*. Department of Geography Research Paper 93. Chicago: University of Chicago, 1964. This is a classic paper that deals with the social-science aspects of settlement on floodplains, including the increasing damages from floods in the face of ever-larger expenditures for flood control.

# Fog

**FACTORS INVOLVED:** Geography, temperature, weather conditions
**REGIONS AFFECTED:** Coasts, especially those where a cool ocean current is present; mountains; cities; towns

## DEFINITION

Fog can be a transportation danger because it reduces visibility. It is particularly hazardous in situations where heavy use of a transportation artery occurs.

## SCIENCE

Fog occurs when the temperature of any surface falls below the dew point of the air directly above it. There are a number of different kinds of fog, depending on the circumstances that lead to its generation. Radiational fog occurs in the early morning hours, when the cooling of the ground has created a temperature differential between the ground and the moist air directly over it. The lower ground temperature (at lower temperatures the air is less able to hold moisture) causes the moisture in the air immediately above it to condense into tiny droplets. Massed, the droplets make visibility impossible. By definition, fog exists when visibility is less than 0.6 mile (1 kilometer).

Advectional fog occurs when moist air moves over colder water. This is the kind of fog common along coasts, especially those where a colder ocean current tends to parallel the coast. If wind speeds increase, the density of this kind of fog also tends to increase, unless the wind speed is such as to blow away the moist air mass constituting the fog. For that to occur, wind speeds greater than 15 knots are needed.

Upslope fog occurs in areas in which the prevailing winds blow over a large surface area from a moist region toward a region of increasing altitudes. As the wind blows upslope, it creates the temperature gradient between the ground and the moister air that can induce fog.

Occasionally, precipitation in the form of drizzle can turn into fog. This can occur if the drizzle is falling through cool air that be-

## MILESTONES

**January 19, 1883:** 357 die in fog-related collision of steamers *Cimbria* and *Sultan.*

**1901:** Transatlantic wireless radio sends first signal to receiver in St. John's, Newfoundland.

**May 29, 1914:** More than 1,000 drown in the sinking of the Canadian liner *Empress of Ireland* following its collision with Norwegian freighter *Storstad* in heavy fog on the St. Lawrence River.

**1925:** First radio signal to warn of fog is sent to ships on the Great Lakes.

**December 23, 1933:** Two trains collide in fog near Paris, killing 230.

**1945:** Radar is used for tracking civilian traffic in ships and planes.

**December 5-9, 1952:** Heavy smog in London kills 4,000 people.

**July 25-26, 1956:** The Italian liner *Andrea Doria* sinks after being struck by Swedish vessel in fog.

**July 31, 1973:** A Delta Airlines jet crashes while attempting to land at Boston's Logan International Airport in fog; 89 die.

**March 27, 1977:** Two airliners collide in fog in Tenerife, Canary Islands; 583 die.

**April 10, 1991:** 138 die in crash of ferry *Moby Prince* and oil tanker *Agip Abruzzo* in Italy.

comes saturated as a result of the drizzle. Such fogs can become very dense and are most apt to occur in places where relatively high rainfall is the norm.

In high latitudes, what are known as ice fogs are rather common. In these cases, below-freezing temperatures cause moisture in the air to become suspended ice crystals that dominate the atmosphere, creating the effect of fog. For such fogs to form, very low temperatures are needed—at least minus 25 degrees Fahrenheit.

The fog that comes off the surface of a body of water in early winter is often warmer than the air above. Even though the vapor pressure of the water is higher (the reverse of the normal condition creating fog) droplets will sometimes move upward from the water creating the effect of fog. Such fog is called steam fog.

## GEOGRAPHY

Radiational fog may occur anywhere if the proper temperature differential exists, but it is most common in areas where there are different elevations. This type of fog tends to concentrate in depressions or river valleys. It tends to burn away during the early morning hours if the day is sunny—the heat of the sun dries up the condensed water vapor.

Advectional fog is most common along coasts and most frequent along coasts where a cold ocean current flows and creates the necessary temperature differential. The cold ocean current is the defining factor, and for this reason fog is very common on seacoasts where such currents exist. The west coast of the United States, from San Francisco northward, is subject to such conditions, with the prevailing wind blowing the moisture off the ocean onto the land. The Pacific coast of North America has at least sixty days of dense fog each year.

The east coast of Canada, especially Newfoundland and Labrador, is notorious for its dense fogs. These fogs result from the cold Labrador current that runs up that coast. Even farther south, on Cape Cod, Massachusetts, fogs are fairly common, although they lack the intensity of those along the east coast of Canada.

Iceland and the British Isles are notorious for their fogs, again resulting from the temperature differential between the land and the surrounding ocean. On the other hand, fogs are rare in the lower latitudes farther south in Europe, although radiational fog may exist in, for example, the Alpine valleys of Switzerland.

Although fog is rare in tropical areas, there are two regions that do experience it. One is the Peruvian coastline, where, although there is little actual precipitation, vegetation can survive in an essentially desert climate from the condensation of the moisture contained in the fogs. Another tropical area that experiences fog is the coast of Somalia, in eastern Africa, where some unusual coastal currents create the necessary temperature differential.

Arctic fogs have created problems for weather-gathering stations in Greenland for a number of years. They are particularly intense on the east coast of Greenland.

Although the reduction in the use of coal-fired steam engines has reduced the amount of steam vented into the atmosphere around cities, auto exhausts and emissions from power plants can, if added to natural fog, produce what is often called smog. This mixture of natural fog and emissions can be a hazard. Some cities, located where prevailing winds cannot disperse such atmospheric collections because of adjacent mountains, have severe problems with smog—Denver and Los Angeles are examples.

## PREVENTION AND PREPARATIONS

Because of the hazard to transportation, especially air transport, at various times efforts have been made to try to disperse fog, especially at transportation hubs. Seeding a fog with salt has been found effective but has some obvious environmental drawbacks. Another method, creating a blast of hot air along the runways of airports, has been used in some critical situations but demands an extremely large fuel input. However, when temperatures are below freezing (below 25 degrees Fahrenheit), success has followed seeding of fog with solid carbon dioxide crystals. Another method occasionally used has been spraying with propane gas. However, when temperatures are above freezing (and most fogs form under such conditions), no satisfactory method has been found to disperse fogs at airports.

Foghorns have been the traditional method of warning vessels both at sea and on large bodies of inland waters, such as the Great Lakes. The most effective antidote to fog has been the development of radar, which sees through fog. This methodology has become increasingly successful in handling air traffic, although the radar devices have had to become more exact as the volume of traffic has grown. Even so, and even though all commercial pilots now must be able to land a plane solely with the use of instrument indicators, fog can shut down air operations. Most pilots prefer being able to see a runway before they land. Even localized fogs can disrupt the schedules of virtually all airlines because they interrupt interconnecting flights.

Although airplane crashes in the United States resulting from fogs are now relatively rare because the flights are regularly shut down when fog closes in at an airport, there is always an intensive investigation by the Federal Aviation Administration (FAA) if there is a crash. Because the federal government controls all the airline flights through its air traffic control system, flights are routinely canceled when a serious fog situation exists.

Fog continues to be a problem in automobile travel, although the development of the interstate highway system, with its dual road structure, has helped reduce the dangers. However, the majority of roads remain two-lane roads, and it is up to the individual motorist to drive with exceptional care in foggy conditions.

As shipping has become more a system for moving freight than for moving people, the risk of marine accidents is no longer what it once was. Still, in certain areas fog continues to be a problem for oceangoing traffic despite the assistance of radar.

## IMPACT

As the amount of air travel has grown, so has the danger posed by fog conditions. The layout and siting of airports can be helpful in mitigating the effects of fog, but the standard response is still to shut down flights until the air clears.

## HISTORICAL OVERVIEW

Although fogs can occur anywhere in the world under the appropriate conditions, they are more common in the northerly latitudes, especially along seacoasts. Consequently, they began to pose a major problem as the inhabited world spread northward from the Mediterranean. They constitute a hazard for travelers, and as the development of new vessels made people more venturesome on the sea, fog became more of a risk factor. At the same time, vessels tended to hug the shoreline, where the lack of visibility in a fog (fog is defined as a condition in which visibility is less than 3,281 feet, or 1,000 meters) posed the risk of running aground on a difficult-to-see coast.

As European fishermen braved the Atlantic to fish in the rich waters of the Grand Banks off Newfoundland, the fogs that often enshroud that peninsula became deadly. Breton fishermen risked their lives in search of cod as early as the fifteenth century, and thousands of fishermen have lost their lives in shipwrecks brought about by the inability of the crewmen to see. In the lobby of one of the principal hotels on the French island of Miquelon, one of the few remaining possessions of France in the Western Hemisphere, there is a chart listing more than 300 wrecks that have occurred along the Newfoundland coastline, most as a result of fog. The locals maintain that the list significantly undercounts the number of wrecks that have cost fishermen their lives.

Throughout the nineteenth century, as residents of coastal areas of New England went to sea to make a living, the risk of shipwreck along the rocky New England coast remained great. In the middle of the nineteenth century the whaling vessels of New England numbered more than 700. Because the ships possessed only relatively rudimentary navigational instruments and navigated by sight, fogs posed a real danger. Even the adoption of foghorns at many risky coastal points did not relieve the danger for sailing vessels.

New technology, especially the invention of wireless radio in the late nineteenth century enabling ship-to-shore communication, reduced some of the risks posed by fog. Radio communication from shore stations to vessels during fog was only introduced gradually, however; the first such signal on the Great Lakes was sent in 1925. The invention of radar in World War II vastly reduced the risks of fog at sea, as it enabled vessels to "see" even under conditions of heavy fog.

Marine disasters under foggy conditions did not disappear with the introduction of wireless radio, however. On May 29, 1914, the *Empress of Ireland* was struck by a Norwegian steam freighter on the St. Lawrence River; when the Norwegian vessel backed off, the *Empress of Ireland* quickly filled with water and went down within fifteen minutes. Although 444 people were saved, more than 1,000 died. All passengers were rescued when the *George M. Cox* struck Isle Royale in Lake Superior in 1933, despite foghorn warnings. Even the presence of radar did not prevent a collision between two vessels on Lake Michigan in October, 1973, although no one was injured.

The most spectacular shipping disaster attributed to fog was, however, the sinking of the Italian liner *Andrea Doria* in July of 1956. The Swedish liner *Stockholm* struck the *Andrea Doria* just after 11 P.M. in heavy fog. The Swedish ship had a reinforced prow, and, despite being equipped with numerous watertight bulkheads, the *Andrea Doria* could not be saved; it sank in the Atlantic eleven hours later. All passengers who survived the impact were saved, however, by other ships that came to the rescue.

Fog, when mixed with suspended particles in the air, can be a killer on its own. The famous London fogs, mixed with suspended particulate matter and called "smogs," proved to be particularly intense between December 5 and 9, 1952. They are thought to be responsible for the deaths of more than 4,000 individuals.

Fog also poses a danger to surface transportation. The greatest problems have arisen in situations where numerous trains use the same track and are dependent on signals that may not be readily visible in heavy fog. London has a history of train disasters due to fog and smog. In 1947, in South Croydon, an overcrowded suburban train was rammed from behind by a faster-moving train. The signaling equipment, only partly automated, failed to alert the faster train to the presence of the suburban train on the same track. In 1957, on a day when fog reduced the visibility to as little as 66 feet (20 meters), an express train struck an electrified suburban train at St. John's, outside of London, killing 92 people. The introduction of fully automated signaling equipment has helped prevent such disasters, although as late as 1966 a passenger train crashed into the rear of a freight train in Villafranca, Italy, causing the death of 27 people.

Fog is a major hazard to airplane traffic. Although most airplane accidents in the United States are not attributable to fog, in part because the stringent rules of the Federal Aviation Administration require that airports with severely reduced visibility be shut down, the danger is great. The crash of a Delta jet attempting to land at Logan International Airport in Boston on July 31, 1973, brought home the dangers posed by fog. Eighty-nine people lost their lives. Since then, airports have been shut down entirely when they are enveloped in fog, and incoming flights are diverted to other airports. The flight control system maintained by the federal government is entirely based on radar, which is unaffected by fog.

*Nancy M. Gordon*

**BIBLIOGRAPHY**

Barry, Roger G., and Richard J. Chorley. *Atmosphere, Weather, and Climate.* 8th ed. New York: Routledge, 2003. A strongly scientific presentation that treats fog as condensation. Provides numerous maps showing water vapor content at various locations.

Gedzelman, Stanley David. *The Science and Wonders of the Atmosphere.* New York: John Wiley & Sons, 1980. Contains numerous diagrams and maps. Provides descriptions of the climate in various geographical areas, with the resulting vegetation. Numerous photographs.

Hidore, John J., and John E. Oliver. *Climatology: An Atmospheric Science.*

2d ed. Upper Saddle River, N.J.: Prentice Hall, 2002. Contains excellent diagrams of the process of fog formation. A solid, scientific-based presentation for the general reader.

Lockhart, Gary. *The Weather Companion.* New York: John Wiley & Sons, 1988. Contains some information on foghorns. Otherwise, a compendium of popular weather lore.

Lydolph, Paul E. *The Climate of the Earth.* Totowa, N.J.: Rowman & Littlefield, 1985. Although a generalized text on climatology, this text contains good material on the different kinds of fogs.

# Heat Waves

**Factors involved:** Chemical reactions, geography, human activity, temperature, weather conditions, wind

**Regions affected:** Cities, coasts, deserts, plains, towns, valleys

## Definition

Heat waves occur when the air temperature remains abnormally high for an extended period of time over a region. Heat waves destroy crops; damage infrastructure, such as roads, buildings, and railroad tracks; and cause both animal and human deaths.

## Science

Heat waves are the result of a combination of natural factors and human activity. Natural factors include the normal heating of the earth's atmosphere by short-wave radiation from the sun and long-wave radiation from the earth, the flows of heat that make up the net radiation balance, the tilt of the earth, and the chemical makeup of the atmosphere above the surface of the earth. Human activity, mainly the burning of fossil fuels, is capable of changing the chemical makeup of the atmosphere and thus affects the heating of the earth's atmosphere.

Normal heating of the earth's atmosphere occurs when radiant heat, or short-wave radiation, from the sun begins to heat the earth shortly after dawn. Radiation is defined as the transmission of energy in the form of electromagnetic waves. The short-wave radiation is absorbed by the earth. The earth then emits long-wave radiation, which is absorbed by the atmosphere as heat. (Wavelength refers to the distance between the wave crests of successive waves.) In summary, the sun's rays heat the earth, the earth passes some of this heat to the air, or atmosphere, that surrounds it, and the atmosphere becomes warm. As the air near the earth warms, it rises, and cooler air descends. This rising and lowering sets air currents in motion in the atmosphere. These air currents carry the heat that under certain circumstances can become a heat wave.

A wide variety of factors can affect the amount of short-wave radiation that is absorbed by the earth. About 30 percent of the short-wave radiation coming to Earth is reflected by clouds or dust particles and never reaches the earth's surface. Another 17 percent of the radiation is absorbed by clouds and other particles in the atmosphere. Thus, a change in the amount of clouds or particles in the atmosphere will affect the amount of radiation that reaches Earth. The condition of the earth's surface also influences how much radiation is absorbed. The color, composition, and slope of the surface determine how much radiation is absorbed or reflected. Rays that strike the earth perpendicularly are less likely to be reflected. Rays that strike dark soil or dark surfaces are more likely to be absorbed than if they strike light-colored areas.

Carbon dioxide, water vapor, and ozone are the three major components of the atmosphere that absorb the long-wave radiation emitted by the earth, with carbon dioxide absorbing the most. The higher the concentration of these substances becomes in the atmosphere, the more heat is absorbed and the hotter the air becomes. High concentrations of these chemicals also provide a blanket effect over the earth, preventing radiation and heat from escaping. This blanket effect results in a phenomenon called the "greenhouse effect." In a greenhouse, the sun's rays pass through the glass and warm the air within the greenhouse. The glass, however, then prevents the heat from escaping. Similarly, the sun's radiation passes through the atmosphere, warming the earth and the air, and then the atmosphere stops the heat from escaping.

Although the greenhouse effect occurs naturally, it can be influenced by human activity. When fossil fuels are burned, enormous quantities of carbon dioxide are produced and released into the atmosphere. Over the last one hundred years, human beings have increased their use of fossil fuels drastically. Generating electricity, heating buildings, and using automobiles are all human activities that currently depend on burning fossil fuels. Debate continues among scientists as to what role the higher levels of carbon dioxide in the atmosphere and the greenhouse effect play in global warming trends.

When the radiation that leaves the earth is subtracted from the radiation that reaches earth, the amount of radiation left over is called the net radiation. Net radiation affects the earth's climates and is a

## MILESTONES

**1348-1350:** Hot summers contribute to the spread of bubonic plague in Europe.

**1665-1666:** Very hot summers in London exacerbate the last plague epidemic.

**1690:** Siberia experiences extreme heat, probably due to southerly winds; at this time, Europe is abnormally cold.

**1718-1719:** Great heat and drought affect most of Europe during the summers of these years.

**1845:** Moist, southerly winds and a hot summer provide the perfect growing conditions for the potato blight fungus, resulting in the Irish Potato Famine.

**1902:** Willis H. Carrier designs the first system to control the temperature of air.

**1906:** The term "air-conditioning" is used for the first time by an engineer named Stuart W. Cramer.

**1936:** Dust Bowl conditions arise in the central United States; 15,000 to 20,000 die.

**1968-1973:** Drought occurs in the Sahel region of Africa.

**1972:** A heat wave affects Russia and Finland.

**1975-1976:** Heat waves are recorded in Denmark and the Netherlands.

**1980:** A heat wave in Texas produces forty-two consecutive days above 100 degrees Fahrenheit.

**1990:** The United Nations' Intergovernmental Panel on Climate Change (IPCC) predicts that, if unchecked, greenhouse gases and carbon dioxide emissions produced by human activity could raise world surface temperatures by 0.25 degree Celsius per decade in the twenty-first century.

**August, 1994:** A severe heat wave and drought parches Japan; blocks of ice are put in subway stations for travelers to rub their heads against.

**1995:** The IPCC predicts carbon dioxide and greenhouse emissions to raise Earth's surface temperature between 0.8 and 3.5 degrees Celsius within one hundred years.

**July, 1995:** A heat wave in the midwestern United States kills almost 500 people in Chicago alone, as well as 4,000 cattle.

> **July, 1998:** A heat wave hits the southwestern and northeastern United States; daytime temperatures in Texas hit 110 degrees Fahrenheit, with forty-one days of above-100-degree weather, causing huge crop losses and 144 deaths.
>
> **July, 1998:** Worldwide, July is determined to be the hottest month in history to date.
>
> **August, 1998:** India reaches 124 degrees Fahrenheit; 3,000 people die in the worst heat wave there in fifty years.
>
> **August, 1998:** As a result of summer heat, 50 people die in Cyprus, and 30 die in Greece and Italy; grapes die on vines.
>
> **August, 1998:** In Germany, record heat produces severe smog, and cars lacking antipollution devices are banned.
>
> **July-August, 2003:** A heat wave grips all of Europe, especially France, Italy, Spain, and Portugal; as many as 40,000 die from heat-related causes, and drought and wildfires follow.

source of heat for earth. Thus, all factors that affect radiation to and from the earth will influence the possible development of heat waves.

### GEOGRAPHY

Heat waves can occur anywhere on Earth. A wide range of countries have reported heat waves, including the United States, Canada, Russia, India, Japan, many European countries, many African countries, Australia, and Cyprus. Heat waves generally occur over land masses rather than over the oceans. More energy is required to raise temperatures over water than over land, so temperature fluctuations are more prevalent over land. Thus, islands that are surrounded by large bodies of water do not experience heat waves. Since air cools as the altitude increases, mountainous areas are less susceptible to heat waves than are lower areas.

Urban areas tend to have higher rates of heat-related deaths than do rural areas. The heat retention of urban structures contributes to the natural heat of the heat wave. Also, the tall buildings and the pollution of urban areas stagnate the movement of air, thus intensifying the effects of a heat wave.

Many areas of the United States have been affected by heat waves.

In 1901, 9,508 heat-related deaths occurred in the midwestern states. During the brutally hot summer of 1936, 15,000 to 20,000 people perished from the heat. As recently as July, 1995, heat in the Midwest killed almost 500 Chicago residents. Heat waves have devastated the southern states and have wreaked havoc in both New England and California. Neither Hawaii nor Alaska has recorded a heat wave. Although Hawaii is located near the equator, the Pacific Ocean surrounding Hawaii moderates its temperatures. Alaskan summer days can be hot, but they only go above 90 degrees Fahrenheit occasionally.

## PREVENTION AND PREPARATIONS

Human beings are powerless to control the natural forces, such as radiation, that affect heat waves. However, human beings can control the amount of fossil fuels they burn, and thus somewhat control the carbon dioxide in the atmosphere. Numerous international conferences have been held to discuss this issue.

Although heat waves are not preventable, both individuals and communities can prepare for heat waves and reduce their harmful effects. Individuals should discuss with family members what they would do during a heat wave and should identify the coolest places to be while at home, at work, or at school. They should learn about places in the community where people can go for help, plan daily activities for the coolest time of day, and refrain from physical activity during the midday hours. Wearing lightweight, light-colored clothing and staying out of the sun can reduce the effects of a heat wave. People should talk to their doctors about any medications or medical conditions that would affect their ability to tolerate heat, as well as learn the signs and symptoms of heat stroke and heat exhaustion and first-aid treatments for these conditions.

Community support programs can greatly reduce loss of life. Those most at risk are the elderly, the poor, and those with health conditions that reduce the ability to tolerate heat. Obtaining air conditioners and fans for those who need them has been effective in saving lives. Establishing "cool centers," areas that are air-conditioned, where people can go to cool down, can also help reduce fatalities. Media announcements, especially television and radio, inform and alert people to the dangers of heat waves. During the Chicago heat wave of 1995, police officers even went door to door to check on elderly citizens.

## RESCUE AND RELIEF EFFORTS

To save lives, rescue and relief efforts must be started as soon as the heat wave hits. The two dangerous medical conditions that result when heat waves occur are heat exhaustion and heat stroke, the latter being the more serious. When someone is exposed to hot weather for an extended time and does not take in adequate water and salt, heat exhaustion occurs. The human body cools itself by sweating; the evaporation of water from the skin reduces body heat. Excessive sweating causes the body to lose large amounts of water and salt. Extended exposure to heat requires the body to sweat profusely in an effort to get rid of heat. If the water and salt lost in this process are not replaced, the body's attempts to cool itself eventually become ineffective, and heat exhaustion occurs.

The symptoms of heat exhaustion include pale, clammy skin, rapid pulse and breathing, headache, muscle cramps, dizziness, and a sick and faint feeling. If heat exhaustion occurs, the victim should lie down in as cool a place as possible with his or her feet raised slightly, loosen tight clothing, and replace lost fluids by drinking water. One level teaspoon of salt added to each quart (or liter) of water will help to replace the salt lost during excessive sweating. Heat exhaustion must be treated immediately or it will progress to heat stroke.

Heat stroke, also called sunstroke, occurs when the body's temperature regulation mechanism fails. This mechanism, which is located in the brain, normally helps the body maintain a constant temperature by telling the body to shiver if it needs to become warmer or to sweat if it needs to cool. If a person suffers a heat stroke, this mechanism stops functioning and the body temperature starts to rise to 104 degrees Fahrenheit (40 degrees Celsius) or higher. This is a medical emergency, and medical help should be sought immediately.

The symptoms of heat stroke include flushed, hot, dry skin; strong, rapid pulse; confusion; and ultimately unconsciousness. To treat heat stroke until medical help arrives, victims should be moved to the coolest place possible. Their clothing should be removed, and they should be sponged with cool or tepid water and fanned by hand or with an electric fan. A blow-dryer set on cool may also be used.

## IMPACT

In the United States alone, heat waves have been responsible for the loss of billions of dollars and thousands of human lives. Heat waves damage property, both privately and publicly owned. They kill cattle and destroy crops. Excessive heat causes roads to buckle and crumble, and it warps metal, causing, for example, railroad tracks to bend, resulting in train derailments. Heat waves have been connected to increased cases of riots, violence, and homicides. Sustained heat waves are very difficult for the human body to tolerate. When heat waves occur, normal daily activity must be adjusted in order for humans to survive.

## HISTORICAL OVERVIEW

Throughout history, extremes in temperature have greatly affected human existence. From 543 to 547 c.e., the entire Roman world suffered from plague. Great heat in the area contributed to the spread of the disease. Hot weather caused the flea that transmitted the bubonic plague to speed up its life cycle. The European countries were also affected by wave after wave of disease from 1348 until 1665. Again, the hot summers furthered the spread of the disease.

Detailed weather records from early times do not exist. Information about weather is inferred from the reports of travelers and food availability. Weather reports from the sixteenth century have survived. However, reports based on instrument readings did not appear until the seventeenth century. These records show that periods of high temperature have been recorded for many areas on earth, including Europe, Africa, China, India, Australia, and North America. As time progressed, the records became much more detailed. Thus, much of the information available on heat waves relates to events occurring after the middle of the nineteenth century.

Heat waves have been a contributing factor in human migration patterns. In Ireland, in 1845, hot summer temperatures favored the growth of the organism that caused the potato blight fungus. Failure of the potato crop resulted in widespread famine. Over the next six years around 1 million people died in Ireland. Although an epidemic of typhus contributed to the death toll, hunger played a significant role. Believing that there were more opportunities elsewhere, thousands of Irish immigrated to the United States.

In the United States, heat waves have been responsible for thousands of deaths and the loss of billions of dollars in the twentieth century alone. The century began with a very hot summer in 1901. It is reported that 9,500 people died that summer. The summer of 1936 was brutally hot; an estimated 15,000 to 20,000 people lost their lives. Those who survived often lost their farms and everything for which they had worked. Again, heat waves influenced migration; families left the "Dust Bowl" area of the middle United States and moved toward the coasts, where more fertile land was to be found.

The air-conditioning of homes began in the 1930's, but it was not in prevalent use. In 1980, only 30 percent of the homes in the United States had air-conditioning, which greatly reduces death tolls during heat waves.

The heat wave of 1980 in the midwestern United States killed 1,265. The heat wave of 1988 resulted in 10,000 casualties. In 1995, almost 500 people in Chicago died within one week. The same heat wave killed 4,000 cattle. The increasing frequency and severity of heat waves worldwide beginning in the last half of the twentieth century generated tremendous concern in the scientific community. Much effort went into studying weather patterns in an attempt to determine whether these heat waves are just part of a natural fluctuation of weather or if human activity is contributing to the warming of the earth.

The damage done by heat waves does not affect all socioeconomic classes to the same degree. The economically disadvantaged suffer more dire consequences when heat waves hit than do those with resources. During the heat wave that struck Chicago in 1995, most of the fatalities were people who were poor and elderly. Most lived in the top floors of old apartment buildings that were not air-conditioned. People with resources obtained air-conditioning or left the city. Farmers are another group of people who are hard hit by heat waves. When heat waves destroy crops or kill cattle, the farmer's livelihood is destroyed as well. Meanwhile, an accountant who lives in an air-conditioned home in the city pays a bit more for hamburger but hardly notices. Thus, heat waves affect some social classes more than others.

In other countries, cultural issues can play a role. In July and August, 2003, a severe heat wave in Europe claimed as many as 40,000 victims, many in France. Most homes in Europe do not have air-conditioning, and the effects of the heat wave were worsened by the tradition of August vacations, with few people around to check on elderly residents.

*Louise Magoon*

## BIBLIOGRAPHY

Abrahamson, Dean Edwin. *The Challenge of Global Warming*. Washington, D.C.: Island Press, 1989. Provides a through discussion of the greenhouse effect.

American Red Cross. *Heat Wave*. Stock Number NOAA/PA 94052. Rev. ed. Washington, D.C.: U.S. Dept. of Commerce, 1998. This pamphlet gives very practical advice on how to survive a heat wave.

Clayman, Charles B. *The American Medical Association Family Medical Guide*. 3d ed. New York: Random House, 1994. Offers a thorough description of heat exhaustion and heat stroke and the first-aid treatments for these conditions.

DeBlij, H. J., and Peter O. Muller. *Physical Geography of the Global Environment*. New York: John Wiley & Sons, 1993. This geography textbook describes the heating of the earth's atmosphere, global distribution of heat flows, the greenhouse effect, and climate changes.

Graedel, T. E., and Paul J. Crutzen. *Atmosphere, Climate, and Change*. New York: W. H. Freeman, 1995. This book gives a very easy-to-read description of weather, temperature, and climatic changes.

_____. *Atmospheric Change: An Earth System Perspective*. New York: W. H. Freeman, 1993. Details the chemistry of the atmosphere and climate and describes ancient climate histories.

Kirch, W., B. Menne, and R. Bertollini, eds. *Extreme Weather Events and Public Health Responses*. Berlin: Springer, 2005. Describes the development of and the damage caused by extreme weather events in Europe since the 1970's.

Lyons, Walter A. *The Handy Weather Answer Book*. Detroit: Visible Ink Press, 1997. Using a question-and-answer format, the author gives short, simple answers to questions that are posed.

Oliver, John E. *The Encyclopedia of Climatology*. New York: Van Nostrand Reinhold, 1987. Provides a good discussion of the effects of temperature extremes.

# HURRICANES, TYPHOONS, AND CYCLONES

**FACTORS INVOLVED:** Geography, gravitational forces, rain, weather conditions, wind
**REGIONS AFFECTED:** Cities, coasts, forests, islands, oceans, rivers, towns

## DEFINITION

Hurricanes, typhoons, and cyclones are storms formed over tropical oceans. A single storm can cover hundreds of thousands of square miles and has interior winds of from 74 to over 155 miles per hour. Hurricanes are known as the "greatest storms on earth," and destruction goes beyond wind damage, as storm surges and subsequent flooding have caused many of the greatest natural disasters in the world. Hurricane damage in the United States continues to rise as more people move to coastal areas; however, the loss of life has decreased because of better forecasting and evacuation methods.

## SCIENCE

A hurricane (from the Caribbean word *huraka'n*), also called a typhoon (a combination of *t'ai feng*, Chinese for "great wind," and *typhon*, Greek for "whirlwind"), requires warm surface water, high humidity, and winds from the same direction at a constant speed in order to form. All hurricanes begin as cyclonic tropical low-pressure regions, having a circular motion that is counterclockwise in the Northern Hemisphere and clockwise in the Southern Hemisphere. These depressions can develop only in areas where the ocean temperatures are over 75 degrees Fahrenheit (24 degrees Celsius). The eye structure of a hurricane, which must be present in order for a storm to be classified as a hurricane, demands temperatures of 79 to 80.6 degrees Fahrenheit (26 to 27 degrees Celsius) to form.

In hurricane formation, heat is extracted from the ocean, and warm, moist air begins to rise. As it rises, it forms clouds and instability in the upper atmosphere. The ascending air then begins to spiral inward toward the center of the system. This spiraling movement

## MILESTONES

**1588:** A major storm destroys the Spanish Armada, which is seeking to escape the English navy under Sir Francis Drake.

**August 15, 1635:** A hurricane strikes Massachusetts and Rhode Island coastal settlements.

**September 27, 1727:** A hurricane strikes the New England coast.

**September 15 and October 1, 1752:** Two hurricanes strike South and North Carolina.

**September 8-9, 1769:** The Atlantic coast, from the Carolinas to New England, is hit by a hurricane.

**October 22-23, 1783:** A hurricane strikes the Atlantic coast, from the Carolinas to New England.

**August 13, 1856:** A hurricane striking Last Island, Louisiana, results in a death toll of 137.

**1890:** The Federal Weather Bureau is created.

**1898:** A hurricane warning network is established in the West Indies.

**September 8, 1900:** A hurricane in Galveston, Texas, leads to the highest death toll from a hurricane to date, from the following storm surge.

**September 15-22, 1926:** The Great Miami Hurricane strikes Florida and the Gulf states, resulting in 243 dead.

**September 10-16, 1928:** A Category 4 storm, the San Felipe, or Lake Okeechobee, hurricane claims over 4,000 lives in the Caribbean and Florida.

**September 21, 1938:** The Great New England Hurricane of 1938 causes high winds, flooding, and a storm surge that leave 680 dead, more than 1,700 injured, and $400 million in damage.

**December 17-18, 1944:** A typhoon in the Philippine Sea kills 790.

**September 4-21, 1947:** A hurricane impacts the Gulf states, leaving over 50 dead.

**1953:** The system of naming hurricanes is adopted.

**October 12-18, 1954:** Hurricane Hazel strikes the Atlantic coast, causing 411 deaths and $1 billion in damage.

**June 27-30, 1957:** More than 500 die when Hurricane Audrey hits the Louisiana and Texas coastlines.

**September 6-12, 1960:** The Atlantic coast's Hurricane Donna results in 168 dead and almost $2 billion in damage.

**August 15-18, 1969:** Hurricane Camille rages across the southern United States; 258 die.

**November 12-13, 1970:** The Bhola cyclone strikes the Ganges Delta and East Pakistan (now Bangladesh), killing at least 300,000 people.

**June 21-23, 1972:** 122 die during Hurricane Agnes.

**September 7-14, 1979:** Hurricane Frederic strikes the Gulf Coast states, causing $1.7 billion in damage.

**September 12-17, 1988:** Hurricane Gilbert kills 260 in the Caribbean and Mexico.

**September 13-22, 1989:** 75 die as Hurricane Hugo strikes the Caribbean, then South Carolina.

**April 30, 1991:** A cyclone hits Bangladesh and kills more than 131,000.

**August 22-26, 1992:** Hurricane Andrew strikes southern Florida, leaving 50 dead and $26 billion in damage.

**July 5-15, 1996:** Hurricane Bertha hits the Caribbean and the Atlantic coast; winds exceed 100 miles per hour.

**November 3, 1997:** Typhoon Linda kills more than 1,100 in Vietnam.

**June 9, 1998:** A cyclone hits the Indian state of Gujarat; more than 1,300 are killed.

**September 16-29, 1998:** 400 die when Hurricane Georges strikes in the Caribbean, then the Gulf Coast; winds exceed 130 miles per hour.

**October 27, 1998:** Hurricane Mitch hits Central America; the death toll exceeds 11,000.

**February 11, 1999:** Cyclone Rona strikes Queensland, Australia; 1,800 are left homeless.

**October 4-9, 2001:** Hurricane Iris kills 31 and does $150 million in property damage in Belize.

**September 18, 2003:** Category 5 hurricane Isabel makes landfall south of Cape Hatteras, North Carolina, leaving 53 dead and property damage of $3.37 million.

**2004:** Four Category 5 storms—Charley, Frances, Ivan, and Jeanne—make landfall in the United States, the most in a hurricane season since 1963.

**August 25-September 2, 2005:** Hurricane Katrina kills 1,500-2,000 people in Louisiana, Mississippi, Alabama, and Florida and leaves hundreds missing; property damage is estimated at $75 billion. The levees protecting New Orleans are breached, and the city is completely flooded. Two other powerful hurricanes, Rita and Wilma, hit the Gulf Coast shortly afterward.

causes the seas to become turbulent; large amounts of sea spray are then captured and suspended in the air. This spray increases the rate of evaporation and helps fuel the storm.

As the vortex of wind, water vapor, and clouds spins at an increasing rate, the eye of the hurricane forms. The eye, which is at the center of the hurricane, is a relatively calm area that experiences only light winds and fair weather. The most violent activity in the hurricane takes place in the area around the eye, called the eyewall. In the eyewall, the spiraling air rises and cools and moisture condenses into droplets that form rainbands and clouds. The process of condensation releases latent heat that causes the air to rise and form more condensation. The air rises rapidly, resulting in an area of extremely low pressure close to the storm's center. The severity of a hurricane is often indicated by how low the pressure readings are in the central area of the hurricane.

As the air moves higher, up to 50,000 feet, it is propelled outward in an anticyclonic flow. At the same time some of the air moves inward and into the eye. The compression of air in the eye causes the temperature to rise. This warmer air can hold considerable moisture, and the water droplets in the central clouds then evaporate. As a result, the eye of the hurricane becomes nearly cloud-free. In the middle and upper levels of the storm, the temperature in the eye becomes much warmer than the outside. Therefore, a large pressure differential develops across the eyewall, which helps to produce the violence of the storm.

The hurricane winds create waves of 50 to 60 feet in the open ocean. Winds in a hurricane are not symmetrical around the eye. Facing the direction the hurricane is moving, the strongest winds are usually to the right of the eye and can move at speeds up to 200 miles per hour. The radius of hurricane winds can vary from 10 miles in small hurricanes to 100 miles in large hurricanes. The strength of the wind decreases in relation to its distance from the eye.

Depending on the size of the eye, which can range from 3 to 40 miles in diameter, a calm period of blue skies and mild winds can last from a few minutes to hours as the eye moves across a given area. The calm is deceptive because it does not mark the end of the storm but a momentary lapse in intensity until the winds from the opposite direction hit.

Storms resembling hurricanes but that are less intense are classified by their central pressure and wind speed. Winds up to 39 miles per hour (34 knots) are classified as tropical depressions, and winds of 40 to 73 miles per hour (35 to 64 knots) are called tropical storms. To be classified as a hurricane, storms must have sustained winds of 74 miles per hour or higher.

All hurricanes in the Northern Hemisphere have a general track, beginning as a westward movement in response to the trade winds, veering northward because of anticyclonic wind flow around subtropical high pressure regions, and finally trending northeastward toward polar regions in response to the flow of the prevailing westerly winds. The specific path that each storm travels is very sporadic. Some will travel in a general curved path, while others change course quite rapidly. They can reverse direction, zig-zag, veer from the coast back to the ocean, intensify over water, stall, return to the same area, make loops, and move in any direction at any given time.

The path of a hurricane is affected by pressure systems of the surrounding atmosphere and the influence of prevailing winds as well as

*A satellite view of a hurricane as it approaches the United States. The cyclonic motion of the "arms" and the eye are visible.* (National Oceanic and Atmospheric Administration)

the earth's rotation. Hurricanes can also be influenced by the presence of high and low pressure systems on the land they invade. The high pressure areas act as barriers to the hurricanes, and if a high is well developed, its outward spiraling flow will guide the hurricane around its edges. Low pressure systems tend to attract hurricane systems.

The greatest cause of death and destruction in a hurricane comes from the rise of the sea in a storm surge. As the hurricane crosses the continental shelf and moves to the coast, the water level may increase 15 to 20 feet. The drop in atmospheric pressure at sea level within the hurricane causes the storm surge. The force of the reduced pressure allows the hurricane to suck up the seas and to allow the winds in front of it to pile up the water against the coastline. This results in a wall of water that can be up to 20 feet high and 50 to 100 miles wide. This wall of water can sweep across the coastline where the hurricane makes landfall. The combination of shallow shore water and strong hurricane winds makes for the highest surge of water.

If the storm surge arrives at the same time as the high tide, the water heights of the surge can increase an additional 3 to 4 feet. The height of the storm surge also depends upon the angle at which the storm strikes the coast. Hurricanes that make landfall at right angles to the coast will cause a higher storm surge than hurricanes that enter the coast at an oblique angle. Often the slope or shape of the coast and ocean bottom can cause a bottleneck effect and a higher storm surge.

Water weighs approximately 1,700 pounds per cubic yard, and when lifted to any great height its weight can be very destructive. The storm surge is responsible for 90 percent of the deaths in a hurricane. The pounding of the waves caused by the hurricane can easily demolish buildings. Storm surges can cause severe erosion of beaches and coastal highways. Often, buildings that have survived hurricane winds have had their foundations eroded by the sea surge or have been demolished by the force of the waves. Storm surges and waves in harbors can destroy ships. The salt water that inundates land can kill existing vegetation, and the residual salt left in the soil makes it difficult to grow new plants.

Precipitation from hurricanes can be more intense than from any other source. The amount of rainfall received during a hurricane depends on the diameter of the rain band within the hurricane and the hurricane's speed. A typhoon in the Philippines in 1944 caused 73.62 inches of rain to fall in a twenty-four-hour period, a world record. Heavy rainfall can cause flash floods or river system floods. Flash floods last from thirty minutes to four hours and are caused by heavy rainfall over a small area that has insufficient drainage. This causes excess water to flow over land and overflow streambeds, resulting in damage to bridges, underpasses, and low-lying areas. The strong currents in flash floods can move cars off roads, destroy bridges, and erode roadbeds.

River system floods develop more slowly. Two or three days after a hurricane, large rivers may overflow their beds because of excessive runoff from the saturated land surface. River floods cover extensive areas, last a week or more, and destroy both property and crops. When the floodwaters retreat, buildings and residences can be full of mud. Often, all furnishings, appliances, wallboard, and even interior insulation within the structure must be completely replaced because of the infiltration of the mud. Rain driven by the wind in hurricanes can cause extensive damage to buildings because of leakage around windows, through cracks, and under shingles.

Hurricanes often spawn tornadoes. The tornadoes associated with hurricanes are usually about half the size of tornadoes in the Midwest and are of a shorter duration. The area these tornadoes affect is small, usually 200 to 300 yards in width and not quite 1 mile long. Yet even though they are smaller tornadoes, they can be very destructive, ruining everything in their path. Tornadoes normally occur to the right of the direction of the hurricane's movement. Ninety-four percent of tornadoes occur within 10 to 120 degrees from the hurricane eye and beyond the area of hurricane-force winds. Tornadoes associated with hurricanes are most often observed in Florida, Cuba, the Bahamas, and the coasts of the Gulf of Mexico and the south Atlantic Ocean.

## GEOGRAPHY

Because hurricanes require temperatures of 79 to 80.6 degrees Fahrenheit (26 to 27 degrees Celsius) to form, they will rarely develop above 20 degrees latitude because the ocean temperatures are never warm enough to provide the heat energy needed for formation. In the Northern Hemisphere the convergence of air that is ideal for hurricane development occurs above tropical waters when easterly moving waves develop in the trade winds. The region around the equator is called the "doldrums" because there is no wind flow. Hurricanes, needing wind to form, can be found as little as 4 to 5 degrees away from the equator. At these latitudes the Coriolis effect, a deflecting force associated with the earth's rotation, gives the winds the spin necessary to form hurricanes.

Hurricanes evolve in specific areas of the west Atlantic, east Pacific, south Pacific, western north Pacific, and north and south Indian Oceans. They rarely move closer to the equator than 4 or 5 degrees latitude north or south, and no hurricane has ever crossed the equator. In the Northern Hemisphere, hurricanes are common from June through November; in the Southern Hemisphere, the hurricane season occurs from December to May.

In the Western Hemisphere, these storms are called hurricanes. They are referred to as typhoons in the western Pacific, cyclones in the Indian Ocean, Willy Willys near Australia, and *baguious* in the Philippines. The swirling motion of these storms is counterclockwise in the Northern Hemisphere and clockwise in the Southern Hemisphere.

## PREVENTION AND PREPARATIONS

Hurricanes cannot be prevented; therefore, steps need to be taken to avoid loss of life and destruction of property. Persons in hurricane areas need to be aware of and respond to hurricane watches and warnings forecast by the National Hurricane Center, National Weather Service, and local media. The National Hurricane Center is responsible for forecasting hurricane watches and warnings for the Atlantic and eastern Pacific north of the equator. Although both warning capacity timing and accuracy have greatly improved, predictions can still be inaccurate by as much as 100 miles in a twenty-four-hour period.

Before a watch or warning is forecast, residents need to prepare a home evacuation plan. This involves determining where the family will go if a hurricane threatens. The options include staying with friends or relatives outside the area or going to public shelters. Evacuation supplies such as extra cash, hygiene products, drinking water, batteries, bedding, clothing for wet and cold conditions, prescriptions, canned foods, and road maps should be kept on hand. A three-week supply for each person and pet is recommended. Restoration supplies should also be organized and stored together for use after residents are able to return home. Restoration supplies include rope and chains, brooms and shovels, rolls of heavy plastic, duct tape, tools, nails, pruning shears and saws, large-capacity garbage bags, nonperishable foods, folding lawn chairs, mosquito spray and netting, and chlorine bleach to be used for purifying water.

In order to protect homes in hurricane areas, shutters should be installed to protect windows. In some cases thin plywood can be used to cover large windows. Masking tape or duct tape applied to windows can help control some of the shattering in window breakage. Gas grills and propane gas tanks should be stored in a safe place so they are not damaged or do not explode during the storm. It is recommended that dead vegetation around the house be cleared and any coconuts removed from the trees so that they will not become destructive debris in the midst of the hurricane. All objects kept outside should be tied down, and all electricity, water, and gas should be turned off at the main panel if a hurricane warning is issued. Insurance policies, inventory records, and important documents should be kept in safe-deposit facilities. Trees and shrubbery should be cut in such a manner as to allow air to flow through them so that they will survive in hurricane winds.

If a hurricane watch is issued, windows should be covered and backup systems such as portable pumps to remove floodwater, alternate power sources, and battery-powered lighting should be made available. Because a hurricane watch means that a hurricane is possible in twenty-four to thirty-six hours, residents should be prepared for evacuation if one is called.

A hurricane warning indicates that a hurricane will reach land within twenty-four hours. All utilities should be turned off and loose items secured. Small items inside the house should be placed on countertops in order to avoid damage in case of flooding. Cash, social security cards, drivers' licenses, wills, medical records, bank account information, small valuables, and photo albums should be put in waterproof bags to ensure their safety. Garbage cans, lawn furniture, and bicycles should be brought inside. Cars should be filled with gas and should contain evacuation maps; if evacuation is called for, then emergency plans should be put into action.

One way to survive a hurricane is to build a "safe room" or shelter in the house. The shelter must be built where it cannot be flooded during a hurricane. It must be anchored to the foundation of the house in such a way as to resist uplift or overturning in the storm. All the connections in the shelter must be strong enough to resist structural failure and penetration by wind-blown debris.

### RESCUE AND RELIEF EFFORTS

Devastation after a hurricane can range from light to catastrophic, depending on the storm's intensity. Millions of cubic yards of debris can be left in a hurricane's wake. Before residents are allowed to return to a hurricane area, emergency management personnel make search and rescue and preliminary damage assessments. Residents are not allowed back until the area is determined safe. Dangling wires, fallen trees, debris, and washed-out roads can make travel into the area difficult or impossible until cleanup has been accomplished.

Debris can consist of trees, shrubs, building materials, and hazardous waste, such as paints, solvents, batteries, and insecticides. As this debris is cleaned up, Emergency Management and Environmental Resource Management personnel, with the help of the U.S. Army Corps of Engineers, will need to authorize and manage the disposal of the debris. Task forces work with regulatory agencies to determine the impact of incineration and other disposal methods.

The Red Cross and other volunteer agencies help provide needed relief. Often there is deterioration or contamination of water supplies, and the Red Cross supplies bottled water as well as nonperishable foods. Shelters may be set up for those left without homes.

Residents are advised not to enter their homes or businesses before officials have checked for structural damage. They are told to beware of such outdoor hazards as downed power lines, weakened limbs on trees, or damaged overhanging structures. People need to be aware that poisonous snakes are often driven from their dens by high water and seek refuge in trees and structures. Residents are encouraged to take as many photographs of the damage to their property as possible for insurance purposes. If their homes are livable, the long process of cleanup begins.

## IMPACT

The Saffir-Simpson Hurricane Scale categorizes the storm intensity of hurricanes into five levels. Category 1 hurricanes are considered weak and have sustained winds of 75 to 95 miles per hour. They cause minimal damage to buildings but do damage unanchored mobile homes, shrubbery, and trees. Normally they cause coastal road flooding and minor damage to piers. Storm surges seen in Category 1 hurricanes are usually 5 to 7 feet above normal.

Category 2 hurricanes, with wind speeds of 96 to 110 miles per hour, damage roofing materials, doors, and windows on buildings. They also cause substantial damage to trees, shrubs, mobile homes, and piers. Utility lines can be blown down, and vehicles may be blown off bridges. Flooding of roads and low-lying areas normally occurs two to four hours before the center of the hurricane arrives. Storm surges are estimated to be 8 to 12 feet high under these conditions.

Category 3 hurricanes are considered strong, with winds of 111 to 130 miles per hour; large trees can be blown down. These storms destroy mobile homes and can cause structural damage to residences and utility buildings. Small structures can be destroyed, and structures near the coastline can sustain damage from battering waves and floating debris. Flooding from this level of hurricane can destroy small structures near the coast, while larger structures normally sustain damage from floating debris. There can be flooding 8 miles or more inland. Coastal areas can sustain storm surges of 11 to 16 feet.

Category 4 hurricanes are categorized as very strong, with winds of 131 to 155 miles per hour. These storms can blow down trees, shrubs, power lines, and antenna towers. They cause extensive damage to single-family structures and cause major beach erosion. They can damage lower floors of structures, and the flooding can undermine foundations. Residences often sustain roof structure failure and subsequent rain damage. Land lower than 10 feet above sea level can be flooded, which would cause massive evacuation of residential areas up to 6 miles inland. Storm surges may reach 14 to 20 feet at this level.

Category 5 hurricanes are classified as devastating, sustaining winds greater than 155 miles per hour. Evacuations of residents living within 5 to 10 miles of the shoreline may be required. Such a strong hurricane can cause complete roof failure on residential and industrial buildings, as well as some complete building failures. Major utilities are usually destroyed in this level of hurricane. Structures less than 15 feet above sea level can sustain major damage to lower floors, and massive evacuations of residential areas usually occur. Storm surges associated with these severe hurricanes can be 18 feet or higher.

The devastation of hurricane winds is exemplified by the fact that the wind force applied to an object increases with the square of the wind speed. A building 100 feet long and 10 feet high that has 100-mile-per-hour winds blowing against it would experience 40,000 pounds of force being exerted against its walls. This is because a 100-mile-per-hour wind exerts a force of approximately 40 pounds per square foot. If the wind speed was 160 miles per hour, the force against the house would be 100,000 pounds. Additionally, winds in a hurricane do not blow at a constant speed. The wind speeds can increase and decrease rapidly. The wind pressure on the house and fluctuating wind speed can create enough stress to cause connections between building components to fail. Often the roof or siding can be ripped off the house, or windows may be pushed in. Structures that fail because of the effects of extreme winds often look as if they have exploded. Rain blown by the wind also contributes to an increase of pressure on buildings and can result in structure failure.

Flying debris, often referred to as "windborne missiles," can be thrown at a building with enough force to penetrate the walls, windows, or roof. A 2-by-4-inch piece of wood that weighs 15 pounds can have a speed of 100 miles per hour when carried by a 250-mile-per-hour wind. This will enable it to penetrate most reinforced masonry.

The impact of hurricanes goes beyond the destruction of homes and property. Agricultural loss, oil platform and drilling rig damage, and destruction of boats can range into millions and even billions of dollars. Property loss alone in 1992's Hurricane Andrew was approximately $25 billion. Agriculture, petroleum industry, and boat losses in Florida and Louisiana amounted to another $1 billion.

The marine environment is also impacted by hurricanes. There can be changes in near-shore water quality, as well as bottom scouring and beach overwash. Fuel from damaged boats can discharge into the water for days. Often, sponges, corals, and other marine life will be severely impacted.

## HISTORICAL OVERVIEW

Hurricanes are major tropical storms that originate in the Atlantic Ocean off the west coast of Africa between June and November. Similar storms can develop in the Pacific Ocean, where they are called typhoons, and in the Indian Ocean, where they are called cyclones. Hurricanes have clearly existed since the end of the last ice age, but their impact on humans has increased markedly with the growth of population in the coastal areas hit by these storms.

The Atlantic Coast and the coastline of the Gulf of Mexico are the two areas most affected by Atlantic hurricanes. The tail end of such a storm may have destroyed the remains of the Spanish Armada in 1588, when it sought to escape the victorious English fleet by sailing around the British Isles.

Hurricanes have had a profound impact on the vegetation of the Atlantic coastline. These "disturbances," as ecologists classify them, have the effect of destroying so much of the vegetation that the process of ecological succession must start over in the areas affected by hurricanes. There is, on average, one hurricane per century at any particular point on the Atlantic coast; in the twentieth century, a Category 4 hurricane struck the Atlantic coast once every six years, on average. Hurricanes are classified according to wind speed from 1 to 5; Category 4 hurricanes have windspeeds of 131-155 miles per hour.

What is known about hurricanes before the twentieth century comes mainly from descriptive records. It is known, for example, that what has been described as a "hurricane" struck the coastline of Rhode Island and Massachusetts in 1635, and another hit about a century later, in 1727. In 1752, the Carolinas were hit, and in 1769 and again in 1783 hurricanes struck the Atlantic coastline from South Carolina to New England. How much destruction was done by these hurricanes, or how many may have lost their lives, is unknown because records of that sort were not kept at that time.

Scientists are sure that a hurricane that missed New Orleans on August 13, 1856, wiped out the settlement on Last Island, off the Louisiana coast. The Federal Weather Bureau was created in 1890, and in 1898 an early warning network was set up in the West Indies—the first steps in the system that, by the end of the twentieth century, succeeded in reducing the loss of life from hurricanes. Notwithstanding, these early warning efforts did not prevent what is still, from the standpoint of loss of life, the most devastating hurricane in U.S. history, the one that struck Galveston, Texas, on September 8, 1900; estimates of the death toll (arising as much from the following storm surge) reach about 12,000.

Deaths by drowning are common features of some of the earlier known hurricanes, a hazard that has been mitigated by the evacuation of communities in the path of a hurricane. A storm that hit the Miami, Florida, area in 1926 left more than 200 people dead. More than 4,000 died in 1928 when, as a consequence of the storm named for it, Lake Okeechobee overflowed. This disaster, also known as the San Felipe hurricane, led to the construction of a levee around the lake.

Only 47 were killed in 1933 when a hurricane struck the mid-Atlantic coast. This hurricane led to further actions on the part of government to prevent the loss of life from hurricanes. Notwithstanding preventive measures, the 1930's had one of the most destructive hurricanes of the twentieth century, when the Great New England Hurricane of 1938 struck New England and pushed inland, killing more than 600 people and causing extensive damage, particularly to the forests of New England. Even though this hurricane qualified as only a Category 2 storm, the extent of the damage etched it permanently in the minds of many New Englanders.

Major changes in the government's handling of hurricane alerts resulted from technological advances in the 1930's and particularly during World War II. The radio made advance warning of large populations much easier as it became popular in the 1930's. World War II, however, with its extensive use of airplanes, revolutionized the handling of hurricane information. With airplanes, it became possible to fly over the disturbances as they progressed from the Atlantic Ocean off the coast of Africa toward the Atlantic coastline of the Western Hemisphere. It thus became customary to follow the path of a hurricane and to forewarn threatened populations by radio. Because the radio message was easier to understand when it had a name attached to it, the practice of naming hurricanes began in 1953.

In 1965 U.S. president Lyndon Johnson reorganized the government's weather monitoring system. Prior to that, in 1955, two new facilities were created: the National Hurricane Center in Miami and the Experimental Meteorology Laboratory, also in Miami. The latter

*Rows of houses in Greenville, North Carolina, are flooded after Hurricane Floyd dumped as much as 20 inches of rain on the coast.* (FEMA)

performs meteorological research, and the former tracks the paths of hurricanes as they develop. They subsequently became part of the National Oceanographic and Atmospheric Administration (NOAA). In 1978 the Federal Emergency Management Agency (FEMA) was added by President Jimmy Carter to the governmental organizations designed to deal with hurricanes and other natural disasters.

The devastation wrought by Hurricane Camille, which struck the Gulf Coast on August 17, 1969, made clear the importance of united societal action. Although Camille caused only 258 deaths—as compared with predecessors Audrey in 1957, in which more than 500 people lost their lives, and Hilda, which killed 304 people in 1964—but the value of the property destroyed by Camille soared into the billions and focused people's minds on the problem of hurricanes.

Hurricanes have been quite erratic in where they strike land (they generally lose force quickly once they move over land), but the Gulf Coast has been a favorite target. In August, 1970, Hurricane Celia struck Texas and Florida; in September, 1979, Hurricane Frederic landed on the Gulf Coast (in 1979 men's names as well as women's began to be used), in 1985 Hurricane Juan struck the Gulf Coast, and in September, 1988, Hurricane Gilbert hit the Caribbean and Mexico. In 1992, Hurricane Andrew hit chiefly South Florida but also went on to Louisiana, and in 1998 Hurricane Georges struck first in the Caribbean and then traveled to the Gulf Coast. In 2005, numerous strong hurricanes formed, with several striking the Gulf Coast. The worst by far was Hurricane Katrina, which devastated Louisiana, Mississippi, and Alabama and left as many as 2,000 dead.

Despite the severity of that season, analysis of the history of hurricanes indicates that, beginning in the second half of the twentieth century, intense hurricanes in the Atlantic Ocean decreased. No conclusive scientific evidence has been found for linking hurricanes to global warming. There is some connection between the formation of hurricanes and the heat over the Sahel in Africa, but it provides no indication as to where any hurricanes that might form will strike land in North America.

It has been found that the number of deaths caused by hurricanes can be reduced dramatically by evacuating the residents of an area in the path of a hurricane. If a hurricane strikes the coast of North America in a relatively uninhabited area, destruction will probably be extensive but few lives will be lost. However, the rapid growth of coastal populations makes it less and less likely that hurricanes will come ashore where there are few people. Even though Hurricane Hugo in 1989 struck a portion of the South Carolina coast that was lightly inhabited, it caused the deaths of 75 people; the more intense Hurricane Andrew resulted in the deaths of only 50. Massive evacuation efforts were made once it became clear where Hurricane Andrew would strike the Florida coast, and no doubt many lives were saved as a result. Evacuating a large city in the path of a hurricane, however, can prove more problematic, as the situation in New Orleans proved with Hurricane Katrina.

In countries where the governmental infrastructure is less well developed than in the United States, the kinds of policies followed in the United States will not particularly help. A cyclone that hit Bangladesh in 1991 killed 131,000 people. A typhoon that landed in Vietnam in November, 1997, killed 1,100. A cyclone in the Indian state of Andhra Pradesh in November, 1996, caused the deaths of more than

1,000 people, and when a cyclone hit the Indian state of Gujarat in June, 1998, more than 1,300 people lost their lives. Hurricane Mitch, which hit Central America in late October, 1998, killed more than 11,000 and totally devastated the economies of Honduras and Guatemala. Experts have estimated that in Asia alone, the number of people at risk for death from cyclones is somewhere between 12,000 and 23,000.

Although actions taken by society have succeeded, at least in the United States, in reducing the effects of hurricanes on humans, the costs of hurricanes have risen dramatically. Hurricane Camille, which struck the Gulf Coast in 1969, and Hurricane Betsy, which landed in the Bahamas, South Florida, and Louisiana in 1965, produced damages estimated to run in the neighborhood of $1 to $2 billion.

In contrast, the damage caused by Hurricane Andrew, in 1992, totaled more than $25 billion. The largest part of this consisted of damage to private property, but many public structures and roads were also affected. The damage caused by Andrew bankrupted a number of insurance companies, and many more restricted the amount of coverage they would provide in hurricane-prone regions. Hurricane Katrina left widespread damage totaling $75 billion. As the value and number of properties in coastal areas grow, the risk of major economic dislocation from future hurricanes grows as well. Although some governments have attempted to restrict development along hurricane-prone shores, this approach has proved unpopular and has not been highly successful. Most experts agree that future disasters caused by hurricanes are inevitable.

*Dion C. Stewart and Toby R. Stewart*
*Nancy M. Gordon*
*R. Baird Shuman*

**BIBLIOGRAPHY**

Bryant, Edward A. *Natural Hazards*. 2d ed. Cambridge, England: Cambridge University Press, 2005. Provides a solid scientific treatment for the educated student. Readers should have a basic understanding of mathematical principles to fully appreciate this book. Contains a glossary of terms.

Emanuel, Kerry. *Divine Wind: The History and Science of Hurricanes*. New York: Oxford University Press, 2005. A hurricane expert describes the science behind these storms and analyzes their historical impact.

Pielke, R. A., Jr., and R. A. Pielke, Sr. *Hurricanes: Their Nature and Impacts on Society.* New York: John Wiley & Sons, 1997. A very informative and well-written book by father and son meteorologists. Focuses on the United States, integrating science and social policies in response to these storms.

Robinson, Andrew. *Earthshock: Hurricanes, Volcanoes, Tornadoes, and Other Forces of Nature.* Rev. ed. New York: Thames and Hudson, 2002. An informative book written for high school students or general adult readers. Provides an interesting mix of science, individual event summaries, and noteworthy facts and figures.

Sheets, Bob, and Jack Williams. *Hurricane Watch: Forecasting the Deadliest Storms on Earth.* New York: Vintage, 2001. Discusses historical methods of prediction as well as modern forecasting techniques.

Simon, Seymour. *Hurricanes.* New York: HarperCollins, 2003. Intended for young people. Discusses how hurricanes are formed, the destruction that they can cause, and the precautions that can be taken.

Tufty, Barbara. *1001 Questions Answered About Hurricanes, Tornadoes, and Other Natural Air Disasters.* Rev. ed. New York: Dover, 1987. This text has a logical flow to it. Excellent illustrations accompany the text.

# ICEBERGS AND GLACIERS

**FACTORS INVOLVED:** Geography, geological forces, gravitational forces, ice, snow, temperature, weather conditions, wind

**REGIONS AFFECTED:** Coasts, forests, lakes, mountains, oceans, rivers, towns, valleys

## DEFINITION

Glaciers are gigantic ice masses flowing down and over land, whereas icebergs, which originate from glaciers, are ice masses that typically float in oceans. Over the centuries, glaciers and especially icebergs have caused much destruction of human property and lives.

## SCIENCE

Glaciers, which cover about 10 percent of the earth's surface, are large masses of freshwater ice formed by the compacting and recrystallization of snow in polar regions and in other regions' high mountains. When the aggregated ice is large and thick enough, it generally starts flowing downhill by gravity and spreading outward because of its increasing volume. Moving glaciers may terminate on land, where their melting ice turns into a river of water, or they may end in a lake or ocean. Various scientists estimate the number of glaciers at 70,000 to 200,000, depending on how their sizes are defined. Glaciers can vary from an area of about one-third of a square mile to nearly 5 million square miles (12.5 million square kilometers), the size of the great Antarctic ice sheet. About three-quarters of the world's freshwater exists as glacial ice.

Climate and topography cause differences in a glacier's size, shape, and physical characteristics. When an ice mass grows so large that it covers an area of about 19,300 square miles (50,000 square kilometers), glaciologists call it an ice sheet, and it usually spreads over vast plateaus, flowing from its center outward. The Antarctic and Greenland ice sheets are the only ones now existing, but during the ice ages of the Pleistocene epoch (1.8 million to 10,000 years ago) ice sheets covered the northern parts of Europe and North America.

If the area covered is less than 19,300 square miles, the glacier is called an ice cap, a flattened, dome-shaped glacier covering both mountains and valleys. In Arctic regions ice caps occur at fairly low altitudes, whereas in such temperate regions as Iceland they occur on high plateaus. In valley glaciers, the flow of ice is confined between a valley's hillsides or mountainsides. These glaciers may originate from ice sheets or ice caps, but they may also flow out of cirque glaciers nestled in the steep-walled hollows of mountain flanks.

Because a glacier is essentially a flowing ice river, it has a tendency to move from its initial high altitude toward sea level. When glaciers are unconfined by geological barriers, they are able to flow to the sea, where, because of erosive action of changing tides and winds, large chunks of ice split from glacial tongues and ice shelves. These floating masses of freshwater ice are called icebergs, and calving is the process of making them by fracture from a glacier's seaward end. Icebergs can be white, blue, green, or even black (from the rock materials they contain).

Scientists have categorized icebergs by their sizes and shapes. Tabular (table-shaped) icebergs, also called "ice islands," are large blocks of ice that protrude several feet above sea level and average 1,640 feet (500 meters) in diameter. Tabular icebergs are rare in the Arctic but common in the Antarctic. Pinnacled icebergs, also called castellated after their castlelike shape, are characteristic of northern polar oceans. Whether tabular or pinnacled, an iceberg has only one-ninth of its mass projecting above the water's surface, though the ratio of an iceberg's vertical height above water to its height below varies because of icebergs' irregular shapes.

Icebergs form mostly during the spring and summer, when warm weather increases the rate of calving. In the Northern Hemisphere glaciers in west Greenland produce about ten thousand icebergs. An average Greenland-born iceberg weighs approximately 2 billion pounds (1 million metric tons) and lasts from two to five years. The West Greenland Current carries these icebergs northward and westward, until eventually many of them are captured by the cold Labrador Current as it moves south to encounter the warm Gulf Stream. They then drift into the region of the Grand Banks, a submarine plateau extending from the Newfoundland coast. Canadian scientists have found a nearly linear decrease in the numbers of icebergs as they wander from northern to southern latitudes. Nevertheless, sufficient numbers survive to populate the North Atlantic shipping lanes with potential hazards to navigation.

## GEOGRAPHY

Glaciers develop in geographical regions of the earth where such precipitation as snow and hail exceeds the aggregated frozen precipitation that melts during the summer. This growing glacial accumulation occurs in polar regions where summers are cool and short, but glaciers are also found in temperate zones on high mountains, such as the Alps in Switzerland, and even in the tropics on very high mountains, such as Mount Kilimanjaro in Tanzania. Glaciers occur on all the earth's continents, except Australia, and on all the world's great mountain ranges. Whether a glacier develops in a certain geographical region depends on both its latitude and its altitude. Approximately 91 percent of the volume of the earth's glacial ice (85 percent of its area) is concentrated in Antarctica, whereas 8 percent of its volume (12 percent of its area) is in Greenland. This means that only 1 percent of the total volume of the earth's glacial ice exists in the world's mountain ranges.

Arctic icebergs are the products of glaciers in Greenland, Canada, Alaska, and Russia, but western Greenland is by far the major source of icebergs in the Northern Hemisphere. Icebergs are rare in the north Pacific Ocean because those that are calved from Alaskan glaciers generally drift northward, whereas in the north Atlantic Ocean icebergs generally drift southward (icebergs have been reported as far south as Bermuda).

Another geographical source of icebergs is the Antarctic. Because the immense weight of the Antarctic's ice sheet has depressed its underlying landmass, most Antarctic ice tends to remain inland rather than flow to the coast. Nevertheless, the sloping coastal edges of the Antarctic ice sheet constantly calve icebergs. For example, in 1927 a section about eight times the size of the state of Rhode Island broke from the Antarctic shore and floated north along the coast of Argentina.

## PREVENTION AND PREPARATIONS

Because glaciers move slowly and because they are located in sparsely populated regions, they do not pose the same threat to human life and property that icebergs do, but they are not devoid of hazard. Glaciers are capable of overrunning buildings or small settlements, as they did in seventeenth century Switzerland during the start of what came to be called the "Little Ice Age." Glacial movements can block streams, and when these ice dams fail, human structures and lives are at risk. Today, remote-sensing mapping techniques are able to identify glacial areas of potential dangers to human communities.

Throughout the period of sailing ships and even during the period of steamships, icebergs caused massive loss of life and property. Because of the tragedy precipitated by *Titanic*'s collision with an iceberg in 1912, an international conference was held in London in 1913 to determine what needed to be done to prevent such disasters in the future. The International Ice Patrol (IIP) began its service in 1914, and through aerial surveillance of icebergs supplemented by observations from commercial ships, the IIP tracked dangerous icebergs, alerted ships to their presence, and prevented collisions. After World War II, radar and sonar techniques were developed to precisely monitor iceberg movements. Canadians were particularly successful in developing airborne ice-mapping sensors, including side-looking airborne radar (SLAR). Scientists from the United States and Canada have also used satellite images to study the loss of glacier mass by calving, and these quantitative data have proved more accurate than estimates based on iceberg reports from ships. A measure of the success of the IIP's efforts is the fact that, since its inception, not a single reported loss of life or property has occurred from a cooperating vessel's collision with an iceberg.

### RESCUE AND RELIEF EFFORTS

Glacier-related disasters are generally neither as dramatic nor as catastrophic as major earthquakes, but their cumulative costs in property loss and human fatalities mean that survival and rescue become important after such disasters occur. When the lobe of a glacier blocks a stream or an iceberg threatens a seabed oil installation off Labrador, sufficient time exists to evacuate people from a potential glacial surge or to lift workers by helicopter from an oil rig.

During the days of sailing ships, rescues were largely matters of chance. When *John Rutledge*, traveling from Liverpool to New York, collided with an iceberg off the Newfoundland banks on February

20, 1856, its 120 passengers and 16 crew members tried to survive in five lifeboats (with one compass among them), but by the time *Germania* picked up one of the lifeboats eight days later, only one young boy remained alive. During the time of the great steamships, the most dramatic rescue of passengers and crew from an iceberg-sunk ship was *Titanic.* Its 705 survivors owed their lives to the wireless telegraph, for the Cunard liner *Carpathia* heard *Titanic*'s SOS messages and sped to the disaster site.

Modern technology has improved survival rates and rescues at sea. Training and drills on ships, emergency alarms, and detailed evacuation systems, as well as superior lifeboats, life rafts, life jackets, and immersion suits, have all facilitated rescues and lessened the loss of life. Because of hypothermia, only 14 people who went down with *Titanic* were pulled alive out of the water, and only half of those survived. Thermal protective suits now enhance the chances that rescue ships will pull survivors rather than corpses out of cold ocean waters.

## IMPACT

In the early twenty-first century, only a small number of glaciers existed near inhabited areas, minimizing their impact on humans. Icebergs cause disasters on a short time scale, such as collisions with ships, but glacier-related hazards can also be serious when considered on a long-term basis. Variations in the amount of glacial ice are crucial to human populations. Throughout geological history, particularly during the ice ages, glaciers have had a powerful effect on humans and their environment, as they forced our species to adapt or migrate. At the height of the last ice age, about twenty thousand years ago, much more ice existed on continents than exists today, preventing humans from using much valuable land in North America and northern Europe. Some scientists predict that the earth will eventually experience another ice age that might last 50,000 years and that this would have devastating effects on human beings.

On the other hand, many scientists are worried about the effects of future global warming on the earth's glacial ice. If all this ice were to melt, the resulting rise in sea level of about 200 feet (60 meters) would submerge every major coastal city. Glaciers are sensitive indicators of climate change, expanding and contracting in response to temperature fluctuations. During the lifetime of our species, humans have adapted to immense expansions and contractions of gigantic polar ice sheets, and if the present understanding of glaciologists about the periodic nature of these fluctuations is correct, humans will need to continue their adaptations well into the future.

*Robert J. Paradowski*

**BIBLIOGRAPHY**

Benn, Douglas I., and David J. A. Evans. *Glaciers and Glaciation.* New York: Arnold, 1998. The authors create a contemporary synthesis of "all important aspects of glaciers and their effects." Particularly valuable is an extensive set of references.

Hoyle, Fred. *Ice: The Ultimate Human Catastrophe.* New York: Continuum, 1981. In this popular account Hoyle presents the arguments of those scientists who believe that an ice age is imminent, while offering practical suggestions about what needs to be done to avoid its catastrophic consequences.

McCall, G. J. H., D. J. C. Laming, and S. C. Scott. *Geohazards: Natural and Man-Made.* New York: Chapman and Hall, 1992. This book, written by geoscientists experienced in the practical problems of natural disasters, enlightens readers through descriptions of geohazards (including glaciers and icebergs), their assessment and prediction, and the mitigation of their effects.

Simon, Seymour. *Icebergs and Glaciers.* New York: HarperTrophy, 1999. Intended for young people. Discusses the formation, movement, and types of glaciers and icebergs. Describes their effect on their surroundings.

Tufnell, L. *Glacier Hazards.* New York: Longman, 1984. The dangers to human life and property posed by ice sheets in glacierized regions can be significant, and the author shows how to identify such high-risk areas and to reduce their dangers.

# LANDSLIDES, MUDSLIDES, AND ROCKSLIDES

**FACTORS INVOLVED:** Geography, geological forces, gravitational forces, human activity, ice, plants, rain, snow, temperature, weather conditions
**REGIONS AFFECTED:** All

## DEFINITION

"Landslide" is a general term referring to any perceptible mass movement of earth materials downslope in response to gravity. The deadly forms of landslides, such as debris avalanches and mudflows, can move at speeds in excess of 249 miles (400 kilometers) per hour and can bury entire cities. The death toll from a single event can be greater than 100,000. Landslides cause more deaths and cost more money each year than all other natural disasters combined.

## SCIENCE

Mass movement is the proper term for any form of detachment and transport of soil and rock materials downslope. Some forms of mass movement have extremely slow velocities, less than 0.4 inch (1 centimeter) a year. Landslides include all forms of mass movement having speeds of greater than 0.04 inch (1 millimeter) a day.

Landslides can be divided into as many as fifteen different classes. The basis for the classification is the type of material that moves (for example, mud) and the general nature of the movement (for example, flow). The names of most of the individual classes are merely a combination of the two terms used in making the classification. For example, when very small particles called mud are saturated with water and flow down a slope like a liquid, the landslide is classified as a "mudflow."

The types of materials that are involved in a mass-movement event are called debris, mud, rock, sand, and soil. These terms refer to the size of the particles that are moving. The word "soil" is used by earth scientists for particles that are less than 0.08 inch (2 millimeters) across. The word "mud" refers to the smaller pieces of soil, whereas

## MILESTONES

**1512:** A landslide causes a lake to overflow, killing more than 600 in Biasco, the Alps.

**September, 1618:** Two villages are destroyed by landslides, and 2,427 are reported dead in Chiavenna Valley, Italy.

**September, 1806:** Portions of Rossberg Peak collapse, destroying 4 villages and killing 800 people in Goldau Valley, Switzerland.

**April, 1903:** A 0.5-mile section of Turtle Mountain near Frank, Alberta, slides down the mountain, killing 70 people in the town.

**December, 1920:** An earthquake shears off unstable cliffs in Gansu Province, China, destroying 10 cities and killing 200,000.

**1959:** Hurricane rains and an earthquake combined with a series of massive landslides bury the 800 residents of Minatitlan, Mexico, and kill another 4,200 in surrounding communities.

**October, 1963:** A landslide caused by an earthquake destroys the Vaiont Dam, drowning almost 3,000 residents of Belluno, Italy.

**November, 1963:** Grand Rivière du Nord, Haiti, is devastated by landslides brought about by tropical downpours; an estimated 500 tourists and residents are killed.

**1964:** Earthquakes and rains cause landslides near Niigata, Japan, killing 108, injuring 223, and leaving more than 40,000 homeless.

**1966:** A slag heap near Aberfan, Wales, collapses and kills 147—116 of them children.

**1968:** More than 1,000 are killed in Bihar and Assam, West Bengal, by floods and landslides.

**January, 1969:** Torrential rains lasting more than a week trigger mudslides that kill 95 and cause more than $138 million in damage in Southern California.

**July, 1972:** Landslides caused by torrential rains kill 370 persons and cause $472 million in property damage throughout Japan.

**1974:** A landslide in Huancavelica, Peru, creates a natural dam on the Mantaro River, forcing the evacuation of 9,000 living in the area and killing an estimated 300.

**September, 1987:** Mudslides wipe out entire sections of the Villa Tina area of Medellín, Colombia, killing 183 residents and leaving 500 missing.

**July, 1998:** Waves created by an undersea landslide caused by an earthquake kill 2,000 in Papua New Guinea.

**August, 1998:** The village of Malpa, India, is destroyed by boulders and mud, leaving 202 dead; only 18 survive.

**February, 2006:** A mudslide buries 16 villages on the island of Leyte in the Philippines; more than 200 are confirmed dead, and 1,800 are missing.

"sand" indicates the larger-sized soil fragments. The term "rock" is used for particles that are greater than 0.08 inch (2 millimeters) across. The term "debris" is used when there is a mixture of soil and rock; however the rock sizes usually predominate in most debris.

Civil engineers, who build highways, bridges, dams, and other construction projects, have slightly modified the classification of materials. They consider "soil" any unconsolidated material, which they divide further into two classes, called "earth" when the particle size is small and "debris" when the particle size is large. The term "rock" is reserved for material that started as distinct, rigid, rock layers within the earth. Rock will usually break up into gravel-size particles during a mass movement.

The nature of the movement can be a "slide," "flow," "fall," or one of a number of special terms in which a mixture of different movements occurs. There are several key characteristic movements associated with a slide, which physically resembles a child's slide in a playground. The material usually moves as a single mass. The moving material is coherent; it does not break apart, nor do the individual fragments take differing contoured paths down the slope. Also, the base of the sliding material is usually a single, well-defined surface. A "translational slide" occurs when the surface at the base of the moving material is a flat plane having a uniform slope, which roughly corresponds to the slope on the land surface prior to the mass movement. A "rotational slide" occurs on a curved basal surface, where the upper part of the surface is steeper and the lower part is gentler, giving the surface a spoon shape.

The mass movement called a "flow" has a motion similar to that of a shallow mountain stream: The entire mass behaves as a fluid. The individual particles of moving material take contoured paths that diverge, converge, and collide with one another as they proceed down the slope. The basal surface beneath the flowing material is more undulating, having higher and lower elevations in different areas of the flow. In most cases flows have higher water content than slides; however, the fluid nature of a flow can also be generated by internally trapped air.

A "fall" occurs when material either free-falls down a cliff face or bounces down a very steep slope. A special movement called a "topple" happens when the material rotates around a fixed pivot axis near the base of the column before the fall occurs. The rotation may proceed slowly over a period of years, but this fall is the fastest of all types of movement.

Two special categories of motion are often associated with natural disasters. An "avalanche" is a special category of flow, in which a highly disaggregated material is fluidized by entrapped air and moves at very fast speeds. A "spread" is a vertical combination of a coherent upper layer that slides downslope on a lower, more fluid layer that flows. Spreads commonly occur during an earthquake, when the dry coherent material above the groundwater table laterally spreads out and sinks into the water-saturated flowing material below the water table.

Often, people are not present at the location of a landslide, and the nature of movement must be deduced from the deposits formed. The standard technique to distinguish a slide from a flow is to make a ratio of the depth (thickness) of the moving material divided by the length (or distance) the material moves down the slope. This ratio is called the depth-length ratio. Flows move greater distances down the slope even though they generally involve less thickness of flowing material. Flows, thus, have small values for the depth/length ratio, compared to slides, which are thick and move a short distance downslope.

Of the fifteen classes of landslides, which are defined by the type of material and the nature of movement, all can be disasters in terms of property loss, but less than half are life-threatening. The most common disaster is when debris moves by a rotational slide; this class is called a "slump." A slump generally moves slowly, taking hours, days, months, or even years to complete its travel down the slope. The main block of material in a slump often breaks into a series of smaller blocks that appear as backward-tilted steps. A small, slow-moving

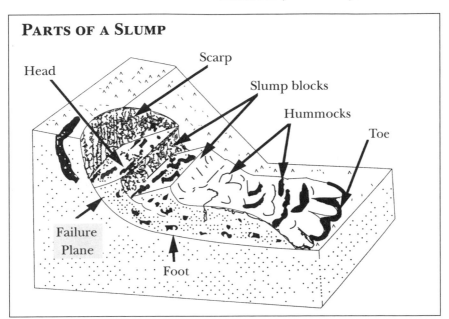

**PARTS OF A SLUMP**

Head · Scarp · Slump blocks · Hummocks · Toe · Failure Plane · Foot

earthflow typically develops at the toe of the slump. Few lives have been lost because of slumps, but when a slump develops in a city or town, every home in a section of several square blocks will have broken foundations and loss of vertical orientation of their walls and will probably need to be razed.

Mudflows and debris flows are the landslides that have generated the greatest death tolls. These events involve thick masses of mud or debris saturated with water and flowing with the consistency of wet cement. They can move at speeds of 31 miles (50 kilometers) per hour and faster. Normally, they develop after a long period of rainfall, which saturates slope materials and causes them to move. These flows also occur after sudden melting of frozen soils, often brought on by spring snowmelt. They are particularly numerous in years with heavy snowfalls and deep snowpack. As the snow melts, the water seeps into the subsurface of the slope, saturating the soil or rock mass and beginning the landslide. Mudflows are usually unexpected, and the slurry of mud and debris rushing down the slope can destroy homes, wash out roads and bridges, fell trees, sweep away cars, and obstruct roads and streams with a thick deposit of mud.

A special class of mudflow or debris flow called a "lahar" is produced when material from a volcanic eruption is ejected onto snow-fields, glaciers, or crater lakes at the summit of a stratovolcano. An eruption of Nevado del Ruiz, an ice-capped Andean volcano in Colombia, in 1985 killed no one. However, the lahar produced by the melting glacier rushed 37 miles (60 kilometers) down the valley and killed 25,000 people in the city of Armero. Lahars can travel at speeds of 93 miles (150 kilometers) per hour, and when these thick deposits of mud come to rest they become as firm as concrete in a matter of a few hours.

Mudslides can be distinguished from mudflows by the coherence of the moving mass. One eyewitness in a mudslide reported that the ground became soft and he sank to his ankles, making walking difficult while he moved several hundred yards downslope on top of a mudslide. People unfortunate enough to be atop a mudflow would immediately sink into it and become part of the churning fluid.

The landslide categories of rockslides, rockfalls, and rock avalanches are also usually lethal. A vivid example is the Vaiont Dam Disaster, where a slab 1.2 miles (2 kilometers) wide by 1 mile (1.6 kilometers) long and 820 feet (250 meters) thick slid into the Vaiont Reservoir in Italy in 1963. The drop into the reservoir took less than one minute. The rockslide splashed a wave over the dam, producing a downstream flood that killed almost 3,000 people in a town 1.5 miles (2.5 kilometers) from the dam. The dam itself survived. A rock avalanche in 1962 in Peru moved 3.9 million cubic yards (3 million cubic meters) of mountain 12.4 miles (20 kilometers) down a valley in seven minutes. Observers said the landslide bounced from one side of the valley to the other at least five times before it spread out over a populated valley at the base of the mountain, killing 60 people. The same valley experienced another rock avalanche in 1970, exacting a death toll of 70,000.

The material of a rockslide differs from that of a rock avalanche in the amount of fracturing found in the rock. Rockslides involve crack development at a specific horizon where there is expansion within the rock mass. Cracks form within the rock over a relatively narrow zone; the fracturing does not penetrate the whole rock mass. Rock avalanches develop when the fracturing is continuous all the way down to the sliding surface. An avalanche involves independent movement of fragments in the entire mass above the sliding surface, as opposed to the rockslide, which involves a single direction of movement for the material above the layer of continuous cracks.

Rockfalls in mountainous regions are often controlled by an increase in temperature, causing a thaw. Rockfalls can be so continuous in mountains that spring climbing on some European peaks must be completed by 10 A.M. Several people are killed each year in the Rocky Mountain region of the United States because of rockfalls, usually motorists struck by bouncing rocks clearing the retaining wall.

All landslides are a form of slope failure. They happen when the shear stress within a slope exceeds the strength of the slope material. Then the slope fails, and millions of cubic feet of rock and soil materials can shear away from the slope and move hundreds or thousands of feet down the hill. There are a half dozen or more factors that can cause shear stresses to exceed the forces that hold the slope in place. The most significant factor promoting landslides is an increase in the angle of the slope: The steeper the slope, the more prone it is to landslides. The angle of the slope always increases directly above any region where construction has cut a relatively flat region into the hillside, such as a road, the leveling for a house foundation, or a quarry site. Fills for roads and waste from mines and quarries are often placed on slopes, making them steeper than the normal angle of rest. Slides will begin until the angle of rest (usually about 35 degrees for coarse material) is attained. The naturally steep walls of river gorges and glaciated valleys are therefore common sites for landslides.

Another common factor contributing to landslides is the addition of water to the area. Water lifts or pushes the grains apart in the soil or rock, reducing the internal friction of the soil and counteracting the gravitational forces that hold the slope in place. Much in the same way air pressure in a car's tires lifts the car, high water pressure in the pores of rock or soil will lower the stability of the slope. This added water can come from heavy rains, melting snow, or even ponds and reservoirs. The area of Southern California is like a desert most of the year; however, it can receive heavy rains in later winter and early spring, which corresponds to the landslide season. Human influence has added water to the ground by construction of septic tanks, ponds, reservoirs, or irrigation canals. In one case in Los Angeles, a man went on vacation leaving his lawn sprinklers running, which caused an earthflow.

Landslides can also be caused by earth tremors. Earthquakes, volcanic eruptions, and even heavy machinery or trains passing on nearby roads or railroads have been known to induce tremors that start landslides. Most of the victims of the 1998 earthquake in Afghanistan were killed not by the earthquake itself but by landslides caused by the quake. In January, 1994, an earthquake in Northridge, California, triggered more than 11,000 landslides over an area of approximately 3,861 square miles (10,000 square kilometers). The largest measured rockslide had a volume in excess of 130,790 cubic yards (100,000 cubic meters). Dozens of homes were destroyed or damaged, roads were blocked, and an oil-field infrastructure sustained damage from the slide.

Another factor that promotes landslides is the removal of lateral or basal support from a slope. In nature, this occurs because of erosion by either meandering rivers or wave action on ocean cliffs. Every year numerous million-dollar homes are lost to earthfalls from wave erosion along the Pacific coastline.

Vegetation changes contribute to landslides in a variety of ways. In high mountain valleys the bedrock is wedged apart by roots of trees. In regions of rockslides the depressions created where small-scale movements have occurred are often the very sites where trees will take root and grow. On gentler slopes vegetation helps to anchor loose soil materials and prevent landslides. Wildfires have been responsible for promoting landslides by destroying tree cover; areas freshly clear-cut by the logging industry or cleared for housing developments have also been reported as sites of increased landslide activity.

The repeated freezing and thawing of water in cracks can be responsible for rockfalls. The process is called frost wedging, in which the expansion during freezing widens the crack and allows the water to penetrate deeper into the rock when the thaw occurs. Individual blocks can be wedged out of the cliff face, falling independently or causing such a loss of cohesion that larger portions of the cliff face can collapse.

## GEOGRAPHY

Mass movement occurs in varying degrees almost everywhere. Huge landslides have been identified on the Moon, on Mars, and beneath the Atlantic Ocean on continental margins. A landslide discovered on Mars in 1978, was about 37 miles (60 kilometers) long and 31 miles (50 kilometers) wide.

The number of landslides increases in regions that have steep slopes, high precipitation, sizable fluctuations in seasonal temperatures, much clay in the soils, and frequent earthquakes and volcanic eruptions. Some countries that are among the hardest hit by landslides are Switzerland, Italy, Japan, China, Peru, and Colombia.

Landslides occur in every state of the United States. California, West Virginia, Utah, Kentucky, Tennessee, Ohio, and Washington have the most severe landslides. Many of the disastrous landslides in the United States have occurred in the West; these states are among the most arid, and the occurrence of landslides is strongly correlated with unusually heavy rainfalls or the melting of winter snowpack.

Once a landslide has occurred in a given area the chances of a repeat occurrence are very high. Governments spend a considerable amount of time and money attempting to identify geographic regions where landslides have occurred. Satellite images are used to

*An undated rockslide in Frank, Alberta, Canada.* (National Oceanic and Atmospheric Administration)

identify large landslides by noting changes in soil and vegetation cover. Photographs taken from planes are used to record the extent of sliding land.

### PREVENTION AND PREPARATIONS

The standard method used to evaluate the potential of a landslide is the determination of the "factor of safety." A numerical value is determined for every factor related to the occurrence of a landslide. The factor of safety is a ratio in which all the values that resist landsliding are divided by the sum of all the values that favor a landslide. The slope is considered stable when the factor of safety has a value that is greater than 1. Landslides are considered imminent when the value is less than 1.

Myriad techniques and equipment are used to assess the instability of a slope. Conventional surveying methods measure and record the development of cracks, subsidence, and uplift on slopes. Tiltmeters are used to record changes in the slope inclination near cracks and areas of weakness. Inclinometers and rock noise instruments are installed to record movements near cracks and ground deformations. Dating cracks and subsidence and upheavals of slope areas can help scientists assess the past changes in climate and denudation, along with rainfall and earthquake and volcanic activities, which can act as triggers for future slope failures.

Recording air-temperature thresholds forecasts the onset of landslides brought on by snowmelt. Research is demonstrating that 85 percent of landslide events occurs within two weeks after the first yearly occurrence of a six-day average temperature of 58 degrees Fahrenheit. This sort of forecasting can allow ample time to prepare persons in the area to evacuate. One of the safety problems of landslides is that they normally happen within seconds, pouring tons of material on homes and buildings in their path, not allowing the populace enough time to evacuate the area.

Trends from past measurement coupled with current monitoring of slopes increase the ability to predict future landslides. Monitoring rainfall and pore water pressure are other ways to try to predict potential landslides. However, predicting landslides is a very inexact science because some cracks can form on slopes and cause landslides within minutes of their formation. Other slopes have been known to sustain cracks, subsidence, or buckling for years and then fail suddenly, with little or no warning.

Local officials are turning more to the development of landslide hazard mapping. Each area is rated as to the potential for movement and assigned to one of six designations. Areas of similar designation are grouped together as regions on a map. Local legislation places restrictions on and develops greater monitoring of the areas having the highest hazard rankings. In San Mateo County in California the hazard maps are used to restrict the number of homes that may be built there. The normal density allowed is one home per 5 acres, whereas high-hazard areas are restricted to one home per 40 acres.

People living in landslide areas need to note common warning signs of potential slope failure. Some signs of landslides are doors or windows sticking or jamming for the first time on a home. New cracks appearing in plaster, tile, brick, or the foundation of houses can be a precursor of earth movement. Widening cracks on paved streets or driveways also indicate movements in landslide areas. Sometimes underground utility lines will begin to break as result of earth movement. Water will sometimes break through the ground in new locations, and fences, retaining walls, utility poles, and trees will tilt more. A faint rumbling sound, increasing in volume, can be heard as the landslide nears. If any of these warning signs are experienced, evacuation plans should be made. It is recommended that there be at least two planned evacuation routes, because roads may become inaccessible from deposit of slide materials.

Japan spends approximately $4 billion annually to try to control mud- and debris flows. The Japanese government has built *sabo* dams along the river systems in urban areas to trap mud and rock that slide down the mountains. In the United States an American version of these dams is found in Los Angeles County, where there is a system of temporary fortifications to protect areas such as Pasadena and Glendale from debris flows that originate in the San Gabriel Mountains and canyons after hard rains.

The best form of landslide prevention is to not build on areas where landslides have occurred, at the base of slopes, at the base of minor drainage hollows, at the base or top of old fill slopes, or on hillside developments where leach-field septic systems are used. Unfortunately, landslide, rockslide, and mudslide areas are very scenic and

*Winter storms in 2005 created a number of fatal mudslides in California, such as this one in the town of La Conchita.* (FEMA)

are known to entice people to build houses. The West Coast, one of the most slide-prone areas in the world, is a prime example of an area that attracts building in spite of the dangers of landslides.

### RESCUE AND RELIEF EFFORTS
A variety of agencies are usually dispatched to the scenes of disastrous landslides. Search and rescue teams are trained in recovery techniques that are appropriate for landslides, such as rescue dogs and proper digging methods. The dangers that are associated with disease, hunger, and lack of water and shelter are handled by entities such as state governments, the Federal Emergency Management Agency (FEMA), and the American Red Cross. The National Landslide Hazards Program, within the United States Geological Survey, responds to emergencies and disasters to provide information on the continuing potential for movement while rescue efforts are taking place.

The National Flood Insurance Program was amended in 1969 to include payment for damage incurred by mudslides caused by flooding. Most homeowners' insurance policies do not cover damage caused by landslides. Federal assistance is available for areas declared a national emergency.

## IMPACT

The United States Geological Survey reported that more people died from landslides in the last three months of 1985 than were killed during the previous twenty years by all other geological hazards (such as earthquakes and volcanic eruptions). In terms of property damage, landslides have cost Americans three times the combined costs from all other natural disasters, including hurricanes, tornadoes, and floods. The average annual statistics for the United States report 25 people killed and $1.5 billion in damage.

Landslides are a major worldwide hazard. Thousands of people are killed each year across the world in landslides. A region of southern Italy experienced a series of landslides in 1973, causing 100 villages to be abandoned and 200,000 people to be displaced. A single mudflow event in the Gansu Province of China in 1920 is thought to have been the deadliest landslide, with an estimated 200,000 people killed. Property damage from landslides worldwide is estimated to be in the tens of billions of dollars.

## HISTORICAL OVERVIEW

Historically, the deadliest landslides have occurred in the mountainous regions of Asia, Europe, and the Americas. While landslides are also frequently experienced in Africa and Australia, the quantity of slides and the resultant loss of life in those regions do not compare to those in other parts of the world. Most landslides occur in hilly or mountainous regions where sloping conditions make such activity more likely, but they can happen almost anywhere.

In the United States, landslides and rockslides have occurred most frequently in the Rocky Mountain region and along the Pacific coast. Utah, Colorado, California, and Washington have been the most susceptible to landslide disasters. West Virginia holds that distinction on the U.S. East Coast, primarily as a result of slope instability caused by mining and the debris and waste that it creates. Alberta, British Columbia, and Quebec are considered the most landslide-prone provinces of Canada.

The largest and most devastating landslides have been caused by earthquakes. Most landslides occur with little or no warning, often in tandem with seismic activity. In one of the worst slides in recorded history, a 1920 earthquake in Gansu Province, China, sheared off unstable cliffs, destroying 10 cities and killing 200,000.

Human activity has also been a major contributor to the death toll caused by landslides. Ground that is normally stable may slide after human activity alters its natural state. Many deadly landslides have occurred when development altered slope and groundwater conditions. In Virginia, a state not considered a prime site for landslide activity, 8 people were killed in 1942 when a coal waste heap slid into a river valley near the city of Oakwood. The worst landslide in the history of Wales occurred when a human-made slag heap outside of Aberfan shifted, sending 2 million tons of rock, coal, and mud downhill into the city and killing 147 people, most of them children. Deforestation was a major factor in the Leyte mudslide that buried villages in the Philippines; more than 2,000 people were missing or confirmed dead.

Scientists were long unaware of the potential for destruction from underwater landslides. A scientific team that visited the site of a 1998 tsunami in Papua New Guinea later concluded that the deadly waves were probably caused by an underwater landslide set in motion by a small earthquake. This theory forced many scientists to seriously consider the possibility of a connection between landslides and tsunamis.

Unlike many other natural disasters, landslides often have a long-lasting effect on the physical environment. Landslides have collapsed mountains, sent rivers on new and destructive courses, and created huge lakes that inundated populated fertile valleys. A 1925 landslide sent some 50,000 cubic yards of debris into the Gros Ventre River of Wyoming, creating a natural dam 350 feet high. A 3-mile-long lake formed behind the dam. It is not unusual for a landslide to permanently displace animals and humans.

Property damage from landslides is a common occurrence throughout the world, resulting annually in billions of dollars in property damage. A variety of methods are now employed throughout the world to prevent landslides. One way of avoiding catastrophe is diversion and drainage of water before it reaches potential problem areas. Building contractors consider the potential for landslide damage to buildings and other structures prior to excavation and construction. The disposal of construction, logging, and mining waste is closely monitored by many governments in efforts to avoid potential slide disasters.

*Dion C. Stewart and Toby R. Stewart*
*Donald C. Simmons, Jr.*

**BIBLIOGRAPHY**

Bloom, Arthur L. *Geomorphology: A Systematic Analysis of Late Cenozoic Landforms.* 3d ed. Upper Saddle River, N.J.: Prentice Hall, 1998. Chapter 9, entitled "Mass Wasting and Hillslopes," provides a low-level technical discussion of factors contributing to landslides.

Bryant, Edward A. *Natural Hazards.* 2d ed. Cambridge, England: Cambridge University Press, 2005. A nontechnical book that cites nearly twenty additional readable references on land instability.

Cooke, R. U., and J. C. Doornkamp. *Geomorphology in Environmental Management.* Oxford, England: Clarendon Press, 1990. This book provides details on hazard assessment and risk calculations. It gives detailed examples from many countries, including the United States.

Easterbrook, Don J. *Surface Processes and Landforms.* 2d ed. Upper Saddle River, N.J.: Prentice Hall, 1999. This college textbook is quite good for a general audience. It provides excellent descriptions, pictures, and accounts of over ten classes of landslides.

Erickson, Jon. *Quakes, Eruptions, and Other Geologic Cataclysms: Revealing the Earth's Hazards.* Rev. ed. New York: Facts On File, 2001. One of the books in the series entitled The Living Earth. Contains a chapter on earth movements that provides a descriptive treatment of landslides.

Plummer, Charles C., David McGeary, and Diane H. Carlson. *Physical Geology.* 11th ed. Boston: McGraw-Hill Higher Education, 2007. A superb introductory textbook. A chapter is devoted to mass wasting and landslides, including descriptions of common forms of landslides and a section on prevention.

Ritter, Dale F., R. Craig Kochel, and Jerry R. Miller. *Process Geomorphology.* 4th ed. Dubuque, Iowa: Wm. C. Brown, 2002. This book provides the technical details of how to evaluate all factors involved in the calculation of the factor of safety. Requires a good background in mathematics, including trigonometry and vectors.

# LIGHTNING STRIKES

**FACTORS INVOLVED:** Chemical reactions, rain,
temperature, weather conditions
**REGIONS AFFECTED:** Cities, coasts, forests, lakes,
mountains, plains, towns, valleys

## DEFINITION

Lightning strikes fatally wound between 50 and 100 persons each
year in the United States, mostly within the thunderstorm season that
occurs during the spring and summer months. Lightning also causes
tens of millions of dollars of damage each year by sparking large forest fires and destroying buildings and various forms of electrical and
communication systems.

## SCIENCE

A lightning bolt is a high-voltage electrical spark which occurs most
often when a cloud attempts to balance the differences between positive and negative charges within itself. Lightning bolts can also be
generated between two clouds, or between a cloud and the ground,
although these conditions occur much less often. A lightning bolt is
generally composed of a series of flashes, with an average of four
flashes. The length and duration of each flash will vary greatly.

Thunder is caused by the heating of air surrounding a lightning
bolt to temperatures as high as 72,032 degrees Fahrenheit (40,000
degrees Celsius), which is approximately five times hotter than the
Sun, causing a very rapid expansion of air. This heated air then
moves at supersonic speeds under a force ten to one hundred times
normal atmospheric pressure, thus forming shock waves that travel
out from the lightning at speeds of approximately 1,083 feet (330 meters) per second.

Thunderstorms are local rainstorms that feature lightning and resultant thunder claps; they sometimes produce hailstones. Much less
often, lightning is created by snowstorms, dust storms, or clouds produced by volcanic eruptions or thermonuclear explosions. The explosive release of electrical energy within a thunderstorm cloud creates a lightning bolt, which is most often produced by accumulations

## MILESTONES

**1769:** 1,000 tons of gunpowder stored in the state arsenal at Brescia, Italy, explode when struck by lightning. One-sixth of the city is destroyed, and 3,000 people are killed.

**1786:** The people of Paris make bell-ringing during thunderstorms illegal. The ringing of church bells was believed to prevent lightning strikes but often proved fatal to ringers.

**April 3, 1856:** 4,000 are killed on the Greek island of Rhodes when lightning strikes a church where gunpowder is stored.

**1900:** The first quantitative measurements of peak current in lightning strikes are conducted.

**1917:** The first photographic record of the spectrum from lightning using a spectroscope is made.

**1918:** In Nasatch National Forest, Utah, 504 sheep are killed by a lightning strike.

**1925:** The U.S. Weather Bureau applies sensors to airplane wings to record atmospheric conditions.

**July 10, 1926:** Explosions triggered by lightning at an ammunition dump in New Jersey kill 21 people, blasting debris 5 miles.

**1927:** French scientists produce the radiosonde, an instrument package designed to measure pressure, temperature, and humidity during balloon ascents and radio the information back to earth.

**1929:** American scientist Robert H. Goddard launches a rocket carrying an instrument package that includes a barometer, a thermometer, and a camera.

**1959:** The first meteorological experiment is conducted on a satellite platform.

**1963:** The first quantitative temperature estimates are made for individual lightning strikes.

**1963:** Lightning strikes a Boeing 707 over Elkton, Maryland, killing all 81 persons on board. This is the first verified instance of a lightning-induced airplane crash.

**December 23, 1975:** A single lightning strike in Umtrali, Rhodesia (now Zimbabwe), kills 21 people.

of electrical charge within the same cumulonimbus cloud. Cloud-to-cloud lightning involves one cloud which is seeking an oppositely charged cloud to neutralize itself. Cloud-to-ground lightning involves a lightning bolt which is seeking the best conducting route to the ground, thus hitting lightning rods, tall buildings, and trees.

Thunderstorms occur when the atmosphere is unstable and moist air at the ground surface rises, creating several small cumulus clouds that initially dissipate while producing rain or electrical charges. As the clouds increase in size and combine, they surge upward and generate rain and lightning. The average storm produces five to ten flashes per minute, whereas larger clouds can produce electrical discharges of over a thousand flashes per minute. A single thunderstorm cloud has the potential to build up an electrical charge of approximately 1 million volts per meter, produced by the action of the rising and falling of air currents. This electrical charge is transferred through the cloud as raindrops, hailstones, and ice pellets collide with smaller water droplets and possibly ice. A falling stream of electrons creates a negative charge, which generally accumulates in the lower part of the cloud, with the positive electrons simultaneously creating a positive charge in the upper part of the cloud. Lightning is essentially the reaction that neutralizes these positive and negative charges.

Other functions of lightning are to enhance rain and snow formation, supply energy to tornadoes, and assist in the fixation of atmospheric nitrogen. Other forms of lightning include ball lightning, also called *kugelblitz*, a rare phenomenon in which round balls of fire appear, often near telephone lines or buildings. Heat lightning involves lightning seen from a distant thunderstorm which is too far away for the thunder to be heard.

American scientist Benjamin Franklin performed the first systematic study of lightning in the late eighteenth century, working from his hypothesis that sparks observed in his laboratory experiments and lightning were both forms of the same type of electrical energy. During a Pennsylvania thunderstorm in 1752, he flew the most famous kite in history, with sparks jumping from a key tied to the bottom of the damp kite string to an insulating silk ribbon tied to Franklin's knuckles. The kite took the place of a lightning rod, and Franklin's grounded body provided the conducting path for electrical currents originating from the storm clouds. Franklin's experiments proved that lightning strikes do contain electricity and determined that the lower parts of the clouds were negatively charged, with Earth providing the positive charge. Franklin's research also laid the groundwork for the implementation of lightning rods as a means of protecting buildings.

## GEOGRAPHY

An estimated fifteen hundred to two thousand thunderstorms occur somewhere on the Earth's surface at any given moment. These thunderstorms are estimated to trigger approximately one hundred or more lightning flashes every second, which corresponds to approximately 8.6 million strikes every day and more than 3 billion every year. Lightning has also been known to occur within atmospheric storms on other planets within Earth's solar system, such as Jupiter and Venus.

Lightning occurs most commonly in warm and moist climates, with the hot and humid climate of Central Florida experiencing the highest occurrence of lightning strikes and the Pacific Northwest seeing the lowest occurrence.

## PREVENTION AND PREPARATIONS

The National Lightning Detection Network was set up in the 1970's to assist meteorologists in locating and tracking thunderstorms and lightning strikes. This intricate computer network utilizes lightning detection images from orbiting satellites and other equipment which reveal precisely where severe storm activity is located, in addition to the exact locations where lightning has occurred and has possibly hit the ground.

Thunder is an important warning signal by nature which reveals that a lightning bolt has just fired within approximately a 10-mile radius. The commonly used "flash-to-bang" method is effective in estimating how far away this most dangerous part of a storm is occurring. Once a flash of lightning is visibly observed, the number of seconds until thunder is heard is counted. The speed of light is 186,300 miles per second, thus enabling lightning to be seen immediately after it flashes. By contrast, sound waves travel about a million times slower at approximately 1 mile every five seconds. To estimate the approximate distance from the location of an individual to the lightning strike, one should divide the number of seconds between the "flash" and the "bang" by five to obtain the distance away that the lightning occurred in miles. If the lightning and thunder are extremely close together, one should divide the difference between the lightning and thunder by 360 to obtain the estimated distance away that the lightning occurred in yards.

Common sense dictates that an individual caught near a thunderstorm should seek safe shelter immediately, particularly if the "flash-to-bang" time is only ten to fifteen seconds, as this means that the lightning is only 2 to 3 miles away. Successive lightning strikes within the same storm can be used to determine if the thunderstorm is approaching one's location or moving away. If the time interval between the lightning and the thunder is getting progressively shorter, the storm is getting closer. If time between the lightning and the thunder is getting progressively longer, the storm is moving away from one's location.

The best defense against getting struck by lightning is prevention, in the form of examining the weather forecast before participating in any outdoor activities. Continually being on the lookout for clouds that appear to be forming into thunderstorms is critical, as is heading for shelter at the first sight of lightning or the first sound of thunder. The occurrence of thunder means that lightning must be present somewhere even if it is not directly visible, with the flash often hidden within thick clouds.

The best shelter from lightning is a large, permanently fixed, and electrically conductive building, staying away from windows and other breakable objects. Sheds and small buildings, particularly those constructed with wood and masonry and that do not contain a lightning rod, do not provide nearly as much protection. In the event that a building is not available, taking refuge in a motor vehicle with a metal roof can provide some protection, as the lightning current has a chance to pass harmlessly down through the vehicle and dissipate into the ground. Regardless of the structure in which a person seeks cover, it is important to refrain from touching any metal surfaces. Locations that contain flammable fuels, such as gasoline, should be avoided during a thunderstorm.

Persons are advised to avoid being exposed in open areas, high places, or near isolated trees during lightning danger periods. Those

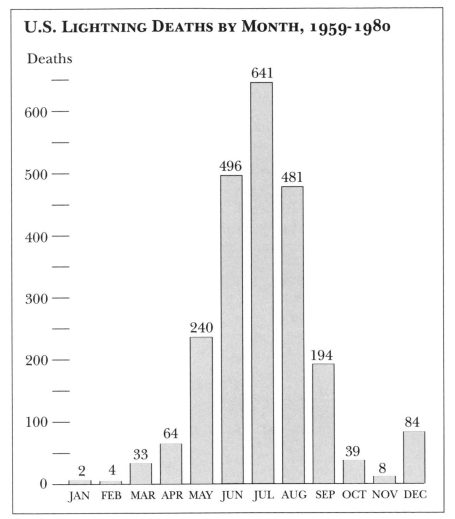

## U.S. LIGHTNING DEATHS BY MONTH, 1959-1980

*This graph represents the deaths caused by lightning in the United States by month from 1959 to 1980. Lightning strikes most often during spring and summer, when the air is warm and moist.*

caught in the water during a storm, such as while swimming, have a much greater chance of experiencing electrical shocks in the event that lightning strikes an area nearby. Saltwater, a better conductor of electricity, is less dangerous than freshwater as the electrical current tends to flow around, rather than through, an individual or boat in the water.

Lightning rods are important protection devices required to be placed within all modern structures. They are made from metal strips that conduct lightning discharges through the building and into the ground. Arresters are often used in locations where power, telephone, and antenna wires enter buildings. Ground wires involve cables that are strung above other wires in an electrical transmission line, in the hope that they will become the preferred target for a lightning surge.

## RESCUE AND RELIEF EFFORTS

The heavy currents of large lightning bolts have been known to shatter masonry and timber, and they often start fires. Lightning has been documented injuring critically or even killing persons talking on the telephone, taking a bath, or sitting near electrical units such as a computer. Cadaver studies on victims of fatal lightning strikes reveal that death can occur from heart damage, inflated lungs, brain damage, and burns.

For those who survive a lightning strike, immediate medical atten-

*Large cities, with their tall buildings, often attract lightning. Because many airports are located in or near cities, lightning poses much danger to airplanes.* (PhotoDisc)

tion is necessary. If the victim is not breathing, artificial respiration can provide adequate short-term life support, though the victim may become stiff or rigid in reaction to the shock. Survivors of electric shock, from lightning or other sources, may suffer from severe burns and permanent aftereffects, including cataracts, angina, or nervous-system disorders. Amnesia and paralysis can also occur.

**IMPACT**

Lightning thunderbolts have long been feared by societies with beliefs in the supernatural, such as the Greeks, Vikings, Buddhists, and Native Americans. Science has confirmed that lightning is one of the strongest forces in nature, with larger bolts generating an average potential difference of 100 million volts of energy, approximately equivalent to the power contained in a middle-sized nuclear reactor.

Data collected by the National Lightning Detection Network reveal that lightning strikes kill an average of 75 people each year in the United States and injure hundreds more, mostly during the spring and summer months. Most fatalities occur from a direct hit, but electrical activity occurring along the ground following a severe strike has also proved fatal.

Lightning is also to blame for over 10,000 forest fires each year in the United States alone, with the total property replacement cost in the tens of millions of dollars. Lightning research greatly increased in the 1960's, motivated by the danger of lightning to both aerospace vehicles and the solid-state electronics used in computers and other technical devices. Commercial airliners performing a normal number of service runs are subjected to an average of one lightning strike per year, and in many cases the lightning is triggered by the airplane itself.

**HISTORICAL OVERVIEW**

Lightning predicted a victory by Gilgamesh, Sumerian hero of an epic dating to the third millennium B.C.E. Zeus, chief god of the Greeks, hurled thunderbolts, and Thor, the thunderer, was the strongest of the Norse gods. Thunderstorms occur throughout the globe, even in Africa's Sahara Desert, and many societies have produced myths that associate lightning, a frightening and long-misunderstood phenomenon, with supernatural power. Thunder and lightning on Mount Sinai preceded presentation of the Ten Commandments to

Moses. The Romans considered the location of lightning to be an omen favoring or discouraging personal and governmental business. Many cultures believed that objects struck by lightning held magical powers, but people's primary concern has been protection from the unpredictability of lightning, with its associated fire and destruction. Romans wore laurel leaves for protection, and, in the Middle Ages, European fire festivals sought protection for communities.

Simultaneously, rational explanations for lightning have encountered superstition. Greek philosopher Socrates described a storm as "a vortex of air." Aristotle theorized that a cooling and condensing cloud forcibly ejects wind which, striking against other clouds, creates thunder. He wrote, "As a rule, the ejected wind burns with a fine and gentle fire, and it is then what we call lightning." Greek historian Herodotus observed that lightning strikes tall objects, and Mongol law recognized the fatal association between lightning and water, forbidding washing of clothes or bathing during thunderstorms. Italian artist and scientist Leonardo da Vinci theorized that clouds forced together by opposing winds could only rise, and he thus connected storm clouds with updrafts.

Not until the eighteenth century was lightning associated with electricity, itself a little-understood phenomenon named in the late 1500's by Elizabethan court physician William Gilbert after the Greek philosopher-scientist Thales of Miletus's experiments with amber, or, in Greek, *electra*. During the seventeenth and eighteenth centuries, electricity and magnetism attracted experimentation and showmanship. Only when knowledge of European experiments and gifts of apparatus, including glass Leyden jars capable of holding and storing electrical charges, came to American Benjamin Franklin in 1746, did a theory of electricity emerge. Franklin determined that there was a single type of electricity, confirmed speculation that lightning was electricity and, in 1749, first proposed that metal rods could protect buildings and ships from strikes. His suggestions for construction, placement, and grounding appeared in the 1753 *Poor Richard's Almanac*.

Practical applications of electricity, beginning with American inventor Thomas Alva Edison's 1879 invention of a durable light bulb, and the subsequent problems of distribution along power lines vulnerable to lightning, encouraged lightning research. Despite lightning rods on poles, lightning struck power lines and disrupted service. Solutions required accurate measurements of lightning voltage and speed of discharge, studies led by Westinghouse and General Electric engineers. German immigrant Charles Steinmetz built high-voltage generators to simulate lightning. Generators produced 50-foot bolts of lightning for New York World's Fair visitors in 1939, but laboratory apparatus could not equal the energy of natural lightning.

In 1925, Sweden's Harold Norinder, using the European-developed cathode-ray oscilloscope, measured a lightning-induced electrical surge of about a ten-thousandth of a second, and Americans measured lightning strikes on power-transmission lines of 5 million volts in under two-millionths of a second. Understanding the magnitude of the problem led to improved protection, reducing power failures.

Research leading to recognition of weather conditions likely to produce lightning, and knowledge of the location of lightning strikes serves military, commercial, and public interest and furthers technological advances. Practical applications of scientist Robert H. Goddard's 1929 Massachusetts launch of a rocket carrying a barometer, thermometer, and camera improved both World War II rocket design and television cameras. In 1959, scientists conducted the first meteorological experiment on a satellite platform. On April 1, 1960, the launch of the polar-orbiting Television Infrared Operational Satellite, TIROS-1, inaugurated the era of satellite meteorology. Capability expanded December 6, 1966, with the launch of the first geostationary meteorological satellite. Research begun at the University of Arizona in the 1970's evolved into the U.S. National Lightning Detection Network under Global Atmospherics Incorporated, the product of a 1995 merger, which supplies data to local forecasters.

Lightning has caused more deaths than tornadoes or hurricanes in the United States but far fewer injuries and less property damage. Despite advances in radar and satellite remote sensing and increasing reliability of forecasts, weather predictions warn only of the potential for lightning, and technology locates lightning only as it occurs. Public and private agencies stress public awareness and education in safety procedures to minimize exposure to strikes and fatalities.

*Daniel G. Graetzer*
*Mary Catherine Wilheit*

213

**BIBLIOGRAPHY**

Dennis, Jerry. *It's Raining Frogs and Fishes: Four Seasons of Natural Phenomenon and Oddities of the Sky.* New York: HarperCollins, 1992. Very readable manuscript highlighting lightning strikes and other natural phenomena within the atmosphere.

Gardner, Robert L., ed. *Lightning Electromagnetics.* New York: Hemisphere, 1990. Text applying examples from physics and electronics to the natural events occurring during a thunderstorm.

Rakov, Vladimir A., and Martin A. Uman. *Lightning: Physics and Effects.* New York: Cambridge University Press, 2003. Covers all aspects of lightning, including physics and protection. Accessible to general readers.

Renner, Jeff. *Lightning Strikes: Staying Safe Under Stormy Skies.* Seattle: Mountaineers Books, 2002. Discusses the risks of lightning, thunderstorm winds, and floods. Offers practical strategies for avoiding lightning.

Salanave, Leon E. *Lightning and Its Spectrum: An Atlas of Photographs.* Tucson: University of Arizona Press, 1980. Document relating the physics principles behind lightning formation and its spectrum.

Uman, Martin A. *The Lightning Discharge.* Mineola, N.Y.: Dover, 2001. Excellent description of the intricate process of lightning discharge in various environments.

Williams, Jack. *The Weather Book.* 2d rev. ed. New York: Vintage Books, 1997. An often-referenced text giving excellent descriptions of various weather patterns such as thunderstorms and catastrophic events such as lightning strikes.

# METEORITES AND COMETS

**FACTORS INVOLVED:** Chemical reactions, geography,
   gravitational forces, temperature, weather conditions
**REGIONS AFFECTED:** All

## DEFINITION
The effects of meteorite and comet impacts on Earth range from the insignificant to the greatest natural disaster humankind may ever face—the extinction of most of the life on Earth.

## SCIENCE
The Moon viewed through even a small telescope is a spectacular sight. It is covered with craters. Samples brought back from the Moon prove that they are impact craters, not volcanic craters. Because Earth and the Moon are in the same part of the solar system, it follows that Earth has been subjected to the same bombardment from space that produced craters on the Moon. Having been largely erased by erosion, Earth's own cratering record is not so obvious. Earth's atmosphere protects it from the rain of smaller meteoroids, a protection the Moon lacks, but the fact remains that Earth has been hit countless times in the past, and no doubt it will be hit countless times in the future.

   Objects that are out in space that might hit Earth include dust, meteoroids, asteroids, and comets. In modern terminology, a meteoroid is a natural, solid object in interplanetary space. A meteor is the flash of light produced by frictional heating when a meteoroid enters a planetary atmosphere. Particularly bright meteors are called fireballs or bolides (especially if they explode). Meteorites are meteoroids that survive their passage through the atmosphere and reach the ground.

   Photographs of three meteorites during their meteor phase—from Pribram, Czechoslovakia, 1959; Lost City, Oklahoma, 1970; and Innisfree, Alberta, 1977—have allowed pre-impact orbits to be calculated. The orbits of all were traced back to the asteroid belt. Beginning in 1969, various workers were able to match the spectra of meteorites with those of asteroids, and it is now widely accepted that most meteorites are chips from asteroids. A few have been identified as having come from the Moon or from Mars.

Rocky or metallic objects larger than about 328 feet (100 meters) across are called asteroids. They are so named because they look like stars—like points of light—in a telescope, but they have more in common with planets than with stars. It is believed that when the Sun first formed it was surrounded by a platter-shaped cloud of gases and dust grains. These grains accreted to form ever-larger objects, and the largest ones became the planets. Asteroids and comets are leftover objects that were never incorporated into planets. Asteroids larger than about 18.6 miles (30 kilometers) in diameter contained enough radioactive elements to melt their insides, allowing nickel and iron to sink to the center and stony material to float to the top. Over the eons, collisions among the asteroids have produced the collection present today. Nickel-iron asteroids are the remnant cores of asteroids whose outer, stony material has been chipped away. To penetrate deeply enough into Earth's atmosphere to cause severe damage, objects must be more than about 131, 164, and 328 feet (40, 50, and 100 meters) in diameter for metallic, stony, or icy bodies, respectively.

The main asteroid belt lies between the orbits of Mars and Jupiter. Farther out in the solar system, beyond the orbit of Neptune, ice was the most abundant solid building material. (Here, ice means mostly frozen water, but it also includes frozen carbon dioxide, methane, and ammonia.) The solid part of a comet, the nucleus, forms from these ices mixed with silicate and hydrocarbon dust grains. An inactive comet looks much like an asteroid, but as a comet nears the Sun, vapor streams from the nucleus as the ices evaporate. Inactive comets are difficult to detect, but a large, active comet is a spectacular sight. The nucleus is surrounded by a vapor cloud 621,400 miles (1 million kilometers) across and has a gas tail up to 62,140,000 miles (100 million kilometers) long.

Asteroids or comets that may hit Earth are of obvious interest. Richard P. Binzel, a professor at the Massachusetts Institute of Technology, developed a scale to help scientists communicate with the media and the public about the perceived risks associated with these objects. This scale is named the Torino Impact Hazard Scale and was adopted by the International Astronomical Union (IAU) in 1999. A Torino scale 0 object is either too small to cause damage or will not

# MILESTONES

**2 billion B.C.E.:** An asteroid impact at Vredefort, South Africa, produces a 186-mile-diameter crater, the largest known on Earth.

**1.85 billion B.C.E.:** An asteroid impact at Sudbury, Ontario, Canada, produces a 155-mile-diameter crater. Groundwater, upwelling through fractured rocks, eventually produces one of the world's richest nickel deposits.

**65 million B.C.E.:** A 6.2-mile-diameter asteroid produces a 112-mile-diameter crater on the Yucatán Peninsula. The associated environmental disaster causes most of the species then living, including the dinosaurs, to become extinct.

**49,000 B.C.E.:** The impact of a huge nickel-iron boulder forms the Barringer meteorite crater in Arizona.

**1680:** Scientist Isaac Newton notes that the comet of 1680 passes less than 621,400 miles (1 million kilometers) from the Sun and deduces that its nucleus must be solid in order to survive.

**December 25, 1758:** The first predicted return of Halley's comet is observed.

**1794-1803:** Scientists prove that meteorites do fall from the sky.

**1861:** Earth passes through the tail of the Great Comet of 1861 with no measurable effects.

**June 30, 1908:** A huge boulder or a small comet explodes over Tunguska, Siberia, causing widespread destruction.

**1920:** Arizona's Barringer Crater is the first Earth feature recognized to have been caused by a meteorite impact.

**January 3, 1970:** The fall of the Lost City, Oklahoma, meteorite is photographed, and its orbit is later traced back to the asteroids.

**August 10, 1972:** A house-sized rock forms a brilliant fireball as it hurtles through Earth's atmosphere and back into space.

**June, 1980:** Luis Alvarez and others at the University of California at Berkeley publish an article in *Science* presenting the hypothesis that an asteroid impact caused the extinction of the dinosaurs.

**March, 1986:** The nucleus of Halley's comet is photographed.

**October 9, 1992:** A meteorite smashes the rear end of a 1980 Chevy Malibu automobile in Peekskill, New York.

**July, 1994:** The impact of the fragmented Comet Shoemaker-Levy 9 on Jupiter is widely observed.

hit Earth. Torino scale 1 objects will probably not hit Earth, but they merit careful watching. Torino scale 2, 3, and 4 objects merit concern, and scale 5, 6, and 7 objects are progressively threatening. Torino scale 8, 9, and 10 objects will hit Earth and are expected to cause local, regional, or global damage, respectively.

## GEOGRAPHY

Any place on Earth may be hit by a meteorite; no location is particularly safe, but seacoasts are the most vulnerable. The 1908 Tunguska impact was a Torino scale 8 event with localized destruction. Had the Tunguska meteorite been just large enough to reach the ground intact, the destruction still would have been largely local. However, if such an object struck the ocean it would generate tsunamis that would cause widespread coastal destruction.

The impact of a Tunguska-scale object on the glaciers of Greenland or Antarctica might melt 35,315 cubic feet (1 cubic kilometer) of ice, but that would produce only an imperceptible rise in the ocean level. However, the impact on Antarctica of a 6-mile-diameter asteroid, such as is thought to have killed the dinosaurs, could melt enough ice to raise the sea level more than 230 feet (70 meters). Another environmentally sensitive site for a giant impact is a thick limestone deposit such as exists on the Yucatán Peninsula. It seems likely that the copious amounts of carbon dioxide released from the Yucatán limestone contributed to a warmer climate for thousands of years after the impact.

## PREVENTION AND PREPARATIONS

The first step in meteorite strike prevention and preparation is to make a survey of objects that come close to Earth. These are called near-earth objects (NEOs). Under the auspices of the International Astronomical Union, the Spaceguard Foundation was established on March 27, 1996, in Rome. The foundation coordinates international efforts to discover NEOs. As of November 2, 2006, 4,338 NEOs had been discovered and their orbits calculated. Considered the most dangerous of these were 814 potentially hazardous asteroids (PHAs). PHAs are larger than 492 feet (150 meters) in diameter and will come within 4.7 million miles (7.5 million kilometers) of Earth. More refined orbital information should eventually tell whether or not

# THE TORINO IMPACT HAZARD SCALE

Assessing asteroid and comet impact hazard predictions.

| | | |
|---|---|---|
| Events Having No Likely Consequences (White Zone) | 0 | The likelihood of a collision is zero, or well below the chance that a random object of the same size will strike Earth within the next few decades. |
| Events Meriting Careful Monitoring (Green Zone) | 1 | The chance of collision is extremely unlikely, about the same as a random object of the same size striking Earth within the next few decades. |
| Events Meriting Concern (Yellow Zone) | 2 | A somewhat close, but not unusual encounter. Collision is very unlikely. |
| | 3 | A close encounter, with 1 percent or greater chance of a collision capable of causing localized destruction. |
| | 4 | A close encounter, with 1 percent or greater chance of a collision capable of causing regional devastation. |
| Threatening Events (Orange Zone) | 5 | A close encounter, with a significant threat of a collision capable of causing regional devastation. |
| | 6 | A close encounter, with a significant threat of a collision capable of causing a global catastrophe. |
| | 7 | A close encounter, with an extremely significant threat of a collision capable of causing a global catastrophe. |
| Certain Collisions (Red Zone) | 8 | A collision capable of causing localized destruction. Such events occur somewhere on Earth between once per 50 years and once per 1,000 years. |
| | 9 | A collision capable of causing regional devastation. Such events occur between once per 1,000 years and once per 100,000 years. |
| | 10 | A collision capable of causing a global climatic catastrophe. Such events occur once per 100,000 years, or less often. |

they will actually hit Earth. There were no known PHAs with more than a minute probability of hitting Earth.

If it is discovered that an asteroid is about to hit Earth, can anything be done about it? The answer depends upon three key factors: the amount of warning time, the size of the asteroid, and the state of readiness of the space program. Taking the third factor first, there are normally no spacecraft on standby that are capable of reaching an asteroid. That means that if the warning time is only a few months, the only thing to be done is to evacuate the probable impact site, or to evacuate coastal areas if an ocean impact is predicted. Such an evacuation will be difficult and disruptive for a Torino scale 8 (local damage) object and will approach the impossible for a Torino scale 9 (regional damage) object. It would be incredibly difficult to evacuate the eastern United States, for example. For a Torino scale 10 object (global catastrophe), preparation efforts will be to provide food, shelter, and energy stores to maximize the number of survivors.

Once an asteroid is discovered and observed for a period of time, its orbit can be predicted accurately for fifty to one hundred years into the future. Deflecting the asteroid into a slightly different orbit becomes an option if there is a ten- to twenty-year warning time. Deflection is probably superior to attempting to destroy the object. Objects small enough to be vaporized with nuclear weapons are small enough to be destroyed by Earth's atmosphere. If an asteroid were not vaporized, but rather only shattered, by a nuclear explosion, the cloud of fragments would continue in the asteroid's orbit and still strike Earth. If there were enough fragments, or if there were large fragments, Earth would still be devastated.

Another solution is to explode a nuclear weapon above the surface of the asteroid. Prior experimentation and manned exploration may be necessary to determine how best to do this. Heat and radiation from the blast will vaporize asteroidal surface material, causing it to push against the asteroid like a rocket engine and thereby change the asteroid's orbit. Only a small change in orbit would be necessary if done far enough in advance. A neutron bomb would be the weapon of choice since neutrons would penetrate deeper beneath the surface and therefore launch more material into space than would the gamma rays and X rays of a conventional thermonuclear weapon.

*Scientists monitor the path of near-Earth objects such as comets in order to identify any collision threats.* (NASA)

If humankind were to develop sufficient space-faring capacity, workers might land on the asteroid. Given enough time and an energy source such as a nuclear reactor, the orbit of the asteroid could be changed by launching rocks from a catapult device (mass driver) acting as a rocket engine. If there were sufficient water available, as ice in a comet nucleus, or combined in minerals as in some carbonaceous asteroids, steam rockets mounted on the object might be used to change its orbit. Three properties of comets make them more difficult to deal with: The vast majority can be discovered only months before their closest approach to Earth, and they are fragile and may break apart if one tries to maneuver them. They also travel faster than asteroids. Typical approach speeds relative to Earth are 9.3 miles (15 kilometers) per second for asteroids, but are 15.5 to 31 miles (25 to 50 kilometers) per second for comets.

## RESCUE AND RELIEF EFFORTS AND IMPACT

If the damage from a meteorite were local, the aftermath would resemble that of other large-scale disasters, such as massive flooding, large earthquakes, destructive hurricanes, volcanic eruptions, or massive bombings. Rescue and aid workers would come from outside the area, but if a large city were destroyed, it would probably take days to bring sufficient resources to bear. As with the Tunguska event, most impacts occur in sparsely inhabited areas, but such events are expected to occur between once every fifty years to once every thousand years.

If the destruction were regional, it might take many weeks to bring in sufficient aid. During that time the tragedy would be greatly compounded. Such regional events are expected to occur between once every thousand years and once every hundred thousand years. If the destruction were worldwide, sufficient aid would not exist. People in steel and stone buildings might survive the sky becoming baking hot (because of the fiery reentry of debris) unless the air became too hot to breathe or too oxygen-depleted by conflagrations. Both Switzerland and China have large systems of underground shelters built for nuclear war, and many other nations have some shelters. Those who survive the initial impact, earthquakes, tsunamis, hot sky, secondary fires, possibly toxic vapors and gases, and rising sea level (from melting ice) will need food and energy to keep warm for a few months to a year until the worldwide dust cloud settles from the air and the Sun shines again. Then they will need crops that will grow in the new, warmer climate. They will also need to deal with greatly increased ultraviolet radiation from the Sun, plagues, and the breakdown of civilization. Yet, except in an extreme worst case, some people should survive. Global climatic catastrophe due to asteroid or comet impact is expected to occur roughly every hundred thousand years.

## HISTORICAL OVERVIEW

Humankind's observations of meteorites and comets surely extend back to the times before recorded history. Some suggest that the ancient Greek myth of Phaethon's ride is based upon a close brush with an active comet. According to the legend, Phaethon, son of the sun god, Helios, receives reluctant permission to drive the sun chariot across the sky. The inexperienced Phaethon drives too close to Earth and scorches it. To curtail further harm to Earth, Jupiter slays Phaethon with a lightning bolt. Helios reclaims the sun chariot, but in his grief, he refuses to bring light to Earth. All of this makes a fairly good description of a small comet rising in the east just before the Sun, a comet fragment producing a Tunguska-like fireball, and dust from an impact blocking sunlight. There is evidence for a destructive blast wave and for wildfires sweeping the Middle East four thousand years ago.

The Greek word *meteoros* means "high in the air." Some ancient Greeks considered comets to be meteors, that is, fiery gases high in the atmosphere. Others thought them to be "long-haired" stars (*astērkomētēs*), properly belonging to the heavens beyond the orbit of the Moon. Because comets often look like swords in the heavens poised to strike Earth, they were usually regarded as ill omens portending drought, famine, or war. Long ago, the term "meteors" also included rainbows, clouds, rain, snow, the aurora borealis, hailstones, and thunderstones. Thunderstones were unusual stones that were imagined to have been formed by lightning fusing dust in the air or by lightning striking the ground and launching stones into the air. Discovered thunderstones actually included some fossils, certain minerals, ancient stone tools, and meteorites.

Throughout history some people claimed to have seen stones fall from the sky, or they have found things they believed to have come from the sky. Certainly, an iron meteorite is different enough from normal rocks that its finder would seek a special explanation. The Assyrian term for iron meant "metal from heaven." The earliest-known iron objects were made from meteoric iron, and it is quite possible that working with this "sky metal" aided the Hittites in ushering in the iron age by smelting iron ore around 1400 B.C.E.

Several meteorites became objects of veneration because they were considered gifts from the gods in the heavens. The temple of Artemis at Ephesus housed a meteorite, and the stone of Emesa in Syria was regarded as an incarnation of the sun god, Heliogebalus. The most famous is the black stone mounted in the corner of the Kaaba in the court of the Great Mosque at Mecca. The black stone of the Kaaba is said to have fallen from the sky as a sign of the divine calling of the prophet Abraham.

By 1790 scientists had shown that most thunderstones did not come from the sky, and they supposed that none did. That supposition changed over a period of only ten years. In 1794 the physicist Ernst Florens Friedrich Chladni published a treatise exploring the evidence for a dozen falls—cases where the meteorite was seen falling and was then recovered. In 1802 the chemist Edward Charles Howard announced that the minerals and chemical constituents of several meteorites were similar to each other but different from terrestrial rocks. In 1803 the physicist Jean-Baptiste Biot reported on a fireball that dropped many stones at L'Aigle in Normandy, proving that meteorites did fall from the sky.

In the 1500's several astronomers noted that because comet tails always pointed away from the Sun, comets must be in heavenly realms and cannot be luminous gases in Earth's atmosphere. Tycho Brahe attempted to measure the distance to the comet of 1577 and showed that it was far beyond the Moon, thereby settling that question. Sir Isaac Newton maintained a lifelong fascination with comets. He eventually proved that the comet of 1680-1681 followed the same laws of motion and gravitation that planets did. It was Edmond Halley who

*Meteor Crater in Arizona was formed by a meteorite more than 150 feet in diameter about 50,000 years ago.* (NASA CORE/Lorain Valley JVS)

fired the public's imagination with his successful prediction of the return of the comet that carries his name. Noting that the comets of 1531, 1607, and 1682 had very similar orbits, Halley supposed that they were the same comet and predicted that it would return near the end of 1758—it did, on Christmas night.

*Charles W. Rogers*

**BIBLIOGRAPHY**

Burke, John G. *Cosmic Debris: Meteorites in History.* Berkeley: University of California Press, 1986. An engaging treatment of how science discovered the truth about meteorites.

Chapman, Clark R., and David Morrison. *Cosmic Catastrophes.* New York: Plenum Press, 1989. This book treats the K/T impact, in which a meteorite hit the earth 65 million years ago, and other disasters.

Cox, Donald W., and James H. Chestek. *Doomsday Asteroid: Can We Survive?* Amherst, N.Y.: Prometheus Books, 1996. A good treatment of the efforts needed to locate and deflect potentially dangerous asteroids and comets.

Lewis, John S. *Comet and Asteroid Impact Hazards on a Populated Earth: Computer Modeling.* San Diego, Calif.: Academic, 2000. An excellent and scholarly treatment of the subject.

_____. *Rain of Iron and Ice: The Very Real Threat of Comet and Asteroid Bombardment.* Reading, Mass.: Addison-Wesley, 1996. A good account of various impacts, including interesting, but less well-known, ones.

Sagan, Carl, and Ann Druyan. *Comet.* New York: Random House, 1985. An excellent book by this very successful husband-wife writing team. It explains what we know about comets and how we learned this. The book is easily read and profusely illustrated.

Steel, Duncan. *Rogue Asteroids and Doomsday Comets: The Search for the Million Megaton Menace That Threatens Life on Earth.* New York: John Wiley & Sons, 1995. A good book for the general reader on mass extinctions and the K/T impact, the Tunguska object, and early detection efforts.

Verschuur, Gerrit L. *Impact! The Threat of Comets and Asteroids.* New York: Oxford University Press, 1996. An excellent and authoritative popular work written by an active astronomer.

Zanda, Brigitte, and Monica Rotaru, eds. *Meteorites: Their Impact on Science and History.* Translated by Roger Hewins. New York: Cambridge University Press, 2001. An accessible, comprehensive guide written by a team of experts.

# SMOG

**FACTORS INVOLVED:** Geography, human activity, temperature, weather conditions
**REGIONS AFFECTED:** Cities, towns, valleys

## DEFINITION

Smog is a common component of urban life in many parts of the world. It was responsible for thousands of deaths after the widespread use of fossil fuels led to damaging emissions in local urban areas. Governments have responded by setting emissions standards in many countries.

## SCIENCE

Smog is one of the major atmospheric problems of modern urban life and is found in two varieties. Until the middle part of the twentieth century, smog was formed by the mixture of particulate matter and sulfurous compounds combined in the atmosphere in regions where coal burning was common. This type of sulfurous smog is commonly called gray air or "London-type" smog. With the increased use of automobiles and trucks, a second type of smog, generated by the impact of sunlight on pollutants, became prevalent in many urban areas. This second type is called photochemical smog and results primarily from exhausts of vehicles in urban areas that have certain meteorological and topographical characteristics. The general term "smog" is a combination of the words "smoke" and "fog" and covers both types of air pollution.

Air pollution formed by the burning of coal is not just a modern phenomenon. As far back as the thirteenth century, laws controlling the burning of coal were enacted to reduce the amount of smoke and haze that formed in London. However, the increased reliance on that common energy source produced more and more episodes of this type of air pollution in Europe and in other areas where coal was burned in quantity.

When coal is burned, large amounts of particulate matter are released into the atmosphere, and these particles can cause health problems when inhaled in sufficient quantity. These small particles

# MILESTONES

**12th and 13th centuries:** Air pollution in London is caused by extensive burning of coal.

**1273:** A law passes in London to restrict the burning of soft coal in an attempt to improve air quality in the area.

**1306:** England's Parliament issues a proclamation requiring citizens to burn wood instead of coal in order to improve local air quality.

**December, 1873:** An air pollution event in London kills between 270 and 700 people.

**February, 1880:** Approximately 1,000 people die in London from an air pollution event.

**December, 1892:** A smog episode kills 1,000 people in London.

**December, 1930:** A thick fog settles in the industrialized area along the Meuse River in Belgium and is trapped for three days; thousands of people become ill and 60 die.

**1943:** A major smog episode in Los Angeles leads local officials to begin to look at regulations to reduce air pollution.

**December, 1948:** Smog accumulates over Donora, Pennsylvania, and is trapped in the valley of the Monongahela River for four days, resulting in 18 deaths above the average number for that time period.

**November, 1949:** A smog forms in Berkeley, California, from the exhaust of automobiles being driven into the area for a football game.

**December, 1952:** A dense fog develops over London and remains stagnant for five days, leading to 4,000 deaths above the average number for that time interval.

**1953:** Smog accumulates in New York City, causing at least 200 deaths.

**1956:** A severe smog episode in London leads to the deaths of 1,000 people.

**November, 1956:** At least 46 people die in a smog episode in New York City.

**1962:** Over 700 people die in a smog event in London.

**December, 1962:** 60 people die from smog in Osaka, Japan.

**January-February, 1963:** Smog kills up to 400 people in New York City.

**1966:** A four-day smog event in New York City results in the deaths of 80 people; Governor Nelson A. Rockefeller declares a state of emergency.

**1970's:** Severe smog conditions are recognized in many Chinese cities; death rates as high as 3,500 people per year are reported in some areas in 1979.

**1980's-1990's:** Reports of increase of deadly air pollution conditions in Eastern Europe, Mexico, and China.

**December, 2005:** In Tehran, Iran, businesses and schools close because of severe smog conditions; hundreds of people are taken to the hospital.

also act as nucleation sites for water vapor to condense and form water droplets, leading to the formation of a fog. In addition, most coals contain a significant amount of sulfur, and, when burned, this sulfur is combined with oxygen and released into the atmosphere as sulfur dioxide. The sulfur dioxide may then combine with the water droplets formed on the particulate matter to create sulfuric acid.

Major episodes of sulfurous smog generally occur when certain topographical and meteorological features coincide. If the urban area is located in a basin, then the pollutants can be easily trapped if an atmospheric inversion develops in the region. An atmospheric inversion forms when winter anticyclonic conditions and low temperatures occur and little low-level atmospheric circulation is produced.

As a result, the pollutants are pumped into a basin sealed by a meteorologic "lid," and there is little to no dispersion of the particulate matter and sulfuric acid droplets. These meteorologic conditions may continue for days, during which time the resultant air pollution will worsen. The smog will be dispersed only if meteorologic conditions change such that breezes can move the pollution over the surrounding hillsides and out of the basin. In some areas, there is no topographic basin that retains the pollutants; rather, the input of pollutants is so great that horizontal flow is not fast enough to remove the smog. The classic examples of this type of smog were the London smogs of the 1950's.

Photochemical smog is formed in very different ways. This type of smog has been recognized since the 1940's in Southern California and is now common in many large urban areas. Once again, the major culprit in the formation of this type of air pollution is the burning of fossil fuels, particularly oil. The combustion of gasoline in motor vehicles and industrial plants produces a wide variety of exhaust particles and compounds. Particularly important in the formation of photochemical smog are hydrocarbons and nitrogen oxides. Through a series of complex chemical reactions, these compounds and others lead to the formation of photochemical oxidants such as ozone and peroxyacetyl nitrate (PAN).

The chemical reactions begin when nitrogen dioxide ($NO_2$) is split by the ultraviolet radiation of sunlight and the oxygen atom released by the reaction, then combines with oxygen ($O_2$) in the air to produce ozone ($O_3$). Ozone is a major component of photochemical smog, causing numerous respiratory health effects. In the absence of other compounds the ozone will decompose, releasing an oxygen atom that will combine with nitrogen oxide (NO), which was produced when nitrogen dioxide was split by sunlight. Thus, the concentration of ozone will generally not rise to high levels unless the latter reaction is not allowed to proceed.

Automobiles and trucks release large quantities of hydrocarbons during operation, and these hydrocarbons are degraded in the atmosphere by oxygen, creating volatile organic compounds. These volatile organic compounds then enter into a number of complex reactions with the NO and thus short-circuit the reaction of NO and ozone that keeps the level of ozone quite low. The reactions of the volatile organic compounds and the nitric oxide may produce numerous compounds, including PAN.

Whereas natural levels of ozone, produced in the absence of volatile organic compounds, may reach background levels of 0.04 parts per million, ozone levels in urban areas may reach over 0.2 parts per million, and levels over 0.6 were recorded in the Los Angeles area during the 1950's. These higher levels of ozone and other pollutants of photochemical smog are usually developed in topographic basins where an atmospheric inversion occurs. In the Los Angeles basin, the effect of descending warm air produced by regional weather patterns tends to seal the air mass into the basin and not allow even coastal breezes to push the pollutants over the mountains to the east and north. These conditions may last for several days and keep the polluted air mass within the region. Pollution will lessen only when the inversion disappears and the smog can be dispersed into the areas east of the basin.

## GEOGRAPHY

Smog has been a significant air-pollution problem in Western countries for centuries because of the development of coal and, later, oil resources as major energy sources that fuel economic development. As a result, the most significant smog episodes have been reported in Europe and the United States. Smog has killed thousands of people in London, Belgium, New York, Pennsylvania, and other industrialized areas in the Western world.

However, photochemical and sulfurous smogs are not confined to the United States and Europe. The industrialization of many other countries and the increase in automobile usage worldwide have created the unwanted side effect of atmospheric pollution. Many of the most severe smog events now occur in Eastern Europe, Mexico, Japan, and China. The number of automobiles operating at the end of the twentieth century was about 700 million, and because the number was expected to climb to over 1 billion in the early part of the twenty-first century, it is apparent that the occurrence of photochemical smog in urban areas will continue to be a significant problem for many years.

## PREVENTION AND PREPARATIONS

Governments have approached the prevention of smog in a number of ways. One approach has been to attempt to control emissions by establishing laws limiting the quantity of emitted pollutants. The United States, France, Japan, Canada, Italy, Germany, Yugoslavia, Norway, and Russia have established air-quality standards. The air-quality standards vary within these countries. In the United States, the Clean Air Act, enacted in 1970 and emended in later years, established national ambient air-quality standards, which set the permissible levels of six pollutants in the air. The six original pollutants were carbon monoxide, lead, ozone, particulate matter, sulfur oxides, and nitrogen oxides.

In many cases the Environmental Protection Agency (EPA) authorized states to monitor and enforce the regulations, which have been aimed at controlling emissions from large point sources, such as coal and oil-fired factories and utilities, in an attempt to reduce the emission of gaseous and particulate pollutants. The localized nature of these point sources makes the control of emissions manageable but often expensive.

However, the formation of photochemical smog is the result of emissions from millions of automobiles, trucks, and buses. Four approaches have been tried to reduce the emission of tailpipe pollutants. One approach has been to set emissions standards that all automobiles must meet in order to be licensed for the road. Smog tests are required for cars, and those not passing the test must be repaired before further use. Second, since the total emission is related to total gasoline usage, an increase in car efficiency would reduce pollutants. Miles-per-gallon standards have been established for automobile manufacturers, although these standards have been modified at times.

The third method of reducing emissions has been alteration of the fuel itself. Gasoline additives such as methyl butyl ether (MTBE) have reduced tailpipe pollutants by helping to burn the fuel more completely. Unfortunately, MTBE has been shown to be a groundwater pollutant and will be phased out of use; alternative compounds will be substituted to reduce emissions. Finally, general conservation methods such as carpooling and mass transit can reduce total fuel use and result in fewer emissions. These regulations have greatly reduced some of the pollutants—lead and particulate matter—but reducing the levels of the other air pollutants has been more difficult.

**IMPACT**

The health impacts of smog are various but are generally associated with respiratory effects. People most affected by sulfurous smogs are children, the elderly, and those with chronic obstructive pulmonary disease. Also affected are people with heart disease. It has been estimated that the London smog event of December, 1952, resulted in an excess of over 4,000 deaths above the average. Most of these deaths were attributed to pulmonary problems, with those having chronic bronchitis resulting in the highest number of deaths. In addition, a significant number died because of heart failure.

Photochemical smogs also affect the young, elderly, and the sick most severely. Epidemiological studies have not shown that photochemical smogs alone cause death, but the combination of smog and high temperatures has resulted in increased mortality. Because ozone is a gas, it most frequently affects respiratory function, and short-term exposure may lead to coughing, wheezing, shortness of

## U.S. AIR POLLUTION TRENDS, 1970-1997
In Thousands of Tons

| Year | PM-10 | PM-10, fugitive dust | Sulfur dioxide | Nitrogen dioxides | Volatile organic compounds | Carbon monoxide | Lead |
|------|-------|----------------------|----------------|-------------------|----------------------------|-----------------|------|
| 1970 | 13,190 | (NA) | 31,161 | 21,639 | 30,817 | 128,761 | 220,869 |
| 1975 | 7,803 | (NA) | 28,011 | 23,151 | 25,895 | 115,968 | 159,659 |
| 1980 | 7,287 | (NA) | 25,905 | 24,875 | 26,167 | 116,702 | 74,153 |
| 1985 | 4,695 | 40,889 | 23,230 | 23,488 | 24,227 | 115,644 | 22,890 |
| 1990 | 5,425 | 24,419 | 23,678 | 23,436 | 20,935 | 95,794 | 4,975 |
| 1995 | 4,306 | 22,454 | 19,189 | 23,768 | 20,558 | 89,151 | 3,924 |
| 1997 | 8,428 | 25,153 | 20,369 | 23,582 | 19,214 | 87,451 | 3,915 |

*Source:* U.S. Department of Commerce, *Statistical Abstract of the United States, 1999*, 1999.

*Note:* PM-10 emissions consist of particulate matter smaller than 10 microns in size.

breath, chest tightness, headaches, nausea, and throat dryness. The long-term effects of ozone exposure are not well understood, but there is some indication of scarring in lung tissue and the development of lung fibrosis. The primary eye irritants found in photochemical smog are PAN, peroxybenzol nitrate, and acrolein.

In the case of both types of smog the advice is the same. All people, particularly those most at risk, should restrict exposure to smog during these air-pollution events by remaining indoors and restricting exercise. Children are particularly at risk to smog because their air intake is higher per unit of body weight than that of adults, and they should be supervised appropriately during a smog event to reduce exposure.

Smog also has significant impacts on agriculture and forests. Ozone, a significant component of photochemical smog, causes an estimated annual economic loss of over $3 billion in the United States because of a reduction in productivity of crops. Particularly susceptible plants include tomatoes, spinach, pinto beans, and tobacco. Ozone and other oxidants also cause damage to forests. Significant tree loss or damage because of ozone has been reported in Southern California, Mexico, Israel, and Europe.

Smog can also cause damage to many consumer products. Stretched rubber exposed to ozone will rapidly degrade and crack, but damage is controlled by adding ozone inhibitors during the production of automobile tires and insulation. Other consumer products affected by ozone include textiles, dyes, and some fabrics.

## HISTORICAL OVERVIEW

Air pollution has been a problem in some parts of the world since the use of coal and oil became important and common. As early as the twelfth and thirteenth centuries in London, the air became so polluted with smoke from coal fires that complaints were frequent, and in 1273 a law was enacted to reduce the amount of soft coal burned. This was followed in 1306 by a proclamation issued by Parliament requiring citizens to burn wood instead of coal in an attempt to rid London of the dreaded gray fogs that periodically caused illnesses and deaths in the city. However, the meteorologic conditions in southern England and the continued use of coal by industries and residents led to numerous smog episodes throughout the years. In the latter part of the nineteenth century, major smog events in London occurred in 1873, 1880, 1881, 1882, 1891, and 1892. An additional major air-pollution episode occurred in 1901.

Smog generated by the industrial use of coal and, later, oil continued to be a significant environmental problem in the twentieth century. In December, 1930, a very heavy fog developed in Belgium along the Meuse River. The fog mixed with the emissions from blast furnaces, fertilizer plants, glass factories, and other industries and created a deadly smog, which caused thousands to become ill and resulted in at least 60 deaths.

In 1948, Donora, Pennsylvania, experienced one of the most deadly air-pollution events in the United States. This area in the Monongahela River Valley was engulfed in a dense polluted fog for four days. The air was polluted with the emissions from coal burning as well as those from a zinc smelter and a steel mill. This stew of air pollutants was responsible for approximately one-half of Donora's population becoming ill and about 20 deaths.

Beginning in the early 1940's in Southern California a new type of smog was recognized. Photochemical reactions produced a type of air pollution that consisted of ozone and other irritants. Initially, it was thought that this smog was produced in much the same manner as those smogs of London or New York. In Los Angeles, politicians thought that the smog could be eliminated within just a few months by restricting the emissions of a number of industries in the city. However, these controls were not successful. In 1949 the role of automobiles in the production of photochemical smog became evident, when such a smog developed in Berkeley, California, where there were no major industrial plants. Fans attempting to reach a football game at the University of California there were stalled in a massive traffic jam, and the idling cars released emissions that were converted into smog.

During the 1950's and 1960's London and New York City continued to suffer very severe, deadly air pollution episodes. Over 4,000 people died in London in December, 1952, and another 1,000 people were killed by smog in the same city in 1956. Killing smogs occurred in New York City in 1953, 1963, and 1966. More than 500 people died from these smog events.

The widespread nature of smog became more evident beginning in the 1970's and continuing throughout the remainder of the century. China revealed the heavy toll air pollution had taken on its population in large cities. It was reported that about 3,500 people died per year in the city of Wuhan alone and that many other Chinese cities suffered severely from the smogs created by the burning of coal.

Air pollution has been extremely damaging in Eastern Europe, although the exact nature of all the damage is not yet known. In addition, Mexico, particularly Mexico City, suffered extreme air pollution in the latter part of the twentieth century. The increasing development of Third World countries will, in all probability, lead to more frequent damaging smog episodes. In December, 2005, hundreds of people had to be taken to the hospital in Tehran, Iran, and businesses and schools were closed as a result of severe smog conditions.

*Jay R. Yett*

**BIBLIOGRAPHY**

Allaby, Michael. *Fog, Smog, and Poisoned Rain.* New York: Facts On File, 2003. Intended for students. Discusses air pollution and its consequences.

Benarde, Melvin A. *Our Precarious Habitat.* New York: John Wiley & Sons, 1989. The author presents information on a wide variety of environmental problems, including smog. Good data are given on specific instances of air pollution and its effects.

Elsom, Derek M. *Atmospheric Pollution: A Global Problem.* Cambridge, Mass.: Blackwell Scientific, 1992. This is an excellent text on all types of atmospheric pollution and includes very informative chapters on smog and its effects. The book covers scientific, economic, political, and social aspects of air pollution.

Graedel, T. E., and Paul J. Crutzen. *Atmospheric Change: An Earth System Perspective.* New York: W. H. Freeman, 1993. The authors are primarily concerned with long-term climate change, but their book is a good introduction to physical and chemical processes of the atmosphere. Also contains an important chapter on urban air quality.

Keller, Edward A. *Environmental Geology.* 8th ed. Upper Saddle River, N.J.: Prentice Hall, 2000. A well-written text that covers atmospheric pollution as well as other geologically important environmental problems.

Soroos, Marvin S. *The Endangered Atmosphere.* Columbia: University of South Carolina Press, 1997. All aspects of air pollution are treated in this book, which includes an informative section on gaseous pollutants.

# TORNADOES

**FACTORS INVOLVED:** Geography, temperature, weather
conditions, wind
**REGIONS AFFECTED:** Cities, coasts, forests, mountains,
plains, towns, valleys

## DEFINITION

Tornadoes are violent, funnel-shaped whirlwinds that extend downward from thunderstorm clouds. Each year, hundreds of tornadoes touch down worldwide, causing billions of dollars in damage and claiming many lives.

## SCIENCE

A tornado is a violently rotating column of air in contact with the ground and extending from the base of a thunderstorm or a towering cumulus cloud. A condensation funnel does not need to reach the ground or even be visible for a tornado to be present. A waterspout is a tornado occurring over water. The word "tornado," a hybrid of the Spanish *tronada* (thunderstorm) and *tornar* (to turn), appeared in sixteenth and seventeenth century English writings but referred to a tropical Atlantic thunderstorm, often with torrential rain and sudden violent gusts (probably a hurricane). Eighteenth and nineteenth century Americans called tornadoes "whirlwinds" or "cyclones." Not until the twentieth century did the word "tornado" define a vortex over land.

A tornado is usually a white, gray, black, or invisible funnel-shaped cloud, but some tornadoes may resemble a wall of smoke rolling across the landscape. Path widths vary from a few yards to more than a mile; path lengths, averaging 4.5 miles, range from 0.25 mile to more than 200 miles. In the United States, the storms move most often from southwest to northeast or west to east at ground speeds from nearly stationary to 70 miles per hour. A tornado may last from a few minutes to more than an hour. Winds in tornadoes generally whirl in a counterclockwise (cyclonic) direction in the Northern Hemisphere and a clockwise (anticyclonic) direction in the Southern Hemisphere, although about one in one thousand whirls in the op-

## MILESTONES

**600-500 B.C.E.:** Perhaps the first recorded tornado is the "whirlwind" mentioned in Ezekiel 2:4 and 2 Kings 2:11 of the Old Testament.

**October 17, 1091:** The earliest British tornado for which there is an authentic record hits London, killing 2 and demolishing 600 houses.

**May 27, 1896:** The Great Cyclone of 1896, an F4 tornado, hits St. Louis, Missouri, leaving 306 dead and 2,500 injured and destroying or damaging 7,500 buildings as well as riverboats and railroads.

**June 30, 1916:** Canada's most lethal twister to date kills 28 in Regina, Saskatchewan.

**March 18, 1925:** The Great Tri-State Tornado, the United States' worst tornado disaster to date, occurs when a 219-mile-long twister destroys entire towns along its path through Missouri, Illinois, and Indiana, causing 689 deaths, more than 2,000 injuries, and $16-18 million in damage.

**March 25, 1948:** Air Force officers Ernest Fawbush and Robert Miller issue the first tornado watch in the United States, but it is for military use only.

**March 17, 1952:** The U.S. Weather Bureau issues the first tornado watch to the American public.

**May 11, 1953:** A tornado destroys much of downtown Waco, Texas, leaving 114 dead and 1,097 injured.

**June 8, 1953:** The last U.S. tornado to date to claim 100 lives devastates parts of Flint, Michigan, killing 120 and injuring 847.

**June 9, 1953:** The worst tornado to date to strike the northeastern United States plows a path greater than a half-mile wide through Worcester, Massachusetts; 94 people are killed, 1,288 are injured, and more than 4,000 buildings are damaged or destroyed.

**April 11, 1965:** The Palm Sunday Outbreak of around 50 tornadoes kills 271, injures more than 3,100, and causes more than $200 million in damages in Illinois, Indiana, Iowa, Michigan, Ohio, and Wisconsin.

**June 8, 1966:** The first $100 million tornado in the United States cuts a path through Topeka, Kansas, killing 16 and destroying more than 800 homes and much of the Washburn University campus.

**May 11, 1970:** A powerful tornado plows through downtown Lubbock, Texas, killing 26 and injuring more than 1,500. This tornado initiates a new interest in tornado studies, including Theodore Fujita's development of a tornado rating scale.

**January 10, 1973:** South America's worst tornado to date destroys parts of San Justo, Argentina; 50 people are killed.

**April 3-4, 1974:** In the Jumbo Outbreak, 148 tornadoes, including 6 rated F5, kill 316 and injure almost 5,500 in 11 midwestern and southern states; an additional 8 deaths occur in Canada. Hardest hit communities include Xenia, Ohio, with 35 deaths and 1,150 injured, and Brandenburg, Kentucky, with 31 deaths and 250 injured.

**June 9, 1984:** Europe's worst tornado to date kills over 400 and injures 213 in Belyanitsky, Ivanovo, and Balino, Russia.

**April 26, 1989:** The world's deadliest tornado to date occurs in Bangladesh when a twister slashes a 50-mile-wide path north of Dhaka; about 1,300 people are killed, more than 12,000 are injured, and almost 80,000 are left homeless.

**May 13, 1996:** A large tornado levels several towns near Tangail, Bangladesh; more than 1,000 are dead and 34,000 are injured, with 100,000 left homeless.

**May 27, 1997:** An F5 tornado hits Jarrell, Texas; 27 are dead, 8 are injured, and 44 homes are damaged or destroyed.

**May 3, 1999:** Part of the Oklahoma Tornado Outbreak, one of the most expensive tornadoes in U.S. history destroys nearly 2,500 homes and kills 49 in Oklahoma City and its suburbs; damage estimates approach $1.5 billion.

**May 15, 2003:** A researcher is able to insert probes called "turtles" into an F4 tornado to measure its pressure.

**February 2, 2007:** A tornado outbreak in central Florida kills 20 people; it is the first event to be measured by the Enhanced Fujita Scale, which factors in storm damage.

posite direction. Scientists do not know the minimum pressure within a tornado but estimate that it may be as low as 60 percent of normal air pressure, or about 600 millibars of mercury. Witnesses have variously described the sound of a tornado as like a freight train, a jet airplane, or a high-pitched squeal.

Wind speeds range from below hurricane strength (75 miles per hour) to more than 300 miles per hour, but about 70 percent of tornadoes produce winds of less than 110 miles per hour. The appearance of a tornado is not an indication of its intensity. No instrument

## THE FUJITA SCALE

| Rating | Strength | Wind Speeds | Damage Levels |
|--------|----------|-------------|---------------|
| F0 | weak | 40-72 mph | light damage |
| F1 | weak | 73-112 mph | moderate damage |
| F2 | strong | 113-157 mph | considerable damage |
| F3 | strong | 158-206 mph | severe damage |
| F4 | violent | 207-260 mph | devastating damage |
| F5 | violent | 261-318 mph | incredible damage |

to measure wind speed has ever survived a strong tornado. Theodore Fujita at the University of Chicago devised a tornado rating scale, called the Fujita scale or F-scale, which examines structural damage to assess the wind speed of a tornado. Meteorologists and engineers assign each U.S. tornado a rating, from F0 to F5, based on the single most intense example of damage in its path. Only 2 percent of tornadoes have received an F4 or F5 rating, but they have caused 70 percent of deaths. An F5 tornado is extremely rare; only twenty of the more than twenty-seven thousand tornadoes from 1970 through 1998 received that rating.

Although tornadoes can appear at any hour of the day, most form between noon and 9 P.M., peaking between 5 and 6 P.M. The majority of tornadoes occur in spring and summer, but they have occurred during every month of the year. A tornado has a distinct life cycle. It is usually born as a thin funnel descending from a parent thunderstorm cloud. As it matures and expands, the rotating column of air picks up material in its path and acquires the color of the circulating debris. In its dying stage the funnel may appear as a long, thin rope. A tornado is capable of massive destruction during all stages. Some tornadoes have multiple vortices, or several small funnels rotating around a central axis. Occasionally, a tornado "outbreak" occurs, when a single weather system produces numerous tornadoes in one day.

Annually, the United States is home to about 100,000 individual thunderstorms; about 1,000 of them produce a tornado. Conditions for formation of a tornadic thunderstorm exist when a layer of warm, moist air becomes trapped beneath a layer of cold, dry air by an intervening layer of warm, dry air. If a cold front or disturbance in the upper levels of the atmosphere disturbs the delicate layering, the warm, moist air pushes upward through the cold air. As the thunderstorm develops, winds of different speeds and directions at varying heights in the atmosphere create an invisible, horizontal spinning effect near the earth's surface, much like a rolling pin moving across a table. The rising warm air tilts the rotating air from horizontal to vertical (stands the rolling pin on end while it is still turning), producing an area of rotation about 2 to 6 miles in diameter within the storm.

Tornadoes appear from this rotating area, called a mesocyclone, but not all mesocyclones produce tornadoes. A majority of tornadoes form in conjunction with cold fronts, but in the central plains many tornadoes develop along a dryline, the dividing line between very moist warm air to the east and hot dry air to the west. Both cold fronts and drylines can produce supercell thunderstorms with clouds towering to 50,000 feet or higher. Supercells produce most of the violent tornadoes. Tornadoes also form when tropical storms or hurricanes move over land, but these tornadoes are usually weak. Scientists have not found the last piece of the puzzle, the exact mechanism that triggers the formation of a tornado.

The capricious nature of tornadoes is well documented. Tornadoes have completely destroyed a house but left food on a table untouched or leveled one house and left the neighboring one intact. The howling winds have carried people and objects great distances and deposited them back to earth unhurt. They commonly drive blades of grass or splinters of wood into trees or houses.

Tornado myths abound. One says that areas near lakes, rivers, and mountains are safe from tornadoes, but in reality these barriers have no effect on tornadoes. They have traveled across lakes and up and down mountains; more than thirty tornadoes have crossed the Mississippi River. Other myths include that tornadoes are always preceded by hail, mobile homes attract tornadoes, and opening windows will keep a building from exploding.

## GEOGRAPHY

More than one-half of the world's tornadoes occur annually in the United States, where the conditions for their formation are ideal: a moisture source to the south, a cold source to the north, mountain ranges to the west, deserts to the southwest, and an active jet stream.

These meteorological conditions converge most often in an area designated "Tornado Alley," which extends from Texas northward to Nebraska.

From 1880 to 1998, more than 35,000 killer tornadoes brought death to virtually every state of the union. The Great Plains, Midwest, and Southeast experienced the greatest loss of life. Only seven states—Alaska, Hawaii, California, Nevada, Utah, Rhode Island, and Vermont—reported no fatalities. Texas led the nation in the number of tornadoes and total deaths. Oklahoma had the greatest tornado concentration per square mile. Mississippi led in deaths per million people.

About twenty other countries, including Canada, Russia, Australia, India, China, Bangladesh, England, Italy, France, and Japan, have conditions favorable for tornadoes. In most of these countries, tornadoes are weak and take few lives. Fujita studied tornado damage reports from throughout the world and concluded that tornadoes rated F4 or greater occur only in the United States, Canada, Bangladesh, and India. Statistics for countries outside the United States may be misleading, however. No standards for identifying and rating tornadoes exist, and no organization compiles international tornado statistics. Countries with large, sparsely populated areas, such as Australia, Canada, and Russia, may experience many more tornadoes than are reported.

Second to the United States in the number of tornadoes is Canada, which averages 80 tornadoes and 1 or 2 deaths annually. Most Canadian tornadoes occur in areas near the U.S. border and in western New Brunswick and interior British Columbia. The United Kingdom, which experiences 33 weak tornadoes in an average year, has the highest frequency of tornadoes per unit area in the world. The most susceptible areas are the Midlands and eastern England; tornadoes are rare in Northern Ireland and Scotland. About 15 tornadoes occur annually in Australia in the summer and winter, particularly in the eastern, southeastern, and western coastal areas.

### PREVENTION AND PREPARATIONS

Humans cannot prevent tornadoes or lessen their destruction, but they can take several steps to lessen loss of life. A successful preparation program includes four integral parts: the issuance of a tornado forecast or watch, the spotting of a tornado, the dissemination of warnings to the public, and the response of an educated public to the warnings.

The United States is the only country to have a national office responsible for issuing severe weather forecasts. The Storm Prediction Center in Norman, Oklahoma, issues a tornado watch (forecast) when atmospheric conditions that could produce a tornado arise. A watch, which usually covers an area of 20,000 to 30,000 square miles, activates spotter networks within the watch area. These volunteers are amateur radio operators, law enforcement officials, or ordinary citizens who receive training in recognizing and reporting tornadoes within their county. A tornado watch also activates emergency procedures at the local National Weather Service (NWS) offices, law enforcement agencies, and emergency management offices. If spotters see a tornado, or if Doppler radar indicates that one may be forming, the local NWS office issues a tornado warning for the affected county. Local television and radio stations break into programming to warn citizens of impending danger, and many communities sound a warning siren. The media, especially television, relay information on the path of the tornado and the safety precautions to take.

In Canada and Australia, provincial and regional weather offices are responsible for tornado forecasts and warnings. Canada has a weather alert system that scrolls severe weather information across television screens, and a Doppler weather radar network was completed in 2003. Most other countries where tornadoes occur have no organized method of forecasting or warning of tornadoes.

Because tornadoes occur so rapidly, all the potential victim has time to do is seek shelter. Doppler radar has increased the average warning time for tornadoes that strike in the United States to about fifteen minutes, but many occur with much less notice. To educate the public about the actions to take when a tornado threatens, the NWS and the Federal Emergency Management Agency (FEMA) distribute millions of tornado-safety brochures to schools and the general public, and states susceptible to twisters have a severe weather safety week each spring. Among the other countries that produce tornado-safety materials are Canada and Australia.

The key to survival in a tornado is to avoid flying and falling debris. The best place to take shelter is in a storm cellar or basement. In homes without basements, the safest place is on the lowest level in an interior room. The idea is to put as many walls as possible between oneself and the tornado and to stay away from windows. People in public buildings should go to an inside hallway on the lowest level and avoid wide-span roofs such as those found in auditoriums, gymnasiums, and shopping malls.

Mobile homes and vehicles are especially vulnerable in a tornado and should be abandoned. In the United States 50 percent of the tornado fatalities from 1985 to 1997 occurred in mobile homes and vehicles. Those caught outdoors should seek shelter inside a building, and if nothing is available they should lie in a ditch. In all cases, arms or pillows should be used to protect the head and neck. Texas Tech University's Wind Engineering Research Center studied building construction for many years in an effort to design homes that could withstand tornado and hurricane winds. In 1998 FEMA made plans for inexpensive home shelters that the Tech Center had designed available to the public and encouraged their construction.

**RESCUE AND RELIEF EFFORTS**
Because tornadoes occur with so little warning, and the odds of their striking one particular locale are so minute, few communities have specific tornado rescue plans. Often the streets are blocked by debris after a tornado, so much of the initial search for victims and rescue of trapped people comes from the survivors themselves. The greatest hazard in a tornado is being buried by falling debris. Frequently, those who seek shelter in a basement have the house fall in on them. When a tornado struck downtown Waco, Texas, in 1953, brick buildings crumbled, burying victims under 20 to 30 feet of rubble. In Saragosa, Texas, in 1987, 22 of the 30 fatalities occurred when the concrete block community center collapsed.

Local law enforcement agencies are usually in charge of search and rescue. When the tornado is of great proportions, the governor may call in the National Guard for assistance, and if a large number of people are unaccounted for, FEMA may send search dogs to sniff through the rubble.

A very strong tornado may hurl victims about like pieces of paper, sometimes many yards from their places of shelter. In the most violent tornadoes, victims may be found in trees or wrapped in telephone or electric lines. Those who remain in mobile homes or cars are often found entangled in twisted metal.

Tornado victims tend to have specific types of injuries. Most fatalities are from crushing injuries and head traumas. Broken bones, gashes, cuts, puncture wounds, and embedded glass are among the most common nonfatal injuries. In nearly all tornadoes, a majority of the victims are the elderly and children.

An immediate concern is to turn off the gas and electricity to prevent fires and electrocutions. The National Guard may be mobilized to restore order and patrol against looting. If many fatalities are involved, law-enforcement officials will order everyone out of the devastated area until the bodies are recovered. When the victims are allowed to return to what remains of their homes and businesses, they usually find very little that is salvageable. What the wind does not destroy, the rain that frequently follows does.

Simultaneously with rescue efforts, national relief organizations, such as the Red Cross and the Salvation Army, begin feeding the victims and rescue workers and setting up shelters for the homeless. A designated agency, often the Red Cross or a local government entity, compiles lists of survivors and fatalities. Within hours of the disaster, religious and civic organizations as well as individuals provide food, clothing, household items, and money for the victims. Many also help in the cleanup and rebuilding process.

If the tornado has left behind substantial property damage, the governor may request a national disaster declaration. This designation, which the president must sign, provides federal assistance to individuals and communities for rebuilding.

#### IMPACT

Tornadoes rarely have a long-lasting effect on the physical environment. Unlike many natural disasters, such as floods or volcanic eruptions, "twisters" do not alter the topography of the area that they strike. The greatest environmental impact of a tornado is on trees, animals, humans, and the artificial environment. Violent tornadoes snap off trees, leaving only stubs, while most smaller tornadoes only break off branches. Occasionally, a twister downs thousands of trees in a forest. More commonly, the greatest damage to vegetation is to agricultural crops, which are readily replanted.

Tornadoes often kill wildlife. Frequently, frogs, fish, and various types of birds "rain" from the sky when they are caught in the rotating winds and dropped some distance away. During a 1978 tornado in Norfolk, England, 136 geese fell from the sky along a 25-mile track. Few reports of tornadoes killing larger wild animals exist, but it is probable that tornadoes killed many bison that once roamed the American Great Plains. Deaths of farm animals are common in tornadoes. Tens of thousands of cows, horses, pigs, and chickens have died through the years when winds carried them distances before dropping them or when barns or chicken houses collapsed. Dogs and cats are also frequent casualties of tornadoes.

Tornadoes cause incredible damage to human-made objects. Stronger storms can reduce brick and wooden buildings to piles of rubble in seconds, and even weak ones can demolish mobile homes. Tornadoes have dumped bridges into rivers and lakes, leaving behind only twisted iron or steel and concrete pillars. A violent tornado can scour pavement from roads, toss cars and trucks like matchsticks, and derail trains. The annual price tag for tornado damage is unknown, but single tornadoes have been known to cause more than $1 billion in damage. The tornado that struck Omaha, Nebraska, on May 6, 1975, left behind $1.135 billion in damage (in 1995 dollars), and the tornadoes that ripped through the Oklahoma City area on May 3, 1999, cost more than $1 billion.

Tornadoes leave their greatest impact on humans. During the twentieth century, these storms killed almost 15,000 and injured approximately 125,000 in the United States. In 1998, a record 1,426 tornadoes touched down in the United States and took 130 lives, the most in twenty-five years. Although they do not keep tornado statistics, India and Bangladesh combined may lead the world in tornado fatalities. A single tornado north of Dhaka, Bangladesh, killed 1,300 and injured 12,000 in 1989, and one in 1996 took more than 1,000 lives in the same area. The number of homeless and bereaved left in the path of tornadoes is uncountable.

## HISTORICAL OVERVIEW

Although Greek philosopher Aristotle, the founder of meteorology, described tornadoes (or what he called "whirlwinds") around 340 B.C.E, few accounts of nature's most violent storms exist before 1600

*A large funnel cloud moves across the plains.* (National Oceanic and Atmospheric Administration)

except in the legends of several American Indian tribes. Tornadoes occurred infrequently in Europe and, except in England, received little notice until settlement began in North America, the prime natural habitat of these storms. Even then, tornadoes were not common occurrences. Only twenty such storms were recorded in pre-Revolutionary War times, including the July 8, 1680, storm in Cambridge, Massachusetts, which claimed the life of John Robbins. This was the first written account of a tornado and a victim within the future United States.

A Jesuit priest's narrative of the tornado that struck Rome in 1749 is one of the few published accounts of a European tornado outside England to appear before the nineteenth century, and after 1800 most of the interest in tornadoes centered in the United States. A twister that struck New Brunswick, New Jersey, on June 19, 1835, stirred an ongoing scientific debate between U.S. meteorologists James Pollard Espy and William Redfield over the origin and nature of the storms. During the 1850's and 1860's, the Smithsonian Institution collected weather data from volunteer observers and military posts, and in 1862 it distributed circulars to the public warning about tornado dangers and asking for reports on these storms. The first weather forecast in the United States, which meteorologist Cleveland Abbe issued on September 2, 1869, raised the possibility of forecasting severe storms and tornadoes in the future.

On February 2, 1870, the federal government created a national weather service and placed it under the jurisdiction of the Army Signal Corps. One corpsman, John Park Finley, began a systematic study of tornadoes in 1877. Based on personal observations of the storms in the Great Plains and historical tornado data, Finley devised a set of rules for forecasting tornadoes. The corps allowed Finley to issue trial tornado predictions in 1884, and he claimed a 95-98 percent success rate. These forecasts never reached the public because the prevailing thought of the time was that people would panic if they thought a tornado might appear. This fear, along with a lack of interest in tornadoes among the scientific community, led to a prohibition on the use of the word "tornado" in any weather forecast until 1938.

During the nineteenth century, four tornadoes in the United States claimed more than 100 lives each: May 7, 1840, in Natchez, Mississippi, 317 deaths; June 3, 1860, in rural Iowa and Illinois, 112 deaths; May 27, 1896, in St. Louis, Missouri, 306 deaths; and June 12, 1899, in New Richmond, Wisconsin, 117 deaths.

The large population increase in the sections of the United States most prone to tornadoes led to greater tornado disasters during the first half of the twentieth century. The worst tornado disaster in U.S. history occurred on March 18, 1925, when a boiling mass of black clouds rolled 219 miles through parts of Missouri, Illinois, and Indiana, killing 689 and injuring more than 2,000 in its path. This "Great Tri-State Tornado," also the holder of the record for the longest path, helped make 1925 the deadliest year (794 deaths) and the 1920's the deadliest decade on record for the United States (3,169 deaths).

Annual deaths during the first half of the century averaged 210, and in addition to the Great Tri-State Tornado, eight tornadoes claimed 100 or more lives each: May 18, 1902, in Goliad, Texas, 114 deaths; April 24-25, 1908, in Louisiana and Mississippi, 143 deaths; March 23, 1913, in Omaha, Nebraska, 115 deaths; May 25-26, 1917, in Mattoon, Illinois, 103 deaths; April 2, 1936, in Tupelo, Mississippi, 216 deaths; April 6, 1936, in Gainesville, Georgia, 206 deaths; June

23, 1944, in Shinnston, West Virginia, 151 deaths; and April 9, 1947, in Woodward, Oklahoma, 181 deaths.

The Weather Bureau lifted the ban on the use of the word "tornado" in forecasts in 1938 and gave its local offices responsibility for issuing severe storm and tornado forecasts, but local offices rarely mentioned the word. World War II brought a change in attitude toward these deadly storms. Many munitions plants and Army Air Corps fields were located in the tornado-susceptible Great Plains and South. To lessen the possibility of many deaths should lightning strike a munitions plant and to decrease the potential loss of airplanes, the bureau organized storm-spotting networks around the crucial facilities. A few of these remained after the war and became the nucleus of a nationwide spotter network organized in the 1950's.

On March 20, 1948, a tornado raked Tinker Field in Oklahoma City. Air Force meteorologists Ernest Fawbush and Robert Miller studied the atmospheric conditions that existed before the storm occurred. Five days later, when they recognized nearly identical conditions, the officers issued a tornado forecast for Tinker Field, the first such forecast in modern history. They were correct—a tornado touched down on the base. Fawbush and Miller continued to issue forecasts for the military, but the civilian population did not receive the same type of advanced notification until 1952. The Weather Bureau issued the first tornado forecast to the American public on March 17 of that year, but no tornadoes occurred within the watch area. Four days later, the bureau issued another tornado watch, and this time it was a "success"—one tornado occurred within the designated area and time—but there was no cause for rejoicing on March 21. The 17 tornadoes that struck Arkansas, Tennessee, and Mississippi that day took 202 lives and injured over 1,200. In May, the Weather Bureau formed a Severe Weather Unit, the ancestor of the Storm Prediction Center, to issue both tornado and severe thunderstorm forecasts for the United States.

In 1953, tornadoes hit three U.S. cities, with terrible consequences. On May 11, a twister plowed through downtown Waco, Texas, taking 114 lives; on June 8, a tornado struck Flint, Michigan, killing 120; and the following day, nature's fury struck Worcester, Massachusetts, leaving 94 dead. These deadly storms ushered in a decade of vast improvements in tornado forecasting and warning, primarily the result of radar and an expanded communications system.

After the Waco tornado, Texas A&M University converted surplus navy radar to weather radar and installed it at various Weather Bureau offices around the state to create the country's first comprehensive tornado warning system. Meteorologists noticed that frequently a tornado formed a distinctive radar pattern, called a hook echo, and they began issuing tornado warnings based solely on radar. During the 1950's, their partner in spreading the warning of approaching danger to the public was radio (95 percent of U.S. households had a radio in 1950), but by the next decade, television had replaced radio as the primary warning medium.

The weather establishment began to realize that one of the best ways to save lives was to educate the public. The Weather Bureau (which became the National Weather Service in 1970), state disaster offices, newspapers, television stations, and schools began a campaign in the late 1950's to teach the public the difference between a tornado watch (meaning a tornado is possible) and a tornado warning (meaning a tornado has been sighted) and the precautions to take to save lives. Most communities in tornado-prone areas organized volunteer spotter networks. Television stations began to acquire radar and to hire professional meteorologists. The White House designated the National Oceanic and Atmospheric Administration (NOAA) Weather Radio as the sole government system to provide direct warnings of natural or nuclear disasters to private homes in 1975, and many Americans bought a special radio that sends out a warning when severe weather threatens their area. In the 1990's, the National Weather Service installed a vastly improved tornado detector, Doppler radar, at all its offices throughout the United States, Puerto Rico, and Guam, and many television stations bought their own Dopplers.

All these advances, along with improved building construction, contributed to a substantial reduction in the U.S. tornado death rate after the 1950's, the last decade to register more than 1,000 tornado deaths. As of 2006, no individual tornado had claimed more than 100 lives since 1953, and the last single tornado to kill more than 50 Americans occurred in 1971. These statistics are remarkable considering that the population in the southeastern and southern plains states, the areas most susceptible to tornadoes, increased more than 60 percent in the second half of the twentieth century.

In spite of all the technological and educational advances that the United States has made, nature's most vicious storm occasionally triumphs. An outbreak (several tornadoes in the same day) of 148 tornadoes on April 3-4, 1974, claimed 316 lives and injured more than 5,000 in 11 states. Other deadly outbreaks occurred on April 11, 1965, when 271 died in 6 midwestern states and on February 21, 1971, when 110 died in Louisiana and Mississippi.

During 1994 and 1995, scientists from many U.S. universities and U.S. and Canadian weather agencies employed an armada of specially equipped vehicles, including aircraft, to gather data from thunderstorms in an effort to unlock the secret of tornado formation. In 2003, researchers were able to insert measuring devices called "turtles" into an F4 tornado.

*Marlene Bradford*

**BIBLIOGRAPHY**

Bluestein, Howard. *Tornado Alley: Monster Storms of the Great Plains.* New York: Oxford University Press, 1999. This book by a leading meteorologist and tornado chaser is a history of tornado research interspersed with magnificent photographs.

Bradford, Marlene. *Scanning the Skies: A History of Tornado Forecasting.* Norman: University of Oklahoma Press, 2001. Traces the history of today's tornado warning system. Explains how advancements in the late twentieth century resulted in the drastic reduction of fatalities.

Eagleman, Joe R. "The Strongest Storm on Earth." In *Severe and Unusual Weather.* Lenexa, Kans.: Trimedia, 1990. The author describes the basic science of tornadoes in terminology that general readers can understand.

Flora, Snowden D. *Tornadoes of the United States.* Norman: University of Oklahoma Press, 1953. This book served as the standard reference work on tornadoes for years. Although outdated in many respects, it offers excellent historical accounts of many destructive tornadoes.

Grazulis, Thomas P. *Significant Tornadoes: 1680-1991.* St. Johnsbury, Vt.: Environmental Films, 1993.

_____. *Significant Tornadoes Update, 1992-1995.* St. Johnsbury, Vt.: Environmental Films, 1997. This massive book and its supplement contain basic tornado information, maps, statistics, and a description of every tornado rated F2 or higher that occurred in the United States from 1680 to 1995.

_____. *The Tornado: Nature's Ultimate Windstorm.* Norman: University of Oklahoma Press, 2003. A comprehensive look at the most destructive tornadoes in the United States and 200 other countries.

Ludlum, David. *Early American Tornadoes: 1586-1870.* Boston: American Meteorological Society, 1970. The author describes every reported tornado that occurred within the present United States until 1870 and discusses early American scientific thought on these storms.

Whipple, A. B. "Thunderstorms and Their Progeny." In *Storm.* Alexandria, Va.: Time-Life Books, 1982. This chapter mixes the science behind tornadoes with excellent meteorological drawings, magnificent photographs, and historical accounts of tornadoes.

# TSUNAMIS

**FACTORS INVOLVED:** Geography, geological forces,
gravitational forces
**REGIONS AFFECTED:** Cities, coasts, islands, oceans

## DEFINITION

A tsunami is an ocean wave, or a series of ocean waves, of enormous energy caused most often by undersea geological disturbances, especially earthquakes. The waves can travel thousands of miles from their source to an island or coastal region, where they can cause great loss of life and massive physical damage to the natural environment and artificial structures.

## SCIENCE

"Tsunami" is a Japanese word that means "harbor wave." Tsunamis are also known popularly as tidal waves, although this is a misnomer because they are not caused by the tides or by Earth-Moon gravitational attraction, as are the tides. Tsunamis are caused by any disturbance under the ocean's surface that causes great movements in the seawater. Tsunamis can be generated by earthquakes as well as landslides or volcanic eruptions on the seafloor. Tsunamis have been called seismic sea waves because they are often caused by earthquakes. They can also be caused by the impact of a large meteorite or large volcanic debris on the surface of the ocean. A tsunami should not be confused with a tidal bore, a storm surge, or a seiche. A tidal bore is a quickly advancing frontal wave of the incoming tide when concentrated into shallow narrow estuaries. Storm surges are associated with hurricanes and cyclones, which superimpose wind-driven waves onto the normal tidal actions and the sea currents created by offshore winds. Seiches are the slow and rhythmic oscillations of water in enclosed or nearly enclosed waters, such as bays or lakes.

Tsunamis, like other waves or wave systems, are collections of energy. At a specific point in time and at a specific location, energy is transferred by a disturbance into a medium at rest, in this case the ocean, is propagated through that medium, and is ultimately dissipated, either slowly through friction with adjacent media or by the sudden transfer of the remaining energy into another medium at a moment and point of disturbance. The vast majority of tsunamis are caused by earthquakes. Earthquakes themselves are caused by the shifting of tectonic plates relative to each other at the lines, either faults or trenches, where the plates meet.

According to plate tectonics, the earth is a dynamic structure in which a dozen or more huge plates, each some 70 to 100 miles thick, float on a semimolten viscous mantle, which covers the entire surface of the earth. The energy dissipated by the circulation of the mantle causes the plates above to shift. Tectonic-plate motion is extremely slow, only an inch or two per year. If the forces that cause this motion are not completely dissipated through this slow movement they will build up and be released at once in a sudden cataclysmic shifting of the plates.

Although earthquakes are the most frequent cause of tsunamis, not all earthquakes will produce such an event. An earthquake must be located under or near the ocean, be large (tsunamis are typically caused by earthquakes measuring 6.5 and above on the Richter scale), have a focal point less than 30 miles below the seafloor, and cause movement in the seafloor. It is the movement of the ocean floor under the water above it which serves as the initial impetus for the creation of the tsunami.

Much more important than the magnitude of the earthquake are the type of earthquake and the type of motion it causes in the seafloor. Vertical shifting of the plates, especially a phenomenon known as subduction, is much more effective than transverse (side-by-side) motion in generating tsunamis. Subduction is the movement of one plate under an adjacent plate. Such subduction earthquakes are especially formative of tsunamis in the Pacific, where the thinner plates underlying the seafloor are moving downward and under the thicker adjacent continental plates. The sudden vertical movement of a subduction earthquake will displace, and thereby upset the equilibrium of, the water above.

Because water is not compressible, the movement will force upwards, or downwards, the entire column of water above the shifted area, which might measure thousands of square miles. Waves form subsequently as gravity pulls the enormous volume of disturbed water back downward to its position of equilibrium. In this type of tsu-

## MILESTONES

**1692:** Tsunamis spawned by an earthquake in Port Royal, Jamaica, kill 3,000.

**1703:** 5,000 die in tsunamis in Honshū, Japan, following a large earthquake.

**1707:** A 38-foot-high tsunami kills 30,000 in Japan.

**1741:** Following volcanic eruptions, 30-foot waves in Japan cause 1,400 deaths.

**1755:** As many as 50,000 lose their lives in the combined earthquake and tsunami in Lisbon, Portugal.

**1783:** A tsunami in Italy kills 30,000.

**1868:** Tsunamis in Chile and Hawaii claim more than 25,000 lives.

**1883:** The Krakatau volcanic explosion and tsunami in Indonesia result in 36,000 deaths.

**1896:** As many as 27,000 die after tsunamis hit Sanriku, Japan.

**1933:** 3,000 are killed by tsunamis in Sanriku, Japan.

**1946:** The Aleutian tsunami creates 32-foot-high waves in Hilo, Hawaii, causing 159 deaths there.

**1946:** 2,000 die in Honshū, Japan, after an earthquake spawns tsunamis.

**1964:** 195-foot waves engulf Kodiak, Alaska, after the Good Friday earthquake; 131 die.

**1998:** A series of tsunamis in Papua New Guinea kills 2,000, mostly children.

**1999:** A tsunami and accompanying earthquake at the island of Vanuatu kills 10, injures more than 100, and leaves thousands homeless.

**2001:** A tsunami in Peru leaves 26 dead and 70 missing.

**2004:** A massive tsunami strikes 11 nations bordering the Indian Ocean, leaving at least 212,000 dead and almost 43,000 missing.

nami generation the amount of vertical drop or uplift of the underlying seafloor and the area over which it occurs govern the size of the resulting tsunami. The physics of the tsunami itself render it possible for the generating energy of the earthquake or other motive disturbance to be propagated across an entire ocean and deposited on shore in powerful destructive forces. The tsunami will move outward in all directions from the point of disturbance in concentric circles, similar to the way ripples fan out in all directions when a stone is dropped into water.

Unlike the ripples on a pond, however, the tsunami waves in the deep ocean are impossible to see from the air, nor can they be felt on a ship by which they pass. It is precisely the dimensions of the tsunami that render that possible. Wave dimensions are height (the distance from the bottom of the trough to the top of the crest), length (the distance from one crest to the next), and period (the time it takes for successive wave crests to reach a fixed point). Waves caused by the wind, which are visible on a lake or at the beach, will have a period of a few seconds, a height of a few feet or less—or more in the case of storms—and a length of a few hundred feet. In such an environment an object or vessel will visibly bob up and down on the surface as successive waves pass. A tsunami wave in the middle of the ocean, however, can have a period ranging from ten minutes to two hours, a height of a few feet or less, but a length of 300 miles or more. The ratio of length to height is thus far greater for a tsunami than for a wind-driven wave. As a tsunami passes in the open ocean an object or vessel will only rise and fall a very short distance over a far greater length of time. The tsunami, for all the destructive power it manifests when striking a shore, is thus impossible to see or feel on the open ocean. To illustrate this irony one need only look to the example of the tsunami that destroyed the village of Sanriku, Japan, on June 15, 1896. About 90 miles offshore, an earthquake caused a tsunami that passed by the town's fishing fleet, then working only 20 miles off the coast, completely unnoticed. The fishermen returned home the next day to find their town destroyed and the bodies of some 27,000 people littering the harbor.

Tsunamis behave as shallow water waves. Such waves are characterized by a very low ratio of water depth to wave length. Although it may be hard to imagine, given the enormous depths found in the open ocean—especially the Pacific—if one considers the dimensions it is not hard to believe. The average depth of the Pacific is between 3 and 4 miles. If a tsunami's length can be some 300 miles, then the ratio of ocean depth to wavelength is on the order of 1 to 100. Very important for the case of a tsunami, the speed of a shallow water wave is the square root of the product of the acceleration of gravity and the depth of the water. That means the deeper the water, the faster the tsunami.

Normal sea waves travel no faster than 60 miles per hour, even in the stormiest of weather over the deepest of seas. A tsunami can travel ten times as fast. The average depth of the Pacific Ocean is 18,480 feet. In water of such a depth a tsunami will travel 524 miles per hour. Through water 30,000 feet deep a tsunami travels at 670 miles per hour—as fast as a jet passenger plane. Furthermore, the rate of energy loss for a wave is inversely related to its length. There-fore, the longer the wave, the more slowly it loses its energy. These two factors, high velocity and slow energy loss, make it possible for a tsunami to deliver a tremendous amount of force across the entire Pacific Ocean, the largest ocean on the earth, in less than one day. A tsunami can carry so much energy that striking a shore will not neces-sarily consume all of its energy. Tsunami waves have been known to bounce back and forth across the Pacific for a week or more while their energy is slowly dissipated.

As a tsunami approaches the perimeter of the ocean or an island and begins to run into increasingly shallow water, the wave's velocity,

*A tsunami capsizes a fishing boat.* (FEMA)

dependent entirely upon the depth of the water, decreases. In 60 feet of water, a tsunami wave will be slowed to 30 miles per hour. However, since the wave's period will remain constant, the height of the wave will increase. Therefore, as the wave approaches land its speed decreases and its height increases. Although tsunami heights of up to 100 feet have been recorded, only very rarely will a tsunami take the form of a towering cresting wave of the sort sought after by surfers. The wave height will increase, however, and the tsunami will be noticeable, unlike on the open ocean.

A tsunami might appear as a quickly changing tide, a series of breaking waves, or even a bore—a steplike wave with a steep breaking front. It is not necessarily the case that the tsunami will cause the water first to rise. If the trough of the tsunami reaches the shore first, the water level can drop and recede to an enormous extent, baring more of the shore bottom than the lowest tide. The crest will still follow, however. It has happened that onlookers, seeing what they thought was an incredibly low tide, have ventured out onto the exposed bottom, only to be caught by the subsequent fast-moving crest and drowned.

## GEOGRAPHY

Although tsunamis can occur in any ocean of the world, approximately 80 percent of tsunamis are found in the Pacific Ocean. Another 10 percent are found in the Atlantic, and the rest are found elsewhere. Most tsunamis occur in the Pacific because that ocean has far more seismic activity than the others. The perimeter of the seafloor of the Pacific, known as the "Ring of Fire," is a series of mountain chains, deep trenches, and volcanic island arcs caused by the movements of the adjoining tectonic plates that cover the surface of the earth. Major mountain ranges, such as the Andes Mountains in South America, and deep trenches, such as the Peru-Chile trench immediately off the west coast of South America, the Aleutian trench south of the Aleutian Islands of Alaska, and the Japan trench east of Japan, were created by the sudden movement of adjoining plates along fault lines.

In the Pacific Ocean at least one tsunami per year has been recorded since 1800, and there is an average of two destructive tsunamis somewhere in the Pacific per year. Hawaii, an easy target in the middle of the Pacific Ocean, suffered 37 tsunamis from 1875 to 2000, while Japan was struck by 15 major tsunamis, 8 of them especially destructive, between 1650 and 2000. Although Pacific-wide tsunamis are somewhat rare, the nations of the Pacific Ocean can expect an oceanwide tsunami on the average of once every ten or twelve years.

Tsunamis are rare in the Atlantic, but they are not unknown. In November of 1928, an earthquake off of the Grand Banks in Newfoundland, Canada, generated a tsunami that caused both loss of life and significant property damage in that region. In terms of local geography, low-lying coastal regions and islands, especially land less than 50 feet above sea level and within 1 mile of the shoreline, are at the greatest risk of damage once a tsunami strikes.

## PREVENTION AND PREPARATIONS

Scientists and public officials are especially keen to lessen the damage and loss of life caused by tsunamis. Mitigation of tsunami damage depends upon three factors: prediction, warning, and preparation. Because earthquakes are the prevalent cause of tsunamis, efforts at tsunami prediction have focused on earthquakes. In spite of significant research, however, scientists remain unable to predict the incidence of earthquakes with real certitude. Tsunami researchers instead focus their efforts on distinguishing as quickly as possible tsunamigenic earthquakes from other earthquakes, thereby decreasing the amount of time necessary to issue a clear warning. The shorter the time period between tsunami generation and the issuance of a warning, the more lives that can be saved. While it remains virtually impossible to warn population centers of an oncoming locally generated tsunami—because of the great speed at which a tsunami travels—it is very possible to warn residents of areas under threat of a tsunami generated by distant seismic disturbances.

The ability to predict the arrival time of a tsunami has been in place for some time. The known physics of tsunami creation and propagation, combined with increasingly accurate mapping of the seafloor over which the tsunamis travel and precise measurements of ocean depths, make it possible to predict with reasonable, even excellent, accuracy the moment and point at which a tsunami will arrive ashore. An earthquake struck off the coast of Chile in 1960, causing enormous damage and loss of life to the local residents, who had been caught completely unaware. Yet once tsunami monitors were able to confirm that a tsunami had been created, they were able to predict its arrival in Hilo, Hawaii, with truly phenomenal accuracy— the tsunami arrived within one minute of its predicted time.

Later, scientists assumed a new challenge, that of ascertaining the amplitude of a tsunami once it is created. This requires a better understanding of how earthquakes create tsunamis and how they are propagated, as well as the creation of better instrumentation to detect and measure them. As part of the Pacific Tsunami Warning System, scientists and engineers have placed throughout the Pacific increasingly sensitive subsurface pressure sensors that measure tsunami amplitude in the open ocean.

The study, understanding, and measurement of coastal runup and impact ashore is an equally important piece of the Tsunami Warning System. Accurate and current surveys of the local topography—both below and above the shoreline—accurate tidal measurement, numerical modeling, and historical data are combined to create worst-case impact and inundation scenarios and define evacuation zones and routes to ensure quick response when a tsunami warning must be issued. This information is also used in long-term public efforts to mitigate public and private property damage and loss of life.

Government agencies can initiate public works projects, such as the construction and maintenance of breakwaters or floodwalls that act as physical barriers to tsunami flooding. Governments can also acquire land or regulate land usage through zoning or taxation policy to prevent, discourage, or regulate areas prone to tsunami impact or flooding. Finally, governments can foster public education and awareness of the dangers inherent in tsunami-prone areas by requiring, for instance, disclosure of such information in real estate transactions.

The final component of efforts to mitigate loss of life from tsunami impact and flooding is the warning itself. Research, monitoring, and understanding of tsunami generation and propagation, and communication of the data relevant to them, are all essential components of any warning effort. Tsunami warnings are issued by the authorities or institutions that monitor the data coming from remote sites and sensors scattered throughout the Pacific. Once a decision to

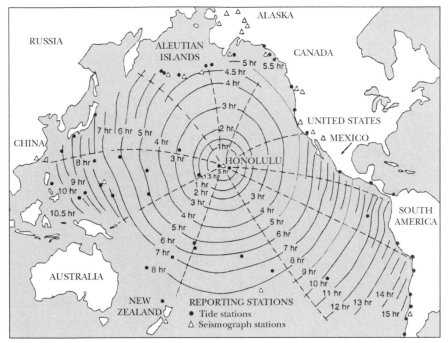

*Tide and seismograph reporting stations of the Pacific Tsunami Warning System. This is a representation of the travel times for tidal waves originating at Honolulu, Hawaii.* (National Oceanic and Atmospheric Administration)

announce a warning has been made, the governmental authorities where a tsunami is expected to come ashore are alerted. The warning is then disseminated to the various appropriate regional and local civil defense organizations and other responsible agencies and broadcast to the public via radio and television.

The effectiveness of such a system, no matter how well devised and maintained, is ultimately dependent upon a well-informed and responsive public. Education and outreach are thus critical components of the work of the organizations responsible for monitoring tsunamis or issuing tsunami warnings and other agencies involved in public safety. Public awareness is essential in the case of locally generated tsunamis, where nearby coastal residents must be taught to seek refuge inland on higher ground upon feeling the tremors of a locally generated earthquake.

Education is, however, no less important in the case of tsunamis generated by distant earthquakes and for which there is thus much time to issue a warning. Residents in areas prone to tsunamis must be educated as to the complexity of the danger. People have drowned because they went out to marvel at what they thought was an incredibly low tide but which in fact was the trough of an oncoming tsunami whose crest followed.

Residents must be likewise alerted to the incidence of multiple waves. Civil defense authorities had managed to evacuate Crescent City, California, in March of 1964 when warned of a tsunami that was on the way from an earthquake that struck near the coast of Alaska. Their work paid off well; there was no loss of life after the arrival of the first two waves of this particular tsunami. Unfortunately, some residents, assuming the danger was over, decided to return to the stricken area before an all-clear signal was given and were drowned by a third wave that was much larger than the first two. It is perhaps an irony that tsunami warnings bring out sightseers interested in viewing the very danger from which they have been instructed to flee. The warnings issued in May of 1960 to Hilo, Hawaii, while instrumental in preventing large-scale loss of life, did bring out a few sightseers, all of whom were drowned.

## RESCUE AND RELIEF EFFORTS

Although the areas of tsunami damage might be small compared to those of other disasters, the damage is particularly thorough. Localities affected by tsunamis are usually devastated, requiring significant short-term and long-term recovery and reconstruction efforts. After a tsunami strikes, the most immediate concern for local civil defense authorities is the public health. While treatment of injured survivors is important, perhaps more critical is the condition of the water supply, typically fouled by tsunami flooding. If sewer lines are broken or the sewage system is overwhelmed, the potential public health hazard is even worse. Additionally, the bodies of the drowned must be located, recovered, and disposed of properly as quickly as possible to prevent further pollution of the water and outbreaks of communicable diseases.

Besides bringing the immediate threats to the public health under control, initial relief efforts require the recovery of the essential infrastructure, especially the water and power supply, as well as communications and transport. Without these basics it is impossible for both individuals and communities as a whole to commence the task of rebuilding. Because the tsunami will have left an enormous amount of debris in its wake, initial cleanup efforts require the removal of everything from trash and building debris to boats and motor vehicles, much of which may have been moved hundreds of yards inland. In the long term, recovery from a tsunami entails reconstruction of homes, businesses, and public spaces and even the rehabilitation of the environment, which often suffers massive damage.

## IMPACT

Tsunamis cause damage in two ways: flooding and exertion of the wave's force against structures. The water that comes onto the shore and proceeds inland is called runup. Its height is the vertical distance measured from the tide level at the time the tsunami strikes the shore to the contour line of highest point on shore reached by the water. A tsunami can easily raise the water level from 20 to 30 yards above normal height and reach, especially if the stricken coastal area is particularly low, hundreds of yards inland, thereby flooding enormous tracts of land. Runup can cause enormous environmental damage, removing years of accumulated beach sand, stripping away coastal vegetation and trees, and drowning animals.

Tsunamis exert a truly powerful force against anything with which they come into contact, including human-made structures. A tsunami wave can easily flatten buildings or remove them from their foundations, wash boats and small ships hundreds of yards ashore, and toss around automobiles and even heavy construction equipment as if they were toys. The movement of such objects, as well as the debris of destroyed structures and even uprooted trees, can cause severe secondary damage when the wave carries them forward and forces them against still-standing structures, and then subsequently when the waters recede and drag the same objects back to strike against what little might still be left standing.

Besides causing severe environmental and property damage, tsunamis cause important and sometimes dangerous infrastructure damage that can threaten public health and delay post-tsunami recovery efforts. Widespread flooding almost always causes polluted water supplies. The local energy grid can be compromised or put out of service entirely if electrical or gas lines are destroyed.

A tsunami's most fearsome toll, however, is always loss of human life, attributable almost exclusively to drowning. Between 1932 and July of 1998, more people died in the United States as a result of tsunamis than as a result of earthquakes. The desire to prevent such loss of life has been the primary motivation behind the establishment of the warning system and preparatory measures now in place throughout the Pacific.

In April of 1946 an earthquake in the Aleutian trench near Alaska generated a tsunami that struck Hawaii unexpectedly, causing 159 fatalities and tens of millions of dollars in damage. Motivated by what is still considered to be Hawaii's worst natural disaster, the United States Coast and Geodetic Survey established in Hawaii the Seismic Sea Wave Warning System, which later became the Pacific Tsunami Warning Center (PTWC). Before the end of the twentieth century, the PTWC would be the operational center of the Pacific Tsunami Warning System, a sophisticated and coordinated international effort comprising 26 member states. These countries of the Pacific region pool their knowledge and resources to monitor the entire Pacific basin for tsunamigenic earthquakes in the hope of giving adequate warnings to population centers under threat of a tsunami and thereby lessening property damage and reducing the loss of human life.

## HISTORICAL OVERVIEW

Tsunamis are caused by sudden seismic shocks that sometimes erupt in coastal waters. When earthquakes accompany tsunamis, as they often do, the loss of life and property in the affected areas can be staggering. Because waterfront land is usually heavily populated, the gigantic waves characteristic of tsunamis are particularly devastating. Unless they have some forewarning of an advancing tsunami, whole populations can simply be swept away in the roiling waters that move with such force that they flatten everything in their paths.

Most large, devastating tsunamis that have resulted in the greatest loss of life have occurred in the Pacific Basin. They have usually been the result of underwater earthquakes caused by the movement of tectonic plates, often in the western reaches of the Pacific Ocean. Japan has often fallen victim to such disasters, although tsunamis have hit Indonesia, eastern Russia, and Alaska with relative frequency as well.

The earliest records of tsunamis date to the end of the fifteenth century, although they undoubtedly occurred but were not recorded before that time. One was thought to have struck Japan in 1498. Two others are known to have occurred there in the early seventeenth century, one in 1605 and the other in 1611. Between 4,000 and 5,000 inhabitants were thought to have died when these tsunamis swamped their oceanside villages.

Tsunami activity in the eighteenth century was substantial. Japan suffered devastation from it in 1707, 1741, and 1792. The Kamchatka Peninsula in the North Pacific was struck by a tsunami in 1737, and one struck the Ryukyu Islands in 1771. Peru was hit by tsunamis in 1724 and 1746.

In 1783, one was recorded in Italy, where tsunamis are experienced only infrequently. This part of the world, however, has not been exempt from them entirely. Indeed, in 1755, the most spectacular tsunami of the eighteenth century hit Lisbon, Portugal, which was struck simultaneously by an earthquake that leveled much of the old city. The waves that engulfed Lisbon almost totally destroyed its port, one of the most active in southern Europe. Memories of this disaster are preserved in the Voltaire's famous novel *Candide* (1759), whose protagonist arrives in Lisbon in time to witness the catastrophe.

The Lisbon disaster claimed as many as 50,000 lives, making it the most destructive such event in recorded history until its loss of life was eclipsed in the twentieth and twenty-first centuries by greater loss of life in tsunamis and earthquakes. When Chile was struck by a tsunami in 1868, its huge waves, traveling at speeds thought to have exceeded 500 miles (800 kilometers) an hour, swirled across the Pacific Ocean and struck Hawaii. Approximately 25,000 lives were wiped out by this event.

Among the costliest tsunamis in loss of life was the eruption of the Krakatau Volcano in Indonesia in 1883, which triggered a wall of water 135 feet high that snuffed out the lives of 36,000 people. In 1896, a tsunami killed 27,000 people in Japan.

In the twentieth century, many tsunamis struck the Pacific rim, the so-called Ring of Fire, but the loss of life was smaller than in many of the tsunamis in earlier centuries, perhaps because early warning systems were in place. The Kamchatka Peninsula suffered tsunamis in 1923 and in 1952. Tsunamis struck the Aleutian Islands in 1946 and 1957. The former devastated Hilo, Hawaii.

Japan suffered tsunamis in 1933, 1944, and 1983, but none of these was so destructive as the one that struck Kodiak, Alaska in 1964, where an earthquake leveled much of the town before the tsunami followed, wiping out the entire community. This tsunami also created the enormous waves that overwhelmed Crescent City, California. Another devastating tsunami of the twentieth century killed more than 5,000 people in the Philippines in 1976.

During the twentieth century, scientists developed the means to prevent the enormous death tolls that tsunamis exacted in earlier centuries. The National Oceanic and Atmospheric Administration (NOAA) set up a tsunami warning system in Hawaii, making it possible to evacuate endangered areas. Following the Alaskan earthquake and tsunami of 1964, this system was extended to Alaska, where it is designated the Regional Tsunami Warning System.

At the Pacific Tsunami Warning System, headquartered in Honolulu, Hawaii, seismologists carefully track seismic activity throughout the Pacific basin and issue warnings whenever there is need. The ability to predict the time and place of landfall has made it possible to protect most residents of coastal areas from tsunamis. So precise is the work of the seismological warning stations that when an earthquake struck off the coast of Chile in 1960, it was possible to predict its arrival in Hilo, Hawaii, to within one minute of the actual landfall.

Despite the remarkable advances that have been made in predicting and giving advanced warnings of tsunamis, the most devastating Indian Ocean tsunami in recorded history occurred on December 26, 2004. The underwater earthquake that created it registered a magnitude of 9.0 on the Richter scale. This tsunami swamped the coastlines of 11 countries that border the Indian Ocean. The immediate death toll was set at 186,983, with another 42,883 missing and unaccounted for. The final death toll may never be known. Many bodies washed out to sea. Thousands eventually died of diseases triggered by the appalling sanitary conditions in the storm areas. Infections from open wounds likely accounted for deaths from blood poisoning and related ills. Dysentery, malaria, typhoid, and dehydration plagued the survivors.

*David M. Soule*
*Nancy M. Gordon*
*R. Baird Shuman*

**BIBLIOGRAPHY**

Lander, James F., and Patricia A. Lockridge. *United States Tsunamis, 1690-1988.* Boulder, Colo.: National Geophysical Data Center, 1989. This is an excellent source for readers looking for more detail regarding specific tsunamis that have struck the United States and its possessions. It includes data and descriptions of individual events, their causes, and the ensuing damages. The many illustrations and tables are helpful.

Lockridge, Patricia A., and Ronald H. Smith. *Tsunamis in the Pacific Basin, 1900-1983.* Boulder, Colo.: National Geophysical Data Center and World Data Center A for Solid Earth Geophysics, 1984. Similar to the work by Lockridge mentioned above, it includes information for the 405 tsunamis that occurred in the Pacific region during the years covered. The number of tsunamis alone is a fascinating statistic.

Myles, Douglas. *The Great Waves.* New York: McGraw-Hill, 1985. This is an excellent and easy-to-read introduction, treating tsunamis throughout history and covering them from the perspectives of science, geography, and impact on people.

Robinson, Andrew. "Floods, Dambursts, and Tsunamis." In *Earth Shock: Hurricanes, Volcanoes, Earthquakes, Tornadoes, and Other Forces of Nature.* London: Thames and Hudson, 1993. This essay gives good, but brief, coverage of the damages a tsunami can cause. Includes some excellent photographs.

Satake, Kenji, ed. *Tsunamis: Case Studies and Recent Developments.* Springer, 2006. A review of current tsunami research. The first part reports on tsunamis generated by volcanic eruptions and earthquakes around the Pacific Ocean, while the second part reports on developments in computations, monitoring, and coastal hazard assessment.

Solovev, Sergei, and Chan Nam Go. *Catalogue of Tsunamis on the Eastern Shore of the Pacific Ocean.* Sidney, B.C.: Institute of Ocean Sciences, Department of Fisheries and Oceans, 1984. This catalogue provides a wealth of data on individual tsunamis.

_____. *Catalogue of Tsunamis on the Western Shore of the Pacific Ocean.* Sidney, B.C.: Institute of Ocean Sciences, Department of Fisheries and Oceans, 1984. The counterpart to the above-mentioned work. Together these two volumes provide the interested reader with great detail on the tsunamis, both real and legendary, that have occurred throughout the centuries in the Pacific Ocean, as well as on the earthquakes or volcanoes or other disturbances that may have caused them.

Whittow, John. *Disasters: An Anatomy of Environmental Hazards.* Athens: University of Georgia Press, 1979. This excellent work covers the mechanics of tsunamis and the earthquakes that cause them. The detailed explanations are superb and are aided by helpful diagrams and tables. Photos are included. This is a great source for those wishing to get a more in-depth understanding of tsunamis.

# VOLCANIC ERUPTIONS

**FACTORS INVOLVED:** Chemical reactions, geography,
   geological forces, wind
**REGIONS AFFECTED:** All

## DEFINITION

A volcanic eruption is the manner in which gases, liquids, and solids
are expelled from the earth's interior onto its surface. Eruptions can
range from calm outflows of lava to violent explosions. About fifty volcanoes erupt every year, and a truly catastrophic eruption occurs
about once a century. Nearly 200,000 people have died over the last
five centuries because of volcanic eruptions. Three-quarters of these
deaths were caused by only 7, extremely violent, eruptions.

## SCIENCE

Volcanic eruptions are induced by and usually propelled by gas. The
most common source of the gas is water, which at the high temperatures associated with volcanic activity is turned to water vapor (steam).
Liquid lava is often involved in an eruption. The ratio of gas to liquid
in an erupting magma (molten rock material within the earth) is extremely variable. Some eruptions are almost entirely gas with minus-
cule amounts of liquid, such as the Salt Lake explosion crater in
Oahu, Hawaii. At the other extreme are eruptions of lava flows that
have less than 1 percent gas, such as the seafloor eruptions at mid-
oceanic ridges.

There are several methods to generate the water and associated
gas in a magma. The gas that causes the eruption can come from the
magma itself. Magmas that are deeply buried (under a high pressure) can dissolve considerable amounts of water. About 10 percent
water can dissolve in a magma that resides 9.3 miles (15 kilometers)
below the earth's surface. The amount of water that can stay dissolved decreases as the magma begins to rise. When the pressure
drops sufficiently, the water comes out of the magma and boils to
make bubbles. This process is called "vesiculation."

Vesiculation occurs in a similar manner to the opening of a champagne bottle: When the cork is removed and the pressure on the liq-

## MILESTONES

**5000 B.C.E.:** Crater Lake, Oregon, erupts, sending pyroclastic flows as far as 37 miles (60 kilometers) from the vent; 25 cubic miles of material are erupted as a caldera forms from the collapse of the mountaintop.

**c. 1470 B.C.E.:** Thera erupts in the Aegean Sea, possibly causing the disappearance of the Minoan civilization on Crete and leading to stories of the lost "continent" of Atlantis.

**August 24, 79 C.E.:** Vesuvius erupts, burying Pompeii and Herculaneum.

**March 11, 1669:** Sicily's Mount Etna begins a series of devastating eruptions that will result in more than 20,000 dead and 14 villages destroyed, including the seaside town of Catania, Italy.

**June 8, 1783-February 7, 1784:** The Laki fissure eruption in Iceland produces the largest lava flow in historic time, with major climatic effects. Benjamin Franklin speculates on its connection to a cold winter in Paris the following year.

**April 5, 1815:** The dramatic explosion of Tambora, 248.6 miles (400 kilometers) east of Java, the largest volcanic event in modern history, produces atmospheric and climatic effects for the next two years. Frosts occur every month in New England during 1816, the Year Without a Summer.

**August 26, 1883:** A cataclysmic eruption of Krakatau, an island in Indonesia, is heard 2,968 miles away. Many die as pyroclastic flows race over pumice rafts floating on the surface of the sea; many more die from a tsunami.

**May 8, 1902:** Pelée, on the northern end of the island of Martinique in the Caribbean, sends violent pyroclastic flows into the city of St. Pierre, killing all but 2 of the 30,000 inhabitants.

**June 6, 1912:** Katmai erupts in Alaska with an ash flow that produces the Valley of Ten Thousand Smokes.

**February 20, 1943:** Paricutín comes into existence in a cultivated field in Mexico. The eruption of this volcano continues for nine years.

**March 30, 1956:** The Russian volcano Bezymianny erupts with a violent lateral blast, stripping trees of their bark 18.6 miles (30 kilometers) away.

**January, 1973:** During an eruption on Heimaey Island, Iceland, the flow of lava is controlled by cooling it with water from fire hoses.

**May 18, 1980:** Mount St. Helens, in Washington State, erupts with a directed blast to the north, moving pyroclastic flows at velocities of 328 to 984 feet (100 to 300 meters) per second (nearly the speed of sound).

**March 28-April 4, 1982:** El Chichón, an "extinct" volcano in Mexico, erupts violently, killing 2,000, injuring hundreds, destroying villages, and ruining over 100 square miles of farmland.

**November 13, 1985:** Mudflows from the eruption of the Nevado del Ruiz, in Colombia, kill at least 23,000 people.

**August 21, 1986:** After building up from volcanic emanations, carbon dioxide escapes from Lake Nyos, Cameroon, killing over 1,700 people.

**June, 1991:** Pinatubo erupts in the Phillipines after having been dormant for four hundred years.

**September-November, 1996:** Eruption of lava beneath a glacier in the Grimsvötn Caldera, Iceland, melts huge quantities of ice, producing major flooding.

**June 25, 1997:** On the Caribbean island of Montserrat, 19 people die and 8,000 are evacuated when the Soufrière Hills volcano erupts.

**January 17, 2002:** The Nyiragongo volcano erupts in the Democratic Republic of Congo, sending lava flows into the city of Goma; 147 die and 500,000 are displaced.

uid is released, the dissolved gas (carbon dioxide in champagne) forms bubbles in the liquid. If an abundance of gas is produced, the bubbles can coalesce and shred the magma into droplets surrounded by turbulent jets of gas. In larger, more explosive eruptions the expanding gases can pulverize preexisting rocks in the throat of the volcano and along the walls of the magma passages. This combination of gases, ash, degasing droplets of liquid, vesiculating clots of lava, and broken fragments of hot rock can erupt as a glowing avalanche (nuée ardente), which is the most destructive and deadly of all forms of eruptions. Numerous nuées ardentes erupted in 1902 from Pelée in the Caribbean, killing 30,000 in St. Pierre within two minutes on May 8 and 800 in Morne Rouge on August 30.

Another source of the water needed to drive an eruption is groundwater. Water that originates as atmospheric precipitation creating lakes, rivers, and oceans is called "meteoric water." Starting at the surface, meteoric water can infiltrate into the ground to produce water-saturated rock, where it is called groundwater. Large quantities of groundwater can be raised to the boiling point as magma rises. The destructive eruption of Vesuvius in 79 C.E., which buried the city of Pompeii and killed over 13,000 people in the region, was initiated by the boiling of groundwater.

Magma reaching the surface of the solid earth can acquire a late-stage explosive nature by interacting with surface water of lakes, rivers, or oceans. The 1963 birth of the island of Surtsey in Iceland produced a pair of violent explosion plumes, a white steam cloud and a black cloud of fragmented lava. The crater region where many volcanoes have their main vent is often a circular depression that becomes filled with meteoric water to make a crater lake. The water in crater lakes is often highly acidic and filled with mud. Kelut, on the Indonesian island of Java has a deep crater lake that has repeatedly been the site of eruptions; a minor eruption in 1919 mixed the lake water and the fragmented lava to make a violent mudflow that killed 5,500 people. The deadliest eruption ever was Krakatau in 1883, which killed 36,000 people from a tsunami that was generated when seawater entered the collapsed side of the island volcano and hit the erupting magma.

An explosion requires two components: the force (expanding gases) and a resistance to the force. To pop a balloon loudly requires that air be blown into it and that the latex rubber exert a force against the inflow of air. The explosion occurs when the pent-up force eventually overcomes the resistance. In a violent eruption the resistance comes from the very sticky nature of the liquid portion of the magma. The stickiness of a liquid is called the viscosity. Highly viscous magmas are the most explosive. The higher the amount of silicon in the magma the greater the viscosity and the more explosive the eruption when water is present.

Nuées ardentes, the most deadly form of volcanic eruptions, usually develop in magmas that have a high silicon content. About 13,000 people were evacuated in Japan in 1991 when a low-gas, high-silicon lava began erupting at Unzen, forming a thick, pasty dome of lava on top of the volcano. When the lava acquired sufficient gas it erupted as a nuée ardente, killing 42 people, mostly journalists and geologists who had stayed to study and photograph the volcano.

Volcanoes are classified into six general categories with several subgroups. The major categories are Hawaiian, Strombolian, Vulcanian, Peléan, Plinian, and Surtseyan. The classification is based upon the volcano's predominant eruptive style, which considers both the violence of the eruption (as indicated by plume height, frequency of event, and volume of material) and the type of material ejected (ranging from the effusion of liquid lava flows to a gaseous mixture that contains ash, fragments of rock, and droplets or clots of liquid). A Volcanic Explosivity Index (VEI) was developed to assist with the classification of an eruption. Calm, effusive lava eruptions are given a VEI value of 0, whereas the most violent eruptions have VEI values of 8.

The most nonexplosive class is the Hawaiian class of eruption. It involves minimal explosions (VEI values of 0 or 1) and a calm outpouring of low-viscosity, low-silicon lava. When these occur on the floor of the ocean at mid-oceanic ridges and ocean basin hot spots they are called submarine eruptions. The pressure of the overlying seawater helps to nullify the explosiveness of the eruption.

A Hawaiian eruption can emerge from a single vent that erupts almost on a daily basis for months on end. These eruptions typically form shield volcanoes with gentle slopes of 3 to 5 degrees. Shield volcanoes may rise from the seafloor to become islands, which can continue growing for another 13,123 feet (4,000 meters) above sea level (Mauna Loa in Hawaii is 13,678 feet above sea level and still growing, as evidenced by a 1984 eruption).

When Hawaiian eruptions occur from long fissures, they can produce large volumes of liquid lava. The Great Tolbachik fissure eruption in Russia in 1975 produced over 70,629 cubic feet (2 cubic kilometers) of lava that covered more than 15.4 square miles (40 square kilometers). In Iceland the Laki fissure eruption of 1783 covered 102 square miles (265 square kilometers), destroyed four-fifths of the sheep and half the cattle, and caused 10,000 residents to starve to death during the ensuing winter.

The Strombolian class of eruptions is weakly explosive (VEI values of 1 or 2). These eruptions usually begin with the volcano tossing out molten debris to form cinders and clots of liquid that solidify in the air to fall as bombs. This high-arching, incandescent portion of the eruption resembles firework fountains. These bursts last only a few

*Lava streams down Mauna Loa in Hawaii.* (National Oceanic and Atmospheric Administration)

seconds, with long pauses of twenty minutes or more between the bursts. Magma can rise from 328 feet (100 meters) to 0.6 mile (1 kilometer) into the air, breaking into lava clots of all sizes. Many Strombolian eruptions are known for throwing bombs hundreds of feet into the air every few seconds. The pyroclastic display is often followed by fluid lava flows. Normally short-lived, the eruptions last a few months before pausing for a year or so. The cinder cones associated with an eruptive phase are rarely over 820 feet (250 meters) in height and the lava flow rarely exceeds 6.2 miles (10 kilometers) in length. The explosion of Etna in Italy in 1500 B.C.E. is thought to be the first historic record of any volcano recorded. Etna has over one hundred recorded eruptions of Strombolian activity, and it still erupts every few years.

The Vulcanian class of eruptions is more explosive, with VEI values ranging from 2 to 4. The magma is usually more viscous and has considerable strength. The eruption column is quite noticeable, rising from 1.9 to 9.3 miles (3 to 15 kilometers) above the volcano. There are few, if any, lava flows; rather, these eruptions are characterized by thick liquid clots being shot far into the air. Vulcanian eruptions' explosiveness is so powerful that it sometimes destroys part of the volcanic edifice.

These volcanoes can lay dormant for over one hundred years and then burst into a noisy, violent eruption. Nuées ardentes are often by-products of Vulcanian explosions, and when the nuée ardente is associated with the collapse or explosion of a volcanic dome sitting over the vent it is classed as a Peléan eruption (often considered a subclass of Vulcanian eruptions).

The dome-building phase of the Peléan eruptions can begin when the center of the crater starts to bulge upward, revealing a spine mantled with explosive debris from the floor of the crater. The dome can grow as much as 98 feet (30 meters) a day to a final height of 1,969 feet (600 meters) or more. The elevation of the crater floor can rise 328 feet (100 meters) above its normal level, changing the shape of the volcano to an almost-level platform. The explosions can shatter the dome, and its pieces can become swept up in the turbulent flow of the nuée ardente. The dome can be rebuilt in the crater again and exist in a quiet phase.

A nuée ardente has so much gas that it is a semifrictionless fluid, and it can race down the slopes of the volcano at velocities of up to 311 miles (500 kilometers) per hour. It is an avalanche of hot, frothy clots of lava, noxious gases, fragments of molten ash, and incandescent boulders. A large cloud of ash and gas rises above the nuée ardente as it moves across the ground, and the clouds can asphyxiate animals and humans that are near the nuée ardente.

*Nevado del Ruiz spawned many mudflows called lahars, which destroyed towns and caused many deaths in northern Colombia.* (National Oceanic and Atmospheric Administration)

The most famous Peléan eruption is the eruption of Pelée in 1902, which became the basis for this subclass of volcanic eruptions. Lamington in New Guinea has produced both Vulcanian and Peléan eruptions. It was not thought to be a volcano until, in 1951, it erupted a nuée ardente that devastated an area of 69.5 square miles (180 square kilometers) and killed 3,000 people. Since then, several volcanic domes have grown in its summit crater and have subsequently been destroyed by later explosions.

Plinian eruptions are the most explosive and rare of the volcanic eruptions of historic record, having VEI values of 4 to 6. Although Ultra-Plinian explosive eruptions (VEI values of 7 and 8) have been deduced from the geological record of their deposits, no Ultra-Plinian eruptions have occurred in recorded history. A powerful eruption shaft develops over the vent, having speeds of several feet per second and shooting volcanic materials in a column that can reach 15.5 miles (25 kilometers) or more in height. As the volcanic fragments falls they can cover a huge area of ground (hundreds of square miles). Plinian eruptive fragments are predominantly made of bubbly pumice and ash. Pumice falling fairly near the volcano can attain thicknesses of close to 100 feet. The Tambora eruption of 1815 in Indonesia is the largest of all historic eruptions. It killed 92,000 people, had an eruption column that was 25 miles (40 kilometers) in height, and deposited 164 feet (50 meters) of pumice in surrounding areas.

The eruption plume of a Plinian eruption will bring an abundance of ash into the stratosphere, which can circle the globe for several years before falling back to the ground. After the 1991 eruption of Pinatubo in the Philippines, the dust clouds became an aviation hazard because neither pilots nor radar could distinguish water-based clouds from dust clouds. In the months following the eruption 14 airliners developed engine problems from dust clouds, and 9 had to make emergency landings.

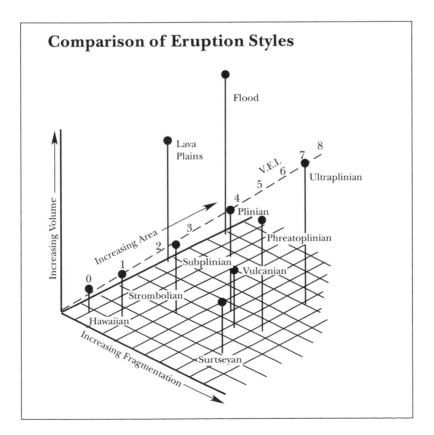

**Comparison of Eruption Styles**

There is a strong correlation between large eruptions and a change in the weather conditions. The eruption of El Chichón (VEI of 4) in Mexico in 1982 was the first eruption cloud to be tracked in the atmosphere by weather satellites. The eruption injected 3.3 million tons of gaseous sulfur into the atmosphere, which converted to sulfuric acid within three months. Following the Laki eruption of 1783 the acid aerosol contaminated the pastures and animals grazing on these grasses, and they died within three days. Once dispersed, the dust and gases can reflect incoming solar radiation and reduce the earth's temperatures. Following the 1815 eruption of Tambora, the coldest summer in over 250 years of record keeping was recorded. The average summer temperature was 2 degrees colder than the second-coldest summer. The Pinatubo eruption of 1991 caused the average world temperature to drop by 0.5 degree.

## GEOGRAPHY

The vast majority of the active volcanoes on Earth are associated with long, narrow belts of fractured rocks. The longest belt and the site of over 75 percent of all the volcanic activity on earth takes place underwater, along the crests of the mid-oceanic ridges. Although the ridge system is over 37,284 miles (60,000 kilometers) in length, the actual number and magnitude of the eruptions are untold. The submarine volcanic events are not counted on the list of active volcanoes until the lava deposits bring the submarine volcano to the surface as an island. Iceland, which is the largest island on the Mid-Atlantic Ridge, has twenty-two active volcanoes. Other notable volcanoes with historic eruptions from the flanks of the Mid-Atlantic Ridge are the Azores, Ascension Island, and Tristan da Cunha.

The longest belt of active volcanoes virtually circles the Pacific Ocean and is commonly called the Pacific "Ring of Fire." Two-thirds of the world's active volcanoes occur in this belt. The volcanic chains making up the Ring of Fire are the Cascades of the United States and Canada (Mount St. Helens), the Mexican Volcanic Belt (El Chichón), the Central American Belt (Santa María), the Andes of South America (Nevado del Ruiz), New Zealand (Ngauruhoe), Tonga (Niuafo'ou), New Guinea (Lamington), Indonesia (Kelut), the Philippines (Pinatubo), the Ryukyu Island arc (Kutinoerabu), the volcanic arc of the Mariana, the Izu and Bonin Islands (Miyakzima), Japan (Unzen), the Kamchatka Peninsula (Bezymianny), and the Aleutian Islands and South Alaska (Katmai).

The third major belt of active volcanoes starts at the Mid-Atlantic Ridge at the Azores and runs east through the Mediterranean Sea (Etna and Vesuvius), across the northern Arabian Peninsula, down the Malaysian Peninsula (Krakatau), and connects with the Ring of Fire in Indonesia. The smallest belt of active volcanoes that is isolated from the other longer belts is the volcanic island arc that occurs along the eastern edge of the Caribbean Sea (Pelée).

There are a number of isolated volcanic centers that occur in the interior of continents and ocean basins, usually a considerable distance from the linear belts. The island of Hawaii in the center of the Pacific basin has experienced over 100 recorded eruptions since 1700, and Nyiragongo in Zaire had a lava lake in its summit crater from the time of its discovery in 1894 until 1977, when it suddenly drained 28.8 million cubic yards (22 million cubic meters) of lava down its flanks and killed 70 people. The active volcanoes outside of the system of belts account for less than 5 percent of all historic eruptions.

## PREVENTION AND PREPARATIONS

Volcanic eruptions are virtually impossible to prevent, but there have been some fairly successful efforts made to divert or control the direction of lava flows and lahars (mudflows) once volcanoes have erupted. Lahars are flash floods, having the consistency of wet cement, which are caused when a volcanic eruption melts glacial ice or occurs in a lava lake. Less than 10 percent of the diversion barriers for lava flows have been successful. In Iceland an advancing lava flow was cooled by a spray of water from hoses, which forced the lava to spread sideways. Aerial bombing to collapse crater walls and disrupt existing magma flows has also been tried. These techniques usually at least slow down the lava flow if they do not divert it, providing for needed evacuation time.

An unusual prevention measure was used on Kelut on Java after the 1919 eruption produced a lahar that killed 5,500 people. The Dutch colonial authorities dug a series of underground tunnels through the crater wall, draining most of the lake. The volcano's next eruption, in 1951, emptied into a lake that was 164 feet (50 meters) lower. There

*A volcano erupts in the middle of Lake Taal in the Philippines in 1965. Islands can be formed by volcanic activity.* (National Oceanic and Atmospheric Administration)

were no lahars produced, but the tunnel system was destroyed. In 1964 the crater again acquired 52.3 million cubic yards (40 million cubic meters) of water, and scientists asked that new tunnels be dug. A 1966 eruption again caused lahars, which killed hundreds of people, and new tunnels were dug to drain the lake. In 1990 prediction techniques forewarned of another eruption, and 60,000 people were evacuated. The eruption did not produce a lahar, but 32 casualties occurred because of roofs collapsing under the heavy weight of the ash and pumice. Steps are now also made to reinforce roofs of homes and buildings in order to support the weight of falling debris.

The best prevention of a high death toll is orderly evacuation. Evacuation plans require a high degree of cooperation between civil authorities and scientists, as well as an amazing amount of preparation. In the scientific arena, the first step to being prepared for a volcanic eruption is to monitor the activity of a volcano. Most volcanoes give some warning signs of an upcoming eruption. Normally, magma will move into the area below the volcano in a reservoir called the magma chamber. The magma then travels up the chamber and begins to release gases. As the magma moves up the chamber it produces small earthquakes and ground vibrations.

There are three forms of seismic activity: short-period earthquakes, long-period earthquakes, and harmonic tremors. Short-period earthquakes are caused by the fracturing of brittle rock as the magma forces its way up the chamber; they signify that the magma is coming near the surface. Long-period earthquakes are thought to be the result of increased gas pressure in the volcano. Harmonic tremors are the result of sustained movement of magma below the surface. Scientists use seismographs to monitor the earthquakes.

As the magma moves toward the surface, a volcano will begin to swell, and the degree of slope of the volcano may change. Fumaroles, which are vents giving off gas, will often increase their sulfur content. Scientists can monitor these events with a number of tools: Tiltmeters measure the change in slope, and geodimeters measure the amount of swelling in the volcano. Gases released near the volcano can be measured by spectrometers.

Many regions have established volcano observatories to monitor ground motion for dangerously active volcanoes. The Rabaul Volcano Observatory in New Guinea recorded two swarms of 1,000 earthquakes in a two-day period in 1984. In June of that month they recorded 13,749 individual earthquakes. They also recorded an uplift of 63 inches (160 centimeters) over the nine months leading up to the earthquakes. With these techniques, scientists are becoming skilled at predicting volcanic eruptions.

Monitoring of volcanoes can save countless live. Communication with the populace is of utmost importance; restricted areas must be drawn, and certain areas must be completely or partially evacuated. In 1985, the eruption of Nevado del Ruiz in Colombia was well monitored, but due to lack of communication the town of Armero was not prepared for evacuation, and a lahar swept down the slope and killed at least 23,000 people, 90 percent of the town's population.

Before the eruption of Pinatubo in June of 1991, scientists worked closely with civil defense authorities in the Philippines to establish a four-stage plan leading to the eruption. They evacuated more than 80,000 people from the area. Each stage of the plan was implemented when the scientists measured a specific level of sulfur in the fumarolic gases, a certain number and strength of earthquakes occurred, or a specified amount of rise and tilt of the volcano came to pass. With each stage the authorities evacuated a larger area and took actions to increase their readiness. The death toll could have run in the tens of thousands, but because of advance preparations and education, only a few hundred people died.

## RESCUE AND RELIEF EFFORTS

More deaths often occur in the aftermath of a violent eruption—from starvation and disease—than from the eruption itself. Survivors usually return to their homes after the eruption has waned. In the historic past, areas around Plinian eruptions were deeply buried, with complete loss of all crops and pastures and severe loss of livestock and potable water supplies. Most countries did not have disaster relief plans, nor was international aid available. This usually led to a higher death toll from starvation and disease than was attributed to the ejected materials from the volcano.

The modern world has vastly differing degrees of readiness. Mexico, with over a dozen active volcanoes, had no civil defense program or contingency plans for evacuation, shelter, or resettlement when El Chichón erupted in 1982. Italy set up its Ministry of Civil Protection in 1981. Many poor countries with active volcanoes have no volcano monitoring programs and no civil defense systems for volcanic eruptions.

Japan is at the other end of the scale in terms of readiness. That country established volcano surveillance and disaster plans in the 1950's. The On-take area is a model of preparation, with concrete volcanic shelters at intervals along all the roads in the area. Within the river systems special dams and canals have been built to impede the progress of lahars. Children wear helmets when they go to school; once a year all citizens in the area participate in a rehearsal of a full-scale evacuation. Temporary lodgings are built and maintained, and the monitoring information from the volcano is computerized and automatically transmitted to the civil authorities.

## IMPACT

Volcanoes are the second most destructive natural disasters on Earth. Historically, two-thirds of all eruptions have caused fatalities. The chief causes of death from violent eruptions are suffocation and drowning. Most catastrophic eruptions occur in populated coastal regions, and tsunamis (tidal waves) generated by eruptions can exact a much greater toll than the actual erupted materials. In the past five hundred years, volcanic eruptions have killed 200,000 people and have cost billions of dollars in damage to homes and property. During the twentieth century, volcanic eruptions killed an average of 800 people per year.

## HISTORICAL OVERVIEW

A dark plume obscures the sun and the sky; acrid fumes irritate the mucous membranes as a sulfurous stench pervades the air. Intermittently, accompanied by deafening noise, lightning, and thunder, eruptions spew fire and brimstone into the air, hurling hot, sputtering chunks of rock far from the mountain. This is the experience of those who have lived near volcanic eruptions and were fortunate enough to survive. In the face of such incredible power, death and destruction, and dramatic changes in landscape, cultures throughout time have attached great religious significance to volcanoes.

Within Western European cultures, objective written descriptions of volcanic events date back to 79 C.E., when Vesuvius, a famous volcano to the northeast of the Bay of Naples in Italy, erupted. The towns of Pompeii and Herculaneum were buried beneath ash and pumice. Pliny the Elder, a well-respected admiral in the Roman navy, perished, and the historian Tacitus, reconstructing the conditions of his death, sought information from his nephew: Pliny the Younger, in two letters, described what had occurred. The volcano had not been active for several centuries, and no one considered it a threat.

Benjamin Franklin was among the first to recognize the global climatic effects of volcanoes when he speculated that the 1783 Laki fissure eruption in Iceland was responsible for the bitter winter of 1783-1784 in Paris. Temperature records for this year from the eastern United States show an average winter temperature 41 degrees Fahrenheit (4.8 degrees Celsius) lower than the 225-year average. The eruption, lasting eight months, produced the largest lava flow in historic time, but much of its deadly effect resulted from the gases that escaped.

Modern analysis of gas samples retrieved from Greenland ice cores reveals a dramatic spike in acidity corresponding to this eruption. It has been estimated that the influx of acid gases into the atmosphere from this one eruption is about equivalent to the annual global anthropogenic input. Sulfur dioxide is responsible for much of the acidity observed in the ice cores, but hydrogen fluoride from the eruption is suspected to have killed most of the cattle in the region, which caused a famine. Three-quarters of the livestock in Iceland, and 25 percent of the human population, died.

The 1815 eruption of Tambora, in Indonesia, produced much greater climatic effects. Whereas the relatively calm basaltic eruption of Laki was probably confined to the lower levels of the atmosphere, where precipitation is constantly removing dust and ash, the very explosive eruption of Tambora injected ash and gases into the stratosphere, far above these elevations. Records from astronomers show that the haze produced by this eruption persisted for at least two and a half years. During 1816, often referred to as the Year Without a Summer, New England experienced a frost every month of the summer. Crops failed, and famines struck much of Europe, Canada, and the United States.

When Krakatau erupted in 1883 it generated intense scientific interest. More than 36,000 people died, most from tsunamis. The eruption was witnessed by many who survived to write about it, and it was the subject of research for the Royal Society and the Dutch government. Heard as far away as 2,990 miles (4,811 kilometers), causing atmospheric pressure fluctuations that circled the globe many times, and lowering temperatures in the Northern Hemisphere by 0.25 degree Celsius for a year or two, this eruption captured the attention of scientists in a way no earlier eruption had. Strange optical effects were observed, including blue tinges on the sun and the moon. Solar energy reaching the earth at an observatory in France decreased initially by 20 percent, then remained 10 percent below normal for many months.

By the second half of the nineteenth century the Neptunist theory, which held that all rocks had precipitated from a primitive ocean, was no longer impeding the development of the earth sciences. Many geologists went into the field to study active and ancient volcanoes. Laboratory techniques evolved rapidly, and by the early twentieth century many of the processes and reactions involved in the melting and freezing of rock had been sketched out.

Pelée erupted in 1902, and suddenly a great deal was learned about pyroclastic flows. Emanating from the volcano after a period of minor eruptive activity, these flows raced down the slopes at velocities of about 99 miles (160 kilometers) per hour, running over and totally destroying the town of St. Pierre. The force of such a blast was devastating in itself, but its temperature, estimated to have been about 1,292 degrees Fahrenheit (700 degrees Celsius), made it particularly deadly. Of the 30,000 people in the town that morning, only 2 survived—and they were horribly burned. These pyroclastic flows, which were given the name nuées ardentes, or "glowing avalanches," had never been witnessed before—at least not by anyone who survived.

Enough was learned, however, to be able to identify this mechanism as having been responsible for similar, but much larger, deposits displaced during the eruption of Katmai a decade later. Only distant ashfalls were directly observed from this volcano, located in a sparsely populated area of Alaska. It was not until 1916 that an expedition actually visited the site of the eruption. Still, there was enough heat left in the deposit to continue to turn water from the soil below it into steam. This region has been called the Valley of Ten Thousand Smokes ever since.

*Cars trapped in a lava flow in Hawaii.* (National Oceanic and Atmospheric Administration)

Over the next sixty years the theory of plate tectonics was developed. It explained why volcanoes occur where they do and why their rocks, shapes, and eruptive styles vary so much. The theory was able to show why some volcanoes, such as all of the Hawaiian islands—other than the big island of Hawaii—are truly dead and pose no risk at all, while most other volcanoes are capable of erupting centuries after their last activity.

One of those that did return to activity was a volcano of the Cascade Range in southwestern Washington, named Mount St. Helens. In 1978 scientists from the U.S. Geological Survey had predicted that this volcano would erupt again, perhaps by the end of the century. In March and April of 1980 it began to exhibit some signs of life. Seismic activity and small ash eruptions indicated that the long-sleeping giant was coming to life. Well aware of the risks it posed, government agencies began restricting access to the region and preparing evacuation plans. The media converged on the region, and there was television news coverage nearly every night.

Peculiar seismic signals, called harmonic tremors, were detected, signaling the ascent of melted rock into the upper reaches of the volcano. This magma caused the mountain to swell, increasing in size by as much as 3 feet a day. Such bulging made the slopes on the mountain steeper and thus less stable. On May 18 a moderate earthquake proved to be the last straw. A major landslide occurred, and as a huge portion of the mountain slid down, the side of the chamber of pressurized magma was exposed. A dramatic lateral blast ensued, devastating vast areas to the north in just a few minutes. This was followed by a vertical blast that transported huge quantities of ash as high as 12.4 miles (20 kilometers) into the atmosphere.

Scientists have estimated that the energy released by Mount St. Helens was the equivalent of one atomic bomb being dropped per second for nine hours. The initial blast was nearly horizontal, which had not been expected, and was far more destructive than anyone had imagined. Still, because of excellent monitoring of the developing events, cooperation between scientists and the government, and strong communication with the populace, only 60 people died.

Similar scientific work and careful monitoring were unable to avoid a calamity a few year later, in 1985, when mudflows, or lahars, from the eruption of Colombia's Nevado del Ruiz killed at least

23,000 people. Scientists had accurately predicted that an eruption would melt much of the glacial ice near the summit, producing huge mudflows that would flow down the river valleys toward the populated towns, including one named Armero. They also knew an eruption was imminent. As with Mount St. Helens, there had been a month of small eruptions in advance of the large one. An hour after the main eruption began authorities urged evacuation of the downstream towns, but the order to evacuate Armero was not given for another five hours. When it was given, radio communication was not established. It is likely that most of the inhabitants would have survived if effective evacuation measures had begun in a timely fashion.

No warning existed for more than 1,700 people in Cameroon, Africa, in 1986, when a cloud of carbon dioxide swept down on them in their sleep. Carbon dioxide enters Lake Nyos from molten rock beneath it. The lake is stratified, and most of the carbon dioxide enters the dense water near the bottom. If the water is suddenly mixed by a landslide, an earthquake, or even stiff breezes, the gas-charged water can rise to the surface, where the pressure is lower and the carbon dioxide comes out of the solution. A cloud of gas, denser than air, builds up and eventually races down the valleys, killing everything in its wake by asphyxiation. Now that this hazard has been identified, efforts are underway to remove the carbon dioxide before it builds up to unstable concentrations.

The successful efforts to mitigate the effects of the eruption of Pinatubo, which occurred in the Philippines in 1991, provide hope. A series of evacuations proceeded in parallel with increasing volcanic activity. Although complicated by the arrival of Typhoon Yunya, the evacuation of more than 200,000 people undoubtedly saved a great many lives. This eruption, the third largest of the twentieth century and occurring in a densely populated area, killed only 320 people.

*Dion C. Stewart and Toby R. Stewart*
*Otto H. Muller*

**BIBLIOGRAPHY**
Bardintzeff, Jacques-Marie, and Alexander R. McBirney. *Volcanology.* 2d ed. Sudbury, Mass.: Jones and Bartlett, 2000. This is a more advanced book that gives details of gas generation and mechanisms for explosive eruptions.

Bullard, Fred M. *Volcanoes of the Earth.* 2d rev. ed. Austin: University of Texas Press, 1984. Still one of the best books on eruption classification, with excellent photographs, line drawings, and illustrations of volcanoes and volcanic processes.

Decker, Robert, and Barbara Decker. *Volcanoes.* 4th ed. New York: W. H. Freeman, 2006. A book for general readers that introduces all aspects of volcanology.

Fisher, Richard V. *Out of the Crater: Chronicles of a Volcanologist.* Princeton, N.J.: Princeton University Press, 1999. This is a personal narrative of visits to many of the volcanic sites mentioned in this article.

Francis, Peter, and Clive Oppenheimer. *Volcanoes.* 2d ed. New York: Oxford University Press, 2004. This book gives information on nearly five hundred volcanic eruptions. It has an interesting chapter on volcanoes and changing weather.

Macdonald, Gordon A. *Volcanoes.* Englewood Cliffs, N.J.: Prentice-Hall, 1972. This college-level textbook contains a map and tabulated data on more than five hundred active volcanoes.

Scarth, Alwyn. *Volcanoes: An Introduction.* College Station: Texas A&M University Press, 1994. This book has a large section on predictions. It also provides many interesting accounts of historic eruptions.

_____. *Vulcan's Fury: Man Against the Volcano.* New ed. New Haven, Conn.: Yale University Press, 2001. Describes 15 notable eruptions in history, from Vesuvius in 79 to Pinatubo in 1991, using firsthand accounts.

# WIND GUSTS

FACTORS INVOLVED: Geography, temperature,
   topography, weather conditions, atmospheric
   pressure, wind
REGIONS AFFECTED: Cities, coasts, forests, mountains,
   plains, towns, and valleys

## DEFINITION

Wind gusts can be violent, with loss of property and life measured in millions, even billions of dollars. They can occur anywhere on earth, sometimes without warning. Wind shear, a localized wind gust, can imperil aircraft, causing collisions with terrain on takeoff and landing.

## SCIENCE

Wind gusts, also called wind shear, occur for a number of reasons, sometimes seemingly at random. No place on the earth's surface is immune to wind gusts, although some areas are more likely to experience them than others. Gusts may be localized differences in atmospheric pressure caused by frontal weather changes. These occur most often in the spring and fall seasons. Normally, fronts having a temperature difference at the surface of 10 degrees Fahrenheit (5 degrees Celsius) or more and with a frontal speed of at least 30 knots are prone to creating wind gust conditions.

These so-called cold fronts contain a wedge of cold air at their leading edge. This wedge of cold air pushes warm air that is ahead of it upward very rapidly. If the warm air is rich in water vapor, as is seen in the southeastern United States, severe storms erupt ahead of the cold front and may continue until it passes. The weather proverb "If the clouds move against the wind, rain will follow" implies a cold front where clouds in the upper wind are moving in a different direction from clouds driven by lower winds. Most experienced aircraft pilots know how to fly cold frontal boundaries for fuel efficiency, in effect gaining a tailwind both ahead of and into the front.

To determine the strength of wind gusts, a good reference is the Beaufort scale. Beaufort numbers vary from 0, no wind, to 12, which

*News photographer Howard Clifford runs from the Tacoma Narrows Bridge as it collapses following a wind gust in 1940.* (University of Washington Libraries, Special Collections, FAR021)

depicts winds in excess of 73 miles per hour. People can start to feel the wind at Beaufort 2. A Beaufort 6 means that an umbrella is hard to control and large tree branches are moving. Serious damage potential arrives with Beaufort 10, when trees are uprooted and considerable structural damage can be incurred by anything in the path of the wind gust.

Thunderstorms, whether a product of a cold front or local air mass heating, are responsible for the majority of wind gusts. Thousands of thunderstorms occur across the earth's surface every day. Typical of thunderstorms are the "first gust," the rapid shift and increase in wind velocity just before a thunderstorm hits, and the "downburst," or rapid downward movement of cooled air in and around the thunderstorm cell. A thunderstorm pulls in relatively warm air near the earth's surface, then sends it skyward at several thousand feet per minute, rapidly cooling it. The cool air, becoming more dense and heavy, then plummets back down to the earth's surface. This downward plunge of 7 to 10 miles creates tremendous inertia that can only be dissipated by outflow when the mass strikes the surface. This effect can be compared to dumping a bucket of water on a concrete surface: The "splash" is the same as the outflow from the downburst.

The gusty winds associated with mature thunderstorms are the result of these large downdrafts striking the earth's surface and spreading out horizontally. Some gusts can change direction by as much as 180 degrees very rapidly and reach velocities of 100 knots as far as 10 miles ahead of the thunderstorm. Low-level gusts, typically between the earth's surface and an altitude of 1,500 feet, may increase as much as 50 percent, with most of the increase occurring in the first 150 feet. This makes them particularly dangerous for aircraft in take-off and landing.

The downburst is an extremely intense localized downdraft from a thunderstorm. The downdraft frequently exceeds 720 feet per minute in vertical velocity at 300 feet above the earth's surface. This velocity can exceed an aircraft's climb capability, even that of large commercial and military jets. This downdraft is usually much closer to the thunderstorm than the first gust. One clue is the presence of dust clouds, roll clouds, or intense rainfall.

Hurricanes and cyclones also breed large wind gusts. Although winds from these weather phenomena have predictable direction and velocity, tornadoes and whirlwinds imbedded in them can produce wind gusts capable of major damage.

Very local gusting is often referred to as wind shear, and it can be horizontal or vertical. Horizontal shear can move an aircraft off the centerline of a precision approach to an airport. While annoying, it is not usually harmful. Vertical shear, however, is potentially lethal to aircraft. The change in velocity or direction can cause serious changes in lift, indicated airspeed, and thrust requirements, often exceeding the pilot's and the aircraft's ability to recover.

A decreasing head wind can cause airspeed and lift of the aircraft to decrease. The pilot reacts with application of power and nose-up attitude of the aircraft. Although overshoots of the intended approach may occur, the pilot is usually able to go around and land safely. Decreasing tailwind causes an increased lift, and the aircraft climbs above the intended approach path.

Modern commercial pilot training devotes significant time to wind shear problems. Using computerized flight simulators, the entire array of wind shear problems can be programmed for flight crews. This increases their awareness and application of wind shear recovery without exposing them to the hazards of ineffective recovery techniques if using actual aircraft.

## GEOGRAPHY

Topographic features, both natural and human-made, can promote wind gusts. Most people have experienced this in cities with tall buildings, where the wind intensity is much greater in the gaps between large buildings and swirling winds are expected.

Conditions peculiar to the southwestern United States prompt the formation of temperature inversions. These inversions are caused by overnight cooling, where a relatively cool air mass hugs the ground and is overlain by warmer air in the low-level jetstream. High winds from the low-level jet sometimes mix with this inversion, and significant wind gusts may occur at the interface with 90-degree shifts in direction and 20- to 30-knot increases in wind velocity common.

On a much larger scale are the gusts resulting from high winds in mountain passes, on the leeward side of large mountains, and across valleys between mountain ranges. A weather phenomenon often called a "mountain rotor" results from differential heating across a valley between two mountain ranges. Air flowing down an upwind mountain during the day is heated, traverses a relatively cool air mass in the valley, then moves across the downwind mountain, causing the turbulence at the boundary of the cooled and heated air masses described above. As the air is heated in the morning, a weak rising motion of the cool air is induced and pulls the air currents attempting to climb the downwind mountain back into the valley. This back-rotation creates a rotary motion that contains both horizontal and vertical wind gusts.

At least one commercial aircraft accident has been tentatively blamed on a rotor. Rotors can be seen, unless the atmosphere is devoid of moisture, as nearly round symmetrical clouds in mountain valleys. Pilots undergoing mountain-flying training are cautioned to steer clear of these rotors. A flight into a dry rotor is usually dangerous.

The roughness of the earth's surface plays a major role in determining wind gust intensity. This roughness can occur from obstacles or terrain contours, called orography. Orography promotes tunnel effects (mountain passes) and hill effects (lee—the side sheltered from the wind—of mountains). Pilots are very familiar with this effect. A very calm outbound flight in the morning after a cold-front passage can mean a bumpy return flight in the afternoon as the frontal wind gains intensity and flows over rough topography.

In general, the rougher the earth's surface, the more the wind will be slowed. Forests and large cities slow the wind more than lakes and prairies. Surface roughness can be classified as to its ability to slow wind. For example, landscapes with many trees and buildings have a roughness class of 3 or 4, while a large water surface has a roughness class of 0. Open terrain has a roughness class of 0.5. Roughness length is used with roughness class, and relates to the distance above ground level where the wind speed theoretically should be 0.

**PREVENTION AND PREPARATIONS**

The aviation industry has been particularly interested in wind gusts, or wind shear, because of their potential effect on aircraft performance in takeoff and landing. According to National Transportation Safety Board (NTSB) records, wind shears contributed to approximately 50 percent of all commercial airline fatalities between 1974 and 1985. The Federal Aviation Administration (FAA) has required some type of wind shear hazard detection systems on scheduled commercial aircraft since 1995.

Pulsed Doppler radar is the primary means of detection of wind gusts for aircraft crews and ground-based air controllers and weather prognosticators. Doppler radar senses speed and direction in the same manner as police traffic radar. A well-understood Doppler effect is a train whistle that is always higher in pitch when the train is approaching than when moving away.

Doppler weather radar bounces its pulses off raindrops in storm clouds. If the raindrops are moving toward the radar set, the reflected signal is higher in frequency than if the rain is falling vertically. Frequencies are compared, and color displays are created to depict areas of precipitation and wind shear. Some Doppler radar sets create an audible warning to aircrews if wind shear is nearby. Effective though dangerous indicators of wind shear are reports from pilots experiencing it. Air-traffic controllers solicit these reports, and many may be received in a short period of time in areas where pilots are experiencing wind shear conditions.

Aside from aviation and its vulnerability to wind gusts, other modes of transportation are frequently disturbed by wind gusts. Mountain valleys and other gust-prone locations often experience upended tractor-trailer rigs, which are typically top-heavy and show a considerable broadside resistance to the wind. Sailing ships and relatively light watercraft are also prone to upset by wind gusts. Even with no sails in the wind, boats are difficult to steer with changing wind speeds bearing against their hulls.

### RESCUE AND RELIEF EFFORTS

Wind gusts produce the same results as tornadoes but are even more localized. Building damage and injury to humans and animals can occur. Trauma-related injuries are typical, including broken bones, excessive lacerations, and imbedded debris. Police and fire officials usually handle the localized nature of wind gust damage, although for widespread damage, the Red Cross and Salvation Army, as well as other relief organizations, may assist victims.

Local authorities also customarily oversee property damage. Clearing may be necessary to restore public utilities and roadways. Insurance adjusters are frequent visitors to damage sites so that they can assess the severity of the damage to client property and recommend compensation.

### IMPACT

Like that of tornadoes, wind gust damage is not long-lasting. It has no significant effect on local topography, but it can cause extensive damage to human-made structures. The famous "Galloping Gertie," or Tacoma Narrows Bridge, was set in motion by wind gusts and ultimately destroyed by its own harmonic frequencies. Windows and trim in large buildings can be damaged or even removed by wind gusts. Large signs and other similar displays are also frequently damaged or dislodged by gusty winds. These articles pose a risk to passersby on the streets below.

Perhaps most important, wind gusts damage aircraft quite easily. Those aircraft on the ground not secured by tie-down lines may be blown around by gusty winds and extensively damaged. However, the most important damage to aircraft occurs when wind gusts overcome the pilot's ability to maintain flying conditions in takeoff or landing configurations. Aircraft collisions with the ground can cause minor damage or extensive loss of life and totally destroy aircraft. Literally thousands of aircraft accidents can be traced to wind gusts as the primary cause of or at least a major contributor to the accident. A portion of the avionics industry is devoted exclusively to assessing the severity of wind shear and its effect on the operation of aircraft. Even local television stations proudly advertise that their weather gurus are equipped with the most modern Doppler radar for the safety and convenience of their viewers.

*Charles Haynes*

**BIBLIOGRAPHY**

Freier, George D. *Weather Proverbs: How 600 Proverbs, Sayings, and Poems Accurately Explain Our Weather.* Tucson, Ariz.: Fisher Books, 1992. A very interesting book on weather phenomena, with modern explanations given to ancient weather lore.

Kimble, George H. T. *Our American Weather.* New York: McGraw Hill, 1955. This is a very readable book, unique in that it depicts U.S. weather by month. Entertaining as well as informative.

National Aeronautics and Space Administration. *Making the Skies Safe from Windshear.* http://www.nasa.gov/centers/langley/news/factsheets/ Windshear.html. A series of NASA documents that detail its research into the causes and detection of wind shear as it affects aircraft.

National Transportation Safety Board. http://www.ntsb.gov/ntsb/query.asp. This is the NTSB's aviation accident/incident database. Although cold and cryptic details are the essence of this Web site, it nevertheless details the mounting toll of aircraft accidents resulting in part from wind gusts.

Palmén, E., and C. W. Newton. *Atmospheric Circulation Systems: Their Structure and Physical Interpretation.* New York: Academic Press, 1969. Although some knowledge of calculus is necessary to master this book, it still has many readable pages concerning global weather at the lower altitudes that can be understood by most individuals.

Wood, Richard A., ed. *The Weather Almanac: A Reference Guide to Weather, Climate, and Related Issues in the United States and Its Key Cities.* 11th ed. Detroit: Thompson/Gale, 2004. Provides a detailed description of the Beaufort number for wind speed and contains much weather data.

# INDEXES

#  CATEGORY LIST

**AVALANCHES**
Avalanches (overview)
1999: The Galtür avalanche, Austria

**BLIZZARDS, FREEZES, ICE STORMS, AND HAIL**
Blizzards, Freezes, Ice Storms, and Hail (overview)
1888: The Great Blizzard of 1888, U.S. Northeast
1996: The Mount Everest Disaster, Nepal

**COMETS.** *See* **METEORITES AND COMETS**

**CYCLONES.** *See* **HURRICANES, TYPHOONS, AND CYCLONES;**
**TORNADOES**

**DROUGHTS**
Droughts (overview)
1932: The Dust Bowl, Great Plains

**DUST STORMS AND SANDSTORMS**
Dust Storms and Sandstorms (overview)
1932: The Dust Bowl, Great Plains

**EARTHQUAKES**
Earthquakes (overview)
526: The Antioch earthquake, Syria
1692: The Port Royal earthquake, Jamaica
1755: The Lisbon earthquake, Portugal
1811: New Madrid earthquakes, Missouri
1906: The Great San Francisco Earthquake
1908: The Messina earthquake, Italy
1923: The Great Kwanto Earthquake, Japan
1964: The Great Alaska Earthquake
1970: The Ancash earthquake, Peru
1976: The Tangshan earthquake, China
1985: The Mexico City earthquake

1988: The Leninakan earthquake, Armenia
1989: The Loma Prieta earthquake, Northern California
1994: The Northridge earthquake, Southern California
1995: The Kobe earthquake, Japan
1999: The İzmit earthquake, Turkey
2003: The Bam earthquake, Iran
2005: The Kashmir earthquake, Pakistan

**EL NIÑO**

El Niño (overview)
1982: El Niño, Pacific Ocean

**EPIDEMICS**

Epidemics (overview)
430 B.C.E.: The Plague of Athens
1320: The Black Death, Europe
1520: Aztec Empire smallpox epidemic
1665: The Great Plague of London
1878: The Great Yellow Fever Epidemic, Memphis
1892: Cholera pandemic
1900: Typhoid Mary, New York State
1916: The Great Polio Epidemic, United States
1918: The Great Flu Pandemic
1976: Ebola outbreaks, Zaire and Sudan
1976: Legionnaires' disease, Philadelphia
1980's: AIDS pandemic
1995: Ebola outbreak, Zaire
2002: SARS epidemic, Asia and Canada

**EXPLOSIONS**

Explosions (overview)
1880: The Seaham Colliery Disaster, England
1914: The Eccles Mine Disaster, West Virginia
1947: The Texas City Disaster

**FAMINES**

Famines (overview)
1200: Egypt famine

## HURRICANES, TYPHOONS, AND CYCLONES

Hurricanes, Typhoons, and Cyclones (overview)
1900: The Galveston hurricane, Texas
1926: The Great Miami Hurricane
1928: The San Felipe hurricane, Florida and the Caribbean
1938: The Great New England Hurricane of 1938
1957: Hurricane Audrey
1969: Hurricane Camille
1970: The Bhola cyclone, East Pakistan
1989: Hurricane Hugo
1992: Hurricane Andrew
1998: Hurricane Mitch
2005: Hurricane Katrina

## ICE STORMS. *See* BLIZZARDS, FREEZES, ICE STORMS, AND HAIL

## ICEBERGS AND GLACIERS

Icebergs and Glaciers (overview)

## LANDSLIDES, MUDSLIDES, AND ROCKSLIDES

Landslides, Mudslides, and Rockslides  (overview)
1963: The Vaiont Dam Disaster, Italy
1966: The Aberfan Disaster, Wales
2006: The Leyte mudslide, Philippines

## LIGHTNING STRIKES

Lightning Strikes (overview)

## METEORITES AND COMETS

Meteorites and Comets (overview)
c. 65,000,000 B.C.E.: Yucatán crater, Atlantic Ocean
1908: The Tunguska event, Siberia

## MUDSLIDES. *See* LANDSLIDES, MUDSLIDES, AND ROCKSLIDES

## ROCKSLIDES. *See* LANDSLIDES, MUDSLIDES, AND ROCKSLIDES

## SANDSTORMS. *See* DUST STORMS AND SANDSTORMS

# ■ Geographical List

**Africa.** *See also individual countries*
1984: Africa famine
2004: The Indian Ocean Tsunami

**Alabama**
2005: Hurricane Katrina

**Alaska**
1964: The Great Alaska Earthquake

**Armenia**
1988: The Leninakan earthquake

**Asia.** *See also individual countries*
2002: SARS epidemic
2004: The Indian Ocean Tsunami

**Atlantic Ocean**
c. 65,000,000 B.C.E.: Yucatán crater
1953: The North Sea Flood of 1953

**Austria**
1999: The Galtür avalanche

**Bahamas**
1992: Hurricane Andrew

**Bangladesh.** *See also* **East Pakistan**
2004: The Indian Ocean Tsunami

**Belgium**
1953: The North Sea Flood of 1953

**California**
1906: The Great San Francisco Earthquake

1928: St. Francis Dam collapse
1989: The Loma Prieta earthquake
1991: The Oakland Hills Fire
1994: The Northridge earthquake
2003: The Fire Siege of 2003

**CAMEROON**
1986: The Lake Nyos Disaster

**CANADA**
1914: *Empress of Ireland* sinking
1974: The Jumbo Outbreak
2002: SARS epidemic

**CARIBBEAN**
1692: The Port Royal earthquake, Jamaica
1902: Pelée eruption, Martinique
1928: The San Felipe hurricane
1989: Hurricane Hugo
1992: Hurricane Andrew
1997: Soufrière Hills eruption, Montserrat

**CENTRAL AMERICA.** *See also individual countries*
1998: Hurricane Mitch

**CHINA**
1959: The Great Leap Forward Famine
1976: The Tangshan earthquake
2002: SARS epidemic

**EAST PAKISTAN**
1970: The Bhola cyclone

**EGYPT**
1200: Egypt famine

**ENGLAND**
1665: The Great Plague of London

1666: The Great Fire of London
1880: The Seaham Colliery Disaster
1952: The Great London Smog

**ETHIOPIA**
1984: Africa famine

**EUROPE.** *See also individual countries*
1320: The Black Death
2003: Europe heat wave

**FLORIDA**
1926: The Great Miami Hurricane
1928: The San Felipe hurricane
1992: Hurricane Andrew
2005: Hurricane Katrina

**FRANCE**
2003: Europe heat wave

**GREAT BRITAIN.** *See also* **ENGLAND; IRELAND; WALES**
1953: The North Sea Flood of 1953

**GREAT PLAINS, U.S.**
1932: The Dust Bowl

**GREECE**
430 B.C.E.: The Plague of Athens

**HAWAII**
1946: The Aleutian tsunami

**HONG KONG**
2002: SARS epidemic

**ICELAND**
1783: Laki eruption

**IDAHO**
1988: Yellowstone National Park fires

**ILLINOIS**
1871: The Great Chicago Fire
1909: The Cherry Mine Disaster
1925: The Great Tri-State Tornado
1995: Chicago heat wave

**INDIA**
2004: The Indian Ocean Tsunami
2005: The Kashmir earthquake

**INDIAN OCEAN**
2004: The Indian Ocean Tsunami

**INDIANA**
1925: The Great Tri-State Tornado

**INDONESIA**
1815: Tambora eruption
1883: Krakatau eruption
2004: The Indian Ocean Tsunami

**IRAN**
2003: The Bam earthquake

**IRELAND**
1845: The Great Irish Famine

**ITALY**
64 c.e.: The Great Fire of Rome
79: Vesuvius eruption
1669: Etna eruption
1908: The Messina earthquake
1963: The Vaiont Dam Disaster

**JAMAICA**
1692: The Port Royal earthquake

**JAPAN**
1657: The Meireki Fire
1923: The Great Kwanto Earthquake
1995: The Kobe earthquake

**KENYA**
2004: The Indian Ocean Tsunami

**LOUISIANA**
1957: Hurricane Audrey
1992: Hurricane Andrew
2005: Hurricane Katrina

**MARTINIQUE**
1902: Pelée eruption

**MASSACHUSETTS**
1872: The Great Boston Fire

**MEDITERRANEAN**
c. 1470 B.C.E.: Thera eruption, Aegean Sea
1669: Etna eruption, Sicily

**MEXICO**
1520: Aztec Empire smallpox epidemic
1982: El Chichón eruption
1985: The Mexico City earthquake

**MIDWEST, U.S.**
1965: The Palm Sunday Outbreak
1974: The Jumbo Outbreak

**MISSISSIPPI**
2005: Hurricane Katrina

**MISSISSIPPI RIVER**
1993: The Great Mississippi River Flood of 1993

**MISSOURI**
1811: New Madrid earthquakes
1896: The Great Cyclone of 1896, St. Louis
1925: The Great Tri-State Tornado

**MONTANA**
1988: Yellowstone National Park fires

**MONTSERRAT**
1997: Soufrière Hills eruption

**NEPAL**
1996: The Mount Everest Disaster

**NETHERLANDS**
1953: The North Sea Flood of 1953

**NEW ENGLAND**
1888: The Great Blizzard of 1888
1938: The Great New England Hurricane of 1938

**NEW JERSEY**
1937: The *Hindenburg* Disaster

**NEW YORK**
1900: Typhoid Mary

**NORTH CAROLINA**
1989: Hurricane Hugo

**NORTH SEA**
1953: The North Sea Flood of 1953

**OKLAHOMA**
1999: The Oklahoma Tornado Outbreak

**PACIFIC OCEAN**
1982: Pacific Ocean El Niño

**PAKISTAN**
2005: The Kashmir earthquake

**PAPUA NEW GUINEA**
1998: Papua New Guinea tsunami

**PENNSYLVANIA**
1889: The Johnstown Flood
1976: Legionnaires' disease, Philadelphia

**PERU**
1970: The Ancash earthquake

**PHILIPPINES**
1991: Pinatubo eruption
2006: The Leyte mudslide

**PORTUGAL**
1755: The Lisbon earthquake

**RUSSIA**
1908: The Tunguska event

**SIBERIA**
1908: The Tunguska event

**SOUTH, U.S.**
1974: The Jumbo Outbreak

**SOUTH CAROLINA**
1989: Hurricane Hugo

**SRI LANKA**
2004: The Indian Ocean Tsunami

**SUDAN**
1976: Ebola outbreaks
1984: Africa famine

**SYRIA**
526: The Antioch earthquake

**TENNESSEE**
1878: The Great Yellow Fever Epidemic, Memphis

**TEXAS**
1900: The Galveston hurricane
1947: The Texas City Disaster
1957: Hurricane Audrey
1997: The Jarrell tornado

**THAILAND**
2004: The Indian Ocean Tsunami

**TURKEY**
1999: The İzmit earthquake

**UNITED STATES.** *See also individual states and regions*
1916: The Great Polio Epidemic
1932: The Dust Bowl, Great Plains
1938: The Great New England Hurricane of 1938
1965: The Palm Sunday Outbreak
1974: The Jumbo Outbreak

**WALES**
1966: The Aberfan Disaster

**WASHINGTON STATE**
1980: Mount St. Helens eruption

**WEST INDIES**
1902: Pelée eruption, Martinique
1928: The San Felipe hurricane

1992: Hurricane Andrew
1997: Soufrière Hills eruption, Montserrat

**WEST VIRGINIA**
1914: The Eccles Mine Disaster

**WISCONSIN**
1871: The Great Peshtigo Fire

**WORLDWIDE**
1892: Cholera pandemic
1918: The Great Flu Pandemic
1980: AIDS pandemic

**WYOMING**
1988: Yellowstone National Park fires

**ZAIRE**
1976: Ebola outbreaks
1995: Ebola outbreak